TEACHER EDUCATION AND CULTURAL CHANGE

Teacher Education and Cultural Change

England, France, West Germany

JAMES LYNCH
H. DUDLEY PLUNKETT

LINNET BOOKS

1973

Library of Congress Cataloging in Publication Data

Lynch, James.
  Teacher education and cultural change: England,
France, and West Germany.

  Includes bibliographical references.
  1. Teachers, Training of – Great Britain. 2. Teachers,
Training of – France. 3. Teachers, Training of – Germany
(Federal Republic, 1949–   ). I. Plunkett, H. Dudley, joint
author. II. Title.
LB1725.G6L96   370'.71'094   73–6720
ISBN 0–208–01398–9

© George Allen & Unwin Ltd, 1973
First published 1973 by George Allen & Unwin Ltd,
London, and in the United States of America under
the imprint Linnet Books by The Shoe String Press, Inc.
Hamden, Connecticut 06514

Printed in Great Britain

Contents

Preface

We have been fortunate in the co-operation we have had in assembling the information needed to prepare this book. A large amount of the material referred to is either published in France or West Germany and largely unavailable in English or in this country, or it consists of unpublished working-papers and mimeographed documents to which access could not have been obtained without guidance and assistance from academic colleagues and officials on the spot.

We extend our thanks to those who have given us their time, advice and inspiration. Among our greatest debts are those to: Pierre Bourdieu, Director of the Centre de Sociologie Européenne, Paris, whose influence on our book will be readily apparent and is even more readily acknowledged; Pierre Laderrière, of the Directorate of Scientific Affairs, Organization for Economic Co-operation and Development; Raymond Lallez, Head of the Pedagogical Centres of the Ecole Normale Supérieure at St Cloud, Paris; Jean Hassenforder of the Service des Etudes et Recherches Pédagogiques, Institut National de Recherches et Documentation Pédagogiques; many officials of the Ministère de l'Education Nationale; Karl Bungardt, General Secretary of the Gewerkschaft Erziehung und Wissenschaft; Franz Letzelter, General Secretary of the German Council for Education; Walter Schultze, formerly Director of the German Institute for International Educational Research; Dr G. Grüner of the Technical University of Darmstadt; many officials of the *Länder* ministries and members of teacher-education institutions; and the many colleagues in England with whom we have been able to discuss our ideas. Responsibility for the interpretation and use made of the information and advice we have received remains with us.

James Lynch
H. Dudley Plunkett
Southampton

Abbreviations

AGDL	Arbeitsgemeinschaft deutscher Lehrerverbände
ATCDE	Association of Teachers in Colleges and Departments of Education
ATO	Area Training Organization
B.Ed.	Bachelor of Education degree
CAPES	Certificat d'aptitude au professorat des enseignements de second degré
CEG	Collège d'enseignement général
CES	Collège d'enseignement secondaire
CET	Collège d'enseignement technique
DES	Department of Education and Science
Dip.Päd.	Diplom-Pädagoge
DUEL	Diplôme universitaire d'études littéraires
DUES	Diplôme universitaire d'études scientifiques
GEW	Gewerkschaft Erziehung und Wissenschaft
HMSO	Her Majesty's Stationery Office
INRDP	Institut National de Recherches et Documentation Pédagogiques
KMK	Ständige Konferenz der Kultusminister
MEN	Ministère de l'Education Nationale
NFER	National Foundation for Educational Research
NUT	National Union of Teachers
OECD	Organization for Economic Cooperation and Development
WRK	Westdeutsche Rektorenkonferenz

Introduction

The educational systems of Europe responded, along with the societies to which they belonged, to the convulsions of the Second World War. While it will require the perspective of history to reveal the significance of the changes that have occurred in these societies in the last quarter of a century, it is undeniable that more widely diffused and even new expectations for welfare, knowledge and participation have changed the consciousness of peoples. Fundamental to the political, social and economic changes that have taken place is that the ways people think and act have a new basis of values. It is hardly disputable that this shift in values is most clearly detectable amongst the young. The way in which young people have made known their expectations for the future has racked even those societies which were formerly the most stable. Protest among students, and the most emphatic and assertive claims have come from the most highly educated, has appeared to be independent of class, ideological or political affiliations. But to say that there has been a spontaneous emergence of youth as a political force on the international scene is not to say that this is simply a traditional response to intergenerational conflict using the technology of modern society to project itself more effectively upon the attention of an adult world. The values and expectations expressed in an increasingly international youth culture are sensed by whole societies, and they are the same values and expectations that are transforming social institutions from empires and churches to the family and the school.

It is inadequate to ascribe such changes amongst the young to the expansion of formal education since 1945, for there are countless other factors that have undoubtedly influenced the directions in which knowledge and values have developed. But it is surely vital to ask to what extent social change corresponds to the social content of current conceptions of what education is for and what it should involve. Or is it the case, on the other hand, that the deliberate formulation of educational objectives and policies is irrelevant to the changing social consciousness of youth? England, France and West Germany, for all their varying characteristics, are alike in that, in the post-war era, they have seen changes in few sectors of their societies as great as those that have occurred in education. In England there has been the transformation of much of primary education involving the widespread adoption of active methods of learning, the development of secondary education on a free and universal basis, the foundation of universities, polytechnics and colleges of further and higher education, and, throughout the educational system, a drift towards comprehensive forms of organization. Less progress has been made in France towards the democratization of secondary education, but a massive expansion has been taking place in higher education, while the events of May 1968 signalled the need for qualitative change throughout the system. In Germany, though progress has been more recent, it has been no less fundamental, with the introduction of comprehensive forms of secondary education and the establishment of new universities including the first *Gesamthochschulen* (comprehensive universities).

In all three societies, these educational changes have represented responses to aspirations of a cumulative nature. There is now a post-war educated generation of parents with children in school, which has acquired high expectations and a keener sense of what value education may have for its children in an increasingly developed and differentiated economy, society and international community. Educational systems are required to expand and alter their functions to meet a new range of objectives. These objectives include those which have long been agreed to be essential to a just society, but which have only in recent years come to be generally regarded as attainable, and others which were previously met by such social institutions as the family or the church, or which represent quite new aspirations of society or of particular groups in society.

The fact of change, its significance among youth and its implications for the future of society all compel a study of education, understood as a process that is oriented by values to create and increase intellectual and social awareness. The question of what the motive forces of education are may be partially an internal one, in that education evidently does create a demand for itself. But looked at in relation to society, education can be seen to respond in countless ways to the prerequisites of such systems as the political or the economic, that are external to itself. It is, thus, the culture of the educational system itself, its own internal organization and the means that it employs to seek to achieve its declared ends, that determine the quality of its response to society by providing an important and particularly manifest link in the chain of causality in the development of knowledge and values. This link is of course secured by the teachers in the schools and, no less evidently, by those who select and train them.

If it seems logical to begin a study of education by focusing upon the quality of the teachers, it is sobering to reflect that, in the undertakings of the educational systems of England, France and West Germany, there is no gap more glaring than the failure to equip the teaching profession for its altered contemporary functions. In England public reports have repeatedly proposed the reforming of the teacher education system,[1] in France similar if more prescriptive arguments were proffered by the *Colloque d'Amiens*[2] in 1968, and in Germany, despite much progress since 1945, dissatisfaction with the system of teacher education has been widespread and in some instances has even provoked student strikes.[3] And yet, if we seek the next logical step to the major advances in the three systems over the last twenty-five years, it must surely involve the transformation of ambitious projects of democratization and extension of public education into truly educational and not merely statistical achievements. The responsibility for this devolves directly upon the teachers. From them must come much of the vision, expertise and cultural sensitivity to interpret and respond to pressure for change and initiate qualitative development in education. This will imply changes in social roles, methods of work and resources of knowledge, and a commitment to an experimental view of education. The study of teachers and their training thus falls into its proper perspective as the study of the evolution in its broader context of an occupation with a key role in fulfilling society's long-term social, economic and cultural aspirations. Any such study must have regard not only to the institutions and programmes upon which the practical operations of teacher education depend, but also to the range of activities which may be expected of teachers and, no less important, to the way in which social values underlying present educational policies and developments are communicated to student teachers.

REFERENCES

1　The most recent such report has been the James Report. See Department of Education and Science, *Teacher Education and Training* (Report by a Committee of Inquiry appointed by the Secretary of State for Education and Science, under the chairmanship of Lord James of Rusholme) (London: HMSO, 1972).

2　The *Colloque d'Amiens* was a conference attended by leading academics and many professionals concerned with teacher education in France. It is reported in Association d'Etude pour l'Expansion de la Recherche Scientifique, *Pour une Ecole Nouvelle: Formation des Maîtres et Recherche en Education* (Paris: Dunod, 1969).

3　A useful overview of the situation in 1969 appears in Bungardt, K., *Schulpolitik in Bewegung 12 Folge: Ein Neuer Anfang und die Ausgangslage* (Material – und Nachrichtendienst der Gewerkschaft Erziehung und Wissenschaft, no. 134) (Bühl-Baden: Konkordia AG für Druck und Verlag, January, 1970).

Part One

Chapter One

The Context and Structure of Teacher Education

EDUCATION IN THE THREE SOCIETIES

However much at the level of the classroom the teacher may feel himself to be making a creative response to a unique situation, he lives in fact in a social environment in which the activities of other individuals constrain his own. It is of the nature of the sociologist's task to seek to objectify such social structures and relationships, but by extension it must be part of any strategy for teacher education to attempt to appraise the educational and sociopolitical context of teaching. We are not at this point concerned with the political content of teacher education, a tendentious topic to which we shall make reference later; rather it is a question of the impossibility of dealing fruitfully with the organization of teacher education without considering its broader setting. Any conceivable aspect of the teacher's eventual work, such as the syllabus, teaching materials, physical and human resources, grouping of pupils or welfare services, will transcend the sphere of influence of the school. These are areas where decisions can be taken for the schools by the public authorities, or through a broader process of decision-making in which numerous expert and lay interest-groups each seek to influence education according to particular values and objectives.

Administrative Control and Organization

While there is no space in a brief study such as this for a historical treatment of the English, French and West German educational systems, it would seem that the conventions and assumptions that characterize them must have deep historical roots to account for the tenacious persistence within socially centripetal post-war Europe, of apparently distinctive educational systems.

The formal institutions for the public control of education in England have never crystallized in such a manner or to such a degree as they have in France. Traditionally financial measures have been applied that made English education authorities at the local level, and even teachers under the nineteenth-century *payment by results* scheme, accountable to the state. But within the margin of such financial limitations, the local authorities have had a wide measure of control, and this in spite of legislation during the present century that has been ever more precise in laying particular tasks at their door. In fact the new tasks that were assigned in this way, such as the provision of secondary education, and the extension of the educational welfare role, consisted largely of the consolidation of what was already under way. This was certainly so in the case of such developments as the successive raising of the school-leaving age, the expansion and differentiation of secondary provision both from the point of view of subject-matter and organization, and the raising of minimum levels of training for qualification as a teacher. In all of these the state has usually established minimum levels of provision while front-running local authorities have gauged the pace of their progress accordingly. One distinctive feature of the English system has been the traditional independent status of the universities. Unlike the training colleges and the technical colleges, which were largely under local authority control, the universities negotiated for their finances from a powerful national position which has only recently been questioned with the expansion of higher educational provision.[1]

The Education Act of 1944[2] effectively set the pattern of organization for English education from the end of the Second World War. The Act laid upon the local education authorities the task of providing education to meet the needs of the population of their areas through three successive stages of education: primary, secondary and further. Though the Act did not formally set down a tripartite provision of secondary education, with the encouragement of the Ministry of Education using the Hadow, Spens and Norwood Reports[3] as authority, this was what was effectively established.[4] For the next twenty years this was the predominant pattern of organization of secondary schools in England and Wales with some 20 per cent of the age cohort attending grammar schools from age 11, 5 per cent attending technical schools and 75 per cent attending modern schools. In fact the percentage provision of these and other types of school varied very considerably between local areas and this was one reason why the system was attacked as unfair.[5] (These figures exclude those 5 to 6 per cent of the child population who attended the independent public schools.)

Not all authorities could provide the three types of secondary school or give them the parity of material and human provision, let alone guarantee them the 'parity of esteem' called for by the educationalists.[6] Some authorities, such as London and Coventry, set up comprehensive schools. Others established multilateral schools incorporating the three types of provision in one building in an additive rather than integrated form. Others introduced bilateral schools: technical-modern, grammar-technical[7] or grammar-modern, either in one building or as separate schools on the same campus, whilst some even introduced selective secondary modern schools. The method of allocation at age 11 to the different types of secondary education came to be known as *the eleven-plus* and was usually based on IQ and tests in English and mathematics. The margin of error in allocation was considerable and the National Foundation for Educational Research (NFER) reported in 1963 that even in the most favourable circumstances this could not be expected to be less than 5 per cent either side of the pass-fail border line.[8] Criticism of misallocations and of other shortcomings in the eleven-plus system were not stilled by the compromise of the 1958 paper *Secondary Education for all: A New Drive*, which paved the way for the establishment of new comprehensive schools 'on genuine educational grounds'.[9]

Dissatisfaction grew to a crescendo by the early 1960s. A Labour Government was returned to power in October 1964 with the avowed aim of abolishing the eleven-plus, and in July 1965 issued Circular 10/65[10] requesting local education authorities to submit, within one year, plans for the comprehensive reorganization of secondary education in their area. The Circular specified six main forms of comprehensive school organiza- tion, including all-through comprehensives (11 to 18 years), three types of two-tier systems, the 11 to 16 years and sixth-form college system and, facilitated by the 1964 Education Act[11] enabling transfer to take place at ages other than eleven-plus, a system of middle schools (8 to 12 years or 9 to 13 years) followed by comprehensive secondary schools. The following year the Department of Education and Science (DES) issued Circular 10/66 restricting future secondary building plan approval to comprehensive schemes. By the time the change of government occurred in 1970 the vast majority of local authorities had submitted comprehensive reorganization plans.[12] Patterns of provision now include all of those advocated by Circular 10/65, as well as variations of these schemes which include 8 to 12 middle schools, followed by secondary comprehensive schools from 12 to 16 years, and sixth form colleges or integrated further education provision from 16 years.[13] In some cases selective systems based on the eleven-plus or similar methods of allocation will continue to operate.

Against this political background we must reassess the notion of the autonomy of the teacher, a hallowed myth of English education which would presumably require that the teacher were free to teach whom, where and how he wished. The persistence of this stereotype is a matter of very great interest in itself, but we shall confine ourselves to the area of curri- culum as the test of the hypothesis. The freedom of choice of the teacher over the content of what he teaches in England diminishes with the age and academic potential of his pupils. The syllabuses and assessment for the various public examinations in England have not, until recently, been responsive to teacher opinion; the teacher in the academic secondary school has had little option but to fit his work into a pre-ordained scheme, often at a cost to his own personal objectives. None the less the terminal character of these examinations allows a little latitude at younger age levels that has vital importance, and the pluralist structure of the examining bodies has permitted some accommodation to the demands of teachers.[14]

The administration of the French educational system since the Napoleonic reforms that established the *Université Impériale* has been described by Minot.[15] All educational institutions, though with the subsequent exception of various private and particularly religious schools, were grouped within the *Université*. The system was controlled from the centre with a meticulous assignment of delegated functions through the regional *académies*. This structure exists in its essentials today, though the central control over the constituent higher education institutions appears to have weakened since May 1968. The various local universities acquired a measure of autonomy by the *Loi d'Orientation*,[16] but the extent of this autonomy remains to be established in practice, and, in any case, under the present legislation cannot be compared to the independence of British and West German institutions.

Teachers are recruited by competitive examination (*concours*) for all levels and types of school and, apart from the staffs of the primary schools which are administered materially by the municipalities, all teachers are employees of the national government. A corps of inspectors (general, academic and departmental) oversees the administration, staffing, curriculum and teaching in the schools. Criticism of this heavily bureaucratized system is found both within and outside the educational system, and at all levels. The question is to what extent such centralized control is compatible with the kinds of teaching and learning that a modern society requires. It is significant that for many this was a central issue in May 1968, and one on which concessions were made by the authorities when a structure of administration was given to individual schools that appeared to promise community representation and freedom of experiment in teaching organization and methods.[17] A potentially very important precedent was being created, in that what was happening educationally was being allowed to affect the administration of the system.

The French school system has evolved to its present rather complex structure from what was essentially a dual system of elementary and higher elementary schooling on the one hand, and academic secondary schooling on the other. Although there existed apprenticeship centres (*centres d'apprentissage*) and technical secondary schools that provided a terminal type of vocational preparation at different levels, the two typical institutions were the primary school and the *lycée*. The present system can best be understood as resulting from the differentiation of these two types of school to meet the needs of an evolving society and economy. Little change of an organizational nature has occurred for pupils under the age of 11, but with the break that has become accepted as the start of secondary education for most French children, a number of possibilities have developed. The higher elementary classes remained in the more rural areas, but in others their pupils were transferred to the *cours complémentaires*, a phase of education in its own right rather than merely a holding operation while the legal age for leaving school had not been reached. Following legislation in 1959[18] this phase, renamed *enseignement général court*, was established in the *collège d'enseignement général* (CEG), a rough equivalent of the English secondary modern school, along with a track (*section*) for the least academically inclined secondary pupils, the *classes de transition et pratique terminale*.

This multilateral system for the first cycle of secondary education was modified under further legislation in 1963.[19] The CEG began to be incorporated into a *collège d'enseignement secondaire* (CES), along with the traditional academic tracks. The CES has preserved the distinct *sections*, though transfer between them is now possible in principle. The Fifth Plan envisaged that by 1978, sufficient CES will be provided to accommodate 80 per cent of children aged 11 to 14.[20] The second cycle (ages 15 to 18/19) takes place in the *lycée*, which is thus in the process of becoming an institution similar to the English sixth-form college as it loses its lower classes. Although comprehensive education is not being sought under current French educational policy,[21] a notable feature of the system as it has operated since the 1963 Law is that the first cycle of secondary education is seen as serving a diagnostic function (*cycle d'observation et d'orientation*). During this four-year period, pupil profiles are established and consultations are routinely held between teachers and parents concerning their children's future educational careers. The extent and effectiveness of control from the centre is far more thorough and direct in France than in the other two countries, mainly because of the responsibility exercised by the Ministry of National Education over the daily curriculum of the schools. The *programme*, a concept which we will examine later in more detail, has been seen as the instrument for the manipulation of education by national policy-makers. Political and educational associations who wish to exert influence over the development of the society have shown sensitivity to this strategic importance of the curriculum. If the Ministry wishes to promote new educational objectives, the best and almost the only direct means available to it is the initiation of new curricular programmes. The power of the programme resides, of course, not merely in the efficiency of the bureaucracy but also in the cultures of the subjects, which have been developed over generations in the *lycées* and *écoles normales*, through one or other of which virtually all teachers will have passed.

In contrast to France, there is a tradition of decentralization in Germany, which was only temporarily checked by the National Socialist regime.[22] In the interests of democratization and denazification, as also for broader political reasons, the war-time Allies were determined that any new German state which might emerge should be politically decentralized.

The eleven states (*Länder*) of West Germany are the legislative and administrative authorities, through their Ministries of Education, for education and cultural provision, including teacher-training institutions and universities, so that there are still marked differences in school provision in the various states. These persist in spite of economic and political pressures that have produced an ever-growing intrusion of the central government into the field of education,[23] and the co-ordinating work and influence of a number of bodies, in particular the Permanent Conference of Ministers of Education (*Ständige Konferenz der Kultusminister*).[24] Education is everywhere compulsory from the age of 6 to 18. Nine years full-time attendance is imposed now in all parts of Germany, Bavaria having been the last to introduce a ninth school year in 1968. In addition many states have introduced a tenth year in general educational secondary schools. Resting on the reform introduced in 1919, primary education extends from grades one through four (six in the City states) although the final years (grades five and six) are considered to be observation and orientation years. After this, pupils may be allocated to the *Hauptschule* (10 to 15/16 years) or the *Realschule* (formerly *Mittelschule*) which may be either the standard type (10 to 16 years or 12 to 16 years in the City states and Bavaria) or the promotion type (*Aufbauform*), following on from the end of the seventh school year at the latest. A third alternative is the *Gymnasium*, either in the ordinary form (10/12 to 18/19 years) or the promotion type (*Gymnasium im Aufbauform* 13 to 18/19 years of age). Pupils from the *Realschule* may transfer to the grammar school for three years at age 16. Both forms lead to the *Abitur* which is an internal examination taken at age 18/19, on the basis of which successful candidates have had, until recently, automatic right of entry to higher education in university, technological university or college of education.[25] Those who leave school at 15 or 16 must continue their education until 18 or until they have successfully terminated their apprenticeship. This further education usually takes place part-time in a vocational school (*Berufsschule*) or in a specialized vocational school (*Fachschule*) or in a full-time specialized vocational school (*Berufsfachschule*).

Arising in part from the recommendations of the German Council for Education,[26] there are now comprehensive schools (*Gesamtschulen*) in many parts of Germany, in addition to the general educational schools already described. These may be either multilateral or integrated (*integrierte Gesamtschule*). Extensive appraisals and reform proposals have been made by the Council[27] and a comprehensive plan has been submitted to the *Bundestag* (Lower Chamber of Parliament) which envisages comprehensive lower secondary education and unitary but differentiated upper secondary education.[28] It will include general and vocational aspects of education, integrated in a pattern of organization similar to that recently introduced in Sweden and in some English local education authority areas. If the Council's recent proposals for the reform of the terminal secondary examination (*Abitur*) are implemented, the work of all secondary pupils and their teachers will be affected.[29]

In West Germany until recently a long and tenacious tradition of programme prescription has functioned to control teacher activity. It has been the practice in Germany, and still is in West Germany, for the Ministries of Education to draft and publish guidelines concerning not only the content of education but also its organization and methods. In the early years of the Federal Republic these guidelines were stringently imposed. Recent years, however, have seen increasing relaxation and democratization of this control and it is now the custom in most *Länder* for working parties of teachers, and interest groups such as the churches and parents, to be associated with the formulation and prescription of curricula at all stages.[30] The guidelines, variously called *Studienpläne, Richtlinien*, etc., are still issued regionally by the eleven Ministries, though they are often published by other agencies such as well-known educational publishers. The Ministries however no longer seek to control the teachers in such detail and to such an extent. There is now much greater sensitivity than formerly to the need to provide the teacher with a guide, a fund of ideas from which he can choose according to his experience, the needs of the children and the context in which he teaches. The whole basis of curriculum formulation has become, particularly in the more progressive states, an exercise in democratic participation. This forward prescription of curriculum obviates the need to use examinations as a means of curriculum formulation and teacher control, as is the case in England, and, although there are Ministry assessors present, the *Abitur* is virtually an internal examination.

Education and Cultural Values

There is little practical difficulty in locating the ideological debate about educational values and policies, or its consequences in types of curricula and schools. And indeed, unless we affirm that there is no correspondence between declared philosophies and actual behaviour, these debates ought to provide us with insight into the dynamics of educational systems. The difficulty lies rather in finding an economical means of conducting such an analysis. As there is at the moment no means of identifying what statements, or which authors of assertions about the aims of education might be judged to require study we propose to begin by using a simple categorization of educational aims that has been developed by Anderson. He has seen policy choices in any educational system as having to be made with respect to efficiency, equity and freedom of choice.[31] A similar view is also taken by a recent OECD document which categorizes demands made upon the educational systems as emphasizing a social-expressive or an economic-instrumental value.[32] For the purpose of our present study such a categorization raises the issue of what the teacher is for. Our analysis can only be carried forward if we are prepared to examine this question conscious that the three societies may favour different answers. There are two aspects to the question; firstly, there is the broad issue as to what cultural values can be inferred to define the role of the teacher; and secondly, there is the more practical problem of the extent to which the role of the teacher may be said to be securely defined. Such questions imply reference to the cultural values of educational systems as well as to those of teacher education. This is not to imply that it is possible to plan all or even most of the outcomes of education, but rather that statements of educational aims must surely provide a basis for discussion of the cultural perceptions which the three societies hold for their teachers.

Traditionally, western societies, including England, France and Germany, have evidenced little concern for equity in education and have accorded educational freedom of choice only to their élites. Education in such societies was quite avowedly founded upon a utilitarian philosophy in terms of both its social and vocational significance. It is only since the Second World War that efforts to quantify the contribution made by education to the society have gained acceptance. A recognizable discipline of the economics of education developed at first in the United States and spread to other countries largely through the channels of the United Nations and other international organizations, particularly the Organization for Economic Co-operation and Development (OECD). The result of the more thorough analysis of measurable aspects of education has been a considerable growth in the rationally planned development of educational systems all over the world. By the late 1950s the assumption that education was an investment in national development was well established and this concept featured in documents produced by governments and international organizations, reflecting closely the progress of academic research. Implementation of human resource investment policies was rapid, because the idea seemed so convincing in developing and industrialized countries alike, though priority tended to be given to the upper levels of formal education.

After a phase of uninhibited expansion, governments began to find demand far outstripping supply at most levels of education, and the question of priorities was more sharply posed. There was a widespread recognition among societies around the world of the potential scale of the economic returns, both private and public, accruing to educational investment. Some researchers attempted to demonstrate statistical relationships between educational investments and national economic growth, and numerous national educational plans were formulated which extrapolated the findings of American research within African and other contexts. It is easily seen that there is a direct continuity between the late Victorian concept of mass education for the workers of the emergent industrial state and the attempt to devise educational systems in the 1960s which would staff the industries and services of a technological society. A stage of runaway utilitarianism characterized most of the highly developed societies by the middle of the decade. Educational systems were becoming increasingly bureaucratized, technological branches of study were favoured, institutions began to seek ways of making education more efficient by the use of teaching aids and programmed learning.

It would be expected that, viewed in a developmental perspective, the notion of equity in education would emerge as an issue at a relatively late stage, and equality of educational opportunity began to be an important proposition in England, France and Germany soon after the First World War and featured prominently in educational reports after the Second World War. Within the educational traditions of the three societies, the Second World War must be seen as ending a massive hiatus. From the latter years of the war in England and France, and from immediately after the war in Germany,[33] much energy was devoted to formulating policies of reform through education. Many of the issues raised, for example, in the Green Book in England in 1941[34] or in the Langevin-Wallon Report[35] in France in 1947 were not themselves new, though the convergence across the societies is remarkable. In fact comprehensive education had been an issue in all three societies from the 1920s. Reform proposals of this kind were espoused by R. H. Tawney[36] in England and by the advocates of the *école unique*[37] in France and the *Einheitsschule* in Germany.[38] However in the post-war societies of the 1940s and 1950s the ideological notions which these policies embraced were soon reinforced or replaced by new demographic, social and economic demands whose effects are still accelerating. The transfer of war technology to civil society, the technologically directed shift in demand for skills by the economies of the three societies, the demographic explosion in the schools, the optimism and concomitant aspirations of people for their own and their children's future, all contributed to inducing substantial expansion in formal public education. The problems were sufficiently drastic to force their recognition and their urgency upon whole societies within a few years.

With the gradual expansion of free secondary education which had taken place since 1945, it had been readily assumed in the three societies that a fairer distribution of opportunities for education was being achieved. However sociological evidence accumulating from the mid-1950s began to reveal that the opportunity gap in education between social groups and classes was still very large in relative terms. It became clear that there were in fact systematic differences in opportunities between individuals of similar measured IQ from different social groups. Support grew for new forms of allocation to schools which were aimed either at retrieving talent or at performing a compensatory function based upon the recognition of a universal right to education.

It now seems that the phase during which the essentially elitist concept of economic investment in education gave way to a notion of social investment was relatively short-lived. It became clear during the later 1960s that this type of school-based social engineering was very limited in its effects. The social structure was being reproduced, or perhaps was being allowed to reproduce itself, through the educational system.[39] More insistently than ever before the real issue of democratization posed itself as a political and cultural problem of the larger community finding expression in the schools and the teaching profession. Such a trend is in fact observable from the shift in OECD reports in recent years from an investment-oriented point of view on education to the expression of the view that equality of educational opportunity may itself be an appropriate policy goal.[40] What followed the 1944 Education Act was a false democratization that has been described as a system of 'sponsored' social mobility;[41] opportunities were provided for those who showed early promise to develop their talents in the grammar school while the remainder of the age group was confined to the more limited horizons of the secondary modern school. The comprehensive or common secondary school was instituted in some areas from the end of the Second World War, but it was not until the failure of the secondary modern school to achieve its official destiny of 'parity of esteem' that comprehensive education became a serious issue. In these developments and especially in Circular 10/65 was a recognition of social priorities going beyond criteria of economic efficiency, as was the case in the United States with the Economic Opportunity Act of 1964 or the Elementary and Secondary Education Act of 1965. The question of equity for the majority of the school population seems henceforward to be defining itself in terms of the internal organization of the common school and the relationship between the value systems upheld by the school and those of the families from which its pupils come. Is the school to give formal recognition to differences of academic aptitude which can be shown to reflect the socio-cultural background of the pupils? And is the school necessarily committed to a function of cultural levelling, or to the imposition of a dominant culture? Social and political arguments were now being raised alongside and in contrast to economic justifications for developing the educational services.

A remarkably similar evolution of educational policy had occurred in France from the time of the Langevin-Wallon Report in 1947 which had proposed the democratization of the secondary school and of the teaching profession. The reforms of 1959 and 1963, instituting the orientation system and the *collège d'enseignement secondaire*, as well as raising the school-leaving age and providing for a wide range of vocational and technical options in secondary education, have successively increased the purely organizational capacity of the educational system to cope with its diversifying social and economic tasks. They represented something of a new idea in French educational legislation, though little advance has been made, within the centralized educational system, towards the diffusion of new pedagogical methods and the humanly efficient utilization of the intellectual and social potentials of the French teaching body.[42] The internal hierarchies of the schools can hardly be said to have been modified. Although there was until recently little documentation of the continuing social inequalities of the French educational system, what research had been done showed them to be considerably greater than in England.[43]

Educational developments in West Germany were stultified for two decades after the Second World War, and even a proposal such as the 1959 *Rahmenplan*[44] could only seek to tie existing forms more closely together rather than propose the type of democratizing reforms then beginning to emerge in the other two countries. Indeed, the rather more progressive *Bremer Plan* was rejected by members of the General German Teachers Association in both selective and intermediate schools precisely because it seemed to propose new school forms and in particular to resurrect the spirit of the *Einheitsschule*.[45] There were educationists and researchers capable of posing the problem, but the writings of Picht, Dahrendorf, Hamm-Brücher and many others about the inadequacies of the educational system and the reports of national bodies such as the Science Council[46] appeared to have little effect until political, economic, social and religious factors emerging in the middle 1960s gave the debate a new context and a new dynamic.[47]

Subsequently the German Council for Education (*Bildungsrat*) responded to the educationists' argument for truly comprehensive reform and initiatives towards greater democratization. Among the latter can be cited the elaboration of new curriculum *guidelines* by several *Länder*,[48] attempting to unify the teaching profession through a common appointments and salary structure for elementary and grammar school teachers, and the introduction of comprehensive schools at least experimentally in all *Länder*.[49]

By the later 1960s there were several social researchers and educationalists who were devoting their attention to these questions, in fact going straight to the issues of equity without passing through the phase of concern with economic efficiency. The more radical approaches that have characterized the definition of the research problems of Bourdieu and his associates have been more concerned with achieving an understanding of the social functions of the educational system than with particular educational reforms.

It remains to be seen what effects the increasingly acute self-consciousness of educationists who are becoming aware of this research, will have upon their perceptions of the teacher's role. Bourdieu argues that it matters little what educators think, that their autonomy is relative and conditional upon their not challenging the interests of the dominant classes, but it is none the less true that the problem has never been so clearly posed, so unavoidably for teachers and policy-makers alike: is the the educational system bound to a dominant culture and to reflecting the interests of a dominant class by reproducing that culture or legitimating its dominance? Bourdieu, in a series of studies, locates the sensitive points of the educational apparatus: the hierarchy of educational institutions, of careers and disciplines within them, the function of the examination and the values maintained by the examination boards. The analysis of the values sustained by these self-reproducing structures and their relations to traditional cultural and social hierarchies constitutes a critique of the Durkheimian idea that the educational system functions to transmit a homogeneous culture rather than, as Bourdieu would argue, to ensure the recognition and acceptance of a hierarchy of cultures and associated social statuses. In a summing-up of the question, Bourdieu argues in effect for a critical sociology of the examination. He thus exposes the problem of social values that lies at the heart of current educational policies, that is, whether problems of equity can really be solved by the educational system.

It appears from the development of educational policies in the three societies that equity as a policy may be socially utopian; it is not a strategy in itself but rather the goal of a range of strategic manoeuvres that succeed one another like the horizons for mountaineers climbing over foothills. To characterize the sum of these strategies as the equalization of opportunities is to beg the question. In fact, what is happening is that demand for education is becoming more diversified. For this reason policy-makers are being pressed to go beyond planning educational systems that are democratic in terms of recognized social groupings in the population, and to provide scope for freedom of choice within the educational system. Since Anderson formulated the notion of a conflict of policy goals between social efficiency, equity and freedom of choice, it has become clearer how much greater the dimensions of the latter may be. In the 1970s we are no longer thinking in terms of the choice to remain in school, the choice to opt for one or other of an arbitrary offering of curricula; already there are colleges and even schools in England, France and Germany where students, parents and others participate in the design of their own curricula, and there is a developing pedagogy that approves the policy of seeking to mobilize the participants in the educational process, both to increase the intrinsic meaning and value of personal learning and to allow an extrinsic significance to emerge from the interaction of curriculum and society. Such a conception implies attaching value to both the manifestation of individual creative choice and action by the learner and, at a political level, the furtherance of ideological positions or group interests within educational systems by learners, teachers and others holding values relating to education. While such activity is not without precedent, the scale, intensity and persistence of new forms of collective activity constitute a new level of politicization of education, a public struggle over its values and their allocation within the system which cannot be without long-term educational consequences. It is within this context of cultural pluralism that the critical issues of teacher education must necessarily be reviewed.

It appears indisputable that the rigidity of educational careers sanctioned by public examinations has effectively restricted freedom of choice to social and intellectual élites in the three societies. The English examination system may have been marginally more restrictive particularly at the upper secondary level and in its effects upon the curricula available to all pupils in the lower secondary schools. It could also be argued that the stronger emphasis upon the idea of a general secondary education in France and Germany, based upon a commitment to *la culture générale* and to *Allgemeinbildung* respectively, has entailed a broader offering of disciplines. The attempt to move closer to this model in England recently, through a formula of required subject combinations in secondary terminal examinations could not find agreement;[50] the principle of increasing the autonomy of the teachers in curriculum planning has been double-edged: it allows teachers the freedom both to subordinate their work to the requirements of institutions of higher education and, as has been happening in England, to design new examinations adapted to what the pupil is learning.

If it is possible to trace a shift in the centre of gravity of educational policies in the three societies from the economic-instrumental along a continuum leading to the social-expressive, this is not to say that such value changes are yet widely evident in their educational systems. The critical point of transfer seems to lie in the expectations held for the teacher's role in education that respond to the values of democratization. It is clear that the traditional authoritarianism of the teacher in the selective secondary school, his trust in his subject as this has been handed on to him, his knowledge-centred approach to teaching and his relative ignorance of the educational sciences in their theories, methods and applications, as well as his social relationship with his clients, left him ill-prepared to promote educational reforms involving social and psychological sensitivities in response to individual, to culturally diverse and particularly to socially disadvantaged pupils. The teacher is necessarily caught in a conflict of values, but we have to consider to what extent different perceptions of both teaching and teacher education reflect this cultural pluralism and are reflected in the strategic decisions of teacher education policy-makers.

TEACHER EDUCATION IN THE THREE SOCIETIES

We are now a generation away from the immediately post-war years of economic and social change and the first experiments of the welfare state. The simple idea of expanding provision to meet shortages of classroom space and teaching personnel continues to arouse concern but in addition the quality and variety of the educational services are gaining ground as matters of political importance. A vital need of the educational system has become its capacity for critical self-appraisal and change. In this respect the structure of the three national systems has predisposed them to change in different ways. In all the systems however it is being recognized that, along with the massive organizational changes that are being proposed or implemented, the test of the educational services will lie in the sensitivity of their operations, or more concretely in the effectiveness and expertise of their personnel. At the same time change is impeded by the fact that teacher-education institutions in all three societies seem to have partially insulated themselves from their social contexts and often from the active experimentation that occurs in the schools. In this sense the challenge that has been felt within many organizations to update information, to question traditional assumptions, to consider new methods of working and possible new structures and relationships, is not being met and in some cases may not even be generally recognized. It is the schools rather than the training institutions that are confronting and grappling with the problems of minorities, environmental disadvantage and poor motivation. In this section we outline the principal features and controversies in the development and current provision of teacher education in England, France and West Germany.

The Dual System of Teacher Education

Although in England there has been teacher training in the universities since 1890, the great majority of trained teachers has always attended the teacher-training colleges and indeed had little or no contact with universities until the establishment of the *joint boards* in 1930, which were then succeeded by the Institute of Education system after the McNair Report of 1944. At that time there were eighty-three colleges granting certificates to students after a two-year post-secondary course. Most of these teachers went into the elementary schools which constituted a separate and, at the secondary stage, parallel provision to that of the grammar schools up to the age of 14. By contrast, university graduates wishing to enter the teaching profession could do so either directly, without any training, or by taking a one-year course at a university department of education. Salaries discouraged such individuals from considering taking a position in the elementary schools.

The *dual system* that resulted from this was commented upon by the McNair Report: 'It is, broadly speaking, true to say that the certificated teacher is to the elementary school what the graduate teacher is to the secondary school'.[51] The Report made specific proposals in an attempt to overcome this cleavage in the teaching body and to unify the education of teachers. Henceforth there would be only one category of teacher, a 'qualified teacher', whose training would be provided by regionally-based associations of colleges and universities. Opinion was divided among the members of the McNair Committee as to how this was to be achieved, whether by establishing university schools of education, which would be directly responsible for all teacher training, or by the retention of greater independence for the training colleges by preserving the existing *joint boards* scheme. In the event, the twenty *institutes of education* which replaced the *joint boards* represented a compromise between these two points of view. All but one are university bodies, though not all the directors have professorial titles. However, in each case the controlling body is representative of the university, training institutions, local education authorities and teachers in the area. The size of the institutes varies considerably as does the number of constituent establishments and students for whom they are responsible. These twenty *area training organizations*, as they are now called, have been responsible, since the end of the Second World War, for conducting examinations and recommending students for qualified teacher status. It is within this broad administrative and organizational context that the descriptions of teacher education in England and Wales in succeeding sections must be understood. More recently the James Report has recognized the predominant role played by the universities in these area training organizations and has recommended the replacement of these latter by *regional councils for colleges and departments of education* which would have wider powers and broader membership including representation from central and local government, the Council for National Academic Awards and the Open University.[52]

In France there is no articulated system of teacher education; instead there are, it might be said, a variety of ways that intending teachers can converge on the profession. The most coherent educational programmes for the preparation of teachers exist at the two extremes of the educational system. The Napoleonic *écoles normales* and *écoles normales supérieures* prepare elementary and higher secondary teachers respectively. There is a gap between that reveals the widespread ambiguity about secondary education which is more pronounced in France and in Germany than in England.[53] Secondary education has been intellectually and socially exclusive in France to the extent that the model secondary teacher is not differentiated from the university teacher. He or she holds the *agrégation*, a diploma attesting high academic competence that is not concerned with teaching, knowledge of child psychology or with social skills. The fact that these latter qualities were and are prized in the *école normale* student, only reinforces the distinction between the elementary teacher, or *instituteur*, and the well qualified secondary *professeur*, despite the fact that they may teach in the same lower secondary school.

In Germany there are certain historical antecedents of the present system which have had a substantial influence in determining the present context. The first of these was the foundation by August Hermann Francke of two separate *Seminare* for the training of elementary and *Gymnasium* teachers in Halle in 1696. It has been argued[54] that this early development was of decisive importance in splitting the teaching profession in Germany. In the second place ecclesiastical control of academic secondary teachers was legally removed in 1810,[55] thus sparing this section of the teaching profession the social and educational odyssey that has been the lot of their elementary colleagues throughout the last century and a half.[56]

The third major historical event in defining the context of the present system was the reform which was introduced by Prussia in 1926 under its Minister of Education, Carl Heinrich Becker.[57] He was able in a short space of time, a time of great intellectual and political ferment in Germany, to build on the Spranger concept of a university-equivalent institution of teacher education (*Bildnerhochschule*)[58] and to develop, for probably the first time in Europe, elementary teacher education of full post-secondary standing in *pädagogische Akademien*.[59] A small group of other *Länder* at that time retained the traditional *Seminar* training, but this form of teacher education has now disappeared everywhere in West Germany. Another group transferred the training of elementary teachers to the university though without combining their training with that of other categories of teacher. This system, though abolished under the National Socialist regime, was reintroduced in the case of Hamburg in 1947,[60] and together with the Prussian solution, is of great importance because it is on the basis of these two models, each containing the separation of teachers into two groups, that post-war West German teacher education was developed.

The Three-Tier System of Teacher Education
The broader changes in the post-Second World War educational systems that were recapitulated in a previous section were only possible with the recruitment of large numbers of teachers to match expanding school enrolments. This expansion had a major consequence for teachers that affected the provision of teacher-education programmes. The presence in the schools of large numbers of adolescents who showed little interest in traditional secondary curricula meant quite new demands upon the teachers in terms of both personal education and professional preparation.[61] In fact, though not without earlier historical precedent, the dual systems have progressively evolved into a three-tier structure of teacher education, as an intermediate type of training and qualification has been strengthened or become available in all three countries. It is, of course, a simplification to characterize teacher education in the three countries in this way, when in fact there are a number of routes to qualification as a teacher in each of the three systems. On the other hand, it is sufficiently accurate to allow us to review the broad lines of the most recent developments in teacher education in relation to the terminal destination of the trainee: primary, lower or non-selective secondary, or academic secondary school. This scheme would need to be broadened to take account of the existence of separate facilities, which have been developing for some time, for the training of teachers for special and vocational schools. A greater diversification is probable in the future as institutions respond to a range of new career tasks for which personnel in the educational service will need to be trained and, no less significantly, retrained.

The Training of Primary Teachers. In the history of English teacher education an important role has been played from the beginning by the religious denominations. It was they who in the early 1840s founded the first formal institutions for the training of elementary teachers, and teacher-training colleges had been operational for half a century before the first public institution was opened in 1904.[62] In 1938 there were 29 public institutions run by the local education authorities and 54 voluntary colleges administered and financed by various religious bodies out of a combination of denominational and public funds. In 1970 there were 157 colleges: the local authorities having the major responsibility with 105 colleges, whilst those maintained by the voluntary bodies numbered 52.

Apart from this increase in the public interest in teacher education the main change in the institutions where almost all the primary teachers are now trained has been the growth in size and diversity of the individual colleges since 1960. It was in that year that the two-year certificate course was lengthened to three years and a decade of expansion of plant, personnel and academic and professional commitment began.[63] The total staff of these institutions was less than 1,000 at the outbreak of the Second World War but had risen to over 10,000 by the academic year 1969.[64] McNair saw the colleges' purpose as the provision of teachers for the elementary schools, but, by 1971, 50 per cent of their students were preparing to be secondary or junior/secondary teachers, and they were in addition providing roughly half of the places on the one-year training courses for graduates. Moreover many colleges now prepare for other professions, such as social and youth work, and more recent proposals for their future envisage for them functions similar to those of the American liberal arts college.[65]

Primary teachers in France are trained in the *écoles normales*, of which there is one for each sex in each of the *départements*. The basic *école normale* training is the teacher-preparation programme with the longest tradition in France. For decades these colleges have been respected as strongholds of the republican values of democratic patriotism and secularism.[66] But, anachronistically in the advanced western countries, the *école normale* course is not entirely post-secondary since it may include preparation for the *baccalauréat*. Prost describes acutely how social changes have led to current criticism and reappraisal of the *écoles normales*.[67] Before the advent of wider opportunities for secondary education, the state bursary for the *écoles normales* gave many students upper- and post-secondary training in return for a pledge to teach for ten years. The disputes in England about the *monotechnic* function of the colleges of education fade into insignificance beside the *école normale* system which, until recently, effectively placed a ceiling upon educational career opportunities for primary school teachers, offering them access only to the occupation of *instituteur* which was itself declining in prestige.

The post-secondary part of the *école normale* training lasts two years,[68] and includes the elements of personal education, professional training and teaching practice that are common to the primary teacher education programmes of England and West Germany. This course ends with an examination, the *certificat de fin d'études normaliennes*, and leads to the *certificat d'aptitude pédagogique* after a test of teaching performance during the first term of teaching. In 1967–8, however, there were only ninety-five teaching staff in the *écoles normales* who held appointments in the psychology of education (*psychopédagogie*), and none listed under any other human or behavioural science rubric.[69] This perhaps gives an indication of the bias of the French institutions. They are strongly affected by the academic culture of the *lycées* which is conveyed to them by the *agrégés de lettres* who form a substantial element (15–20 per cent) of their staff in spite of the fact that students are destined very largely for primary teaching. By no means all primary teachers receive this training, however. Over the past fifteen years a shortfall of trained recruits amounting to a third or more of the teaching vacancies has been made up by the appointment of unqualified personnel many of whom are able to qualify through experience. The proportion of unqualified *remplaçants* climbed to 15·8 per cent of the primary teaching force in 1961–2, but now represents probably not more than 5 per cent of teachers in permanent primary posts.[70] However, the available statistics do not reveal what proportion of primary teachers now teaching have obtained their qualification through formal training.

In most of the *Länder* of West Germany elementary school teachers are trained at *pädagogische Hochschulen* (colleges of education). These institutions contained some 69,000 students in the academic year 1969–70, roughly double the total of a decade previously. In some cases these institutions, as in Bremen, are autonomous. In others, as in North Rhine-Westphalia, they have been grouped to form university-equivalent institutions. In Bavaria and Hessen after a period of autonomy, they have been incorporated into the university system, in the latter case into development of *Gesamthochschulen* (comprehensive universities). There is yet another pattern in Hamburg where there has been a long and vigorous tradition of university preparation of teachers of all kinds, in which prospective elementary teachers are now enrolled as full members of the university attached to an institute of education. In all *Länder* the course lasts six semesters (three years) to the *first state examination*, after which there is a varying period of more or less formal preparation before the *second state examination* and final appointment as a permanent civil servant. The basis of entry to all these courses is now the *Abitur*, although a small proportion of the entrants in some *Länder* is made up of those who have had either an adequate general education or practical experience, and who in addition are able to pass a special examination. In general the course to the *first state examination* includes both theory and practice (except in Hamburg) and in some *Länder* it includes a *social practice*.[71] The theoretical elements within the course are usually the study of education and auxiliary disciplines including political education, the study of one or more main subjects and associated methodologies, and basic subjects which are usually treated from a didactic point of view with knowledge of subject-matter being largely presupposed. The examination at the end of the first phase usually includes theoretical and practical, oral and written sections. The period of the second phase of teacher education is of particular importance to our theme and is increasingly being formally organized and supervised as a *Referendariat* for elementary teachers.[72] After a varying period of time the young teacher may take his second teachers' examination including both theoretical and practical aspects and specialist subject and educational elements. On passing this examination, the teacher is appointed as a permanent civil servant.

The Training of Intermediate Teachers. Intermediate or lower secondary teachers have not formed as clearly indentifiable a category in England as in the other two countries. However, before the Second World War the English teacher-training colleges were providing almost all the staff for the upper sections of the elementary schools which took pupils up to the age of 14. With the reorganization of schools and salary structures after the 1944 Education Act, and the raising of the school-leaving age to 15 in 1947, this teaching force together with a small proportion of graduates was employed in the secondary modern schools. With the change of teaching commitment in these schools from class to subject teaching, the need rapidly arose for teachers to have a more extensive training than the two-year courses provided at that time, and gradually additional one-year specialist courses (wing courses) were instituted. Some of the teachers thus trained undertook grammar school teaching but most joined two-year-trained colleagues in secondary modern schools.

With the introduction of three-year courses in 1960 much greater emphasis was given to the study of one or two main teaching-subjects. Such courses began to erode the differences between the studies of student-teachers in colleges and courses taken by university undergraduates, and this in spite of the additional, professional commitments of the college student. It was in part in recognition of this fact that the Robbins Committee proposed the change in name from 'teacher-training college' to 'college of education'.[73] The colleges of education continued to supply the bulk of the staff for the secondary modern schools and for the lower and non-academic sections of comprehensive schools. This function was further strengthened when, with the introduction of the four-year Bachelor of Education (B.Ed.) degree for students in colleges from 1965, a further sub-categorization of the teaching profession took place. It is as yet early to say what role will be allocated in the teaching profession to these new graduates, but it is not unlikely that they will take the place of the products of specialist wing courses, although the original intention was that they would largely be recruited into the primary schools. The trend in appointments is increasingly disadvantageous to the two-year and three-year certificated teachers.

The major source of teachers for the first cycle of secondary education in France is from among the *instituteurs*. Just as the English colleges of education trained teachers for the senior elementary forms and then later for the secondary modern schools, so the *écoles normales* trained for the terminal classes in the elementary schools and, more recently, for the *collèges d'enseignement général* and for the less academic tracks of the *collèges d'enseignement secondaire*.[74] These teachers are known as *bivalent*, that is, as opposed to university trained teachers with a single specialist subject. University towns have centres, or sections in their *écoles normales*, where the *certificat d'aptitude pédagogique des collèges d'enseignement général* can be obtained. Candidates for this course could be students in initial training as primary teachers, students from university faculties or *instituteurs* with five years of teaching experience. The course is a three-year one with the normal three elements, except that the academic education of the students consists in following the first two years of university studies leading to the *diplôme universitaire d'études littéraires/scientifiques* (DUEL/S) with modification to allow them to take two main subjects. Obtaining this diploma also opens the way to taking a full degree course.

Another category of teacher of intermediate status in France is the teacher of the transitional classes (*classes de transition et pratiques terminales*). Some of the work of these teachers, who are concerned with the academically weakest pupils up to school-leaving age, would be described in other systems as remedial or compensatory. An innovatory training programme leading to a special *certificat d'aptitude professionnelle* has been established to train these teachers, who must have had five years' experience as *instituteurs*, but it has been functioning in only nine centres since 1966. The availability of both these courses has led to a drain upon the personnel of the primary schools. Berger has documented the widespread disillusionment of the *instituteurs*[75] and this has been historically accounted for by Prost.[76] Because of the reorganization and expansion to which the secondary schools have been subject, the process of assimilation, by which primary teachers get a foothold in the secondary schools, has gathered momentum. Given the latter's need, this development is hardly likely to be checked.

There are basically two ways of training to become a teacher in the intermediate schools in the *Länder* of West Germany, although of course the detailed organization and regulations are prescribed by the eleven educational authorities and thus vary from *Land* to *Land*. A certain uniformity was, however, introduced into the labyrinthine complexity of organization, regulation and prescription of the different *Länder* by the recommendations of the Permanent Conference of Ministers of Education of Feb. 17, 1953.[77] These proposed two basic ways of training to become an intermediate school teacher. The first route was via elementary school teacher training. After completion of the first and second examinations and at least three years' practice the teacher could apply for a course involving preparation in at least two specialist subjects (and in some *Länder* educational studies) in the teachers' colleges. The second recommended mode of entry was via the university, where the study of two specialist subjects for six semesters was followed by educational studies combined with practice teaching. This has in some cases been followed by a practical preparatory course of varying periods as in North Rhine-Westphalia and Bavaria. Increasingly, however, the category of intermediate teacher is being superseded and some *Länder* now have no intermediate teacher training, as they move towards a tripartite *grade-teacher* system of training.

The Training of Selective Secondary Teachers. In both England and France it has been quite common for secondary teachers, particularly the more prestigious, to receive no training as teachers. They gave evidence of knowing their academic field by obtaining a university degree and that was sufficient. But since 1890 in England there has been a system of training consisting of a one-year full-time course, now usually called the post-graduate certificate of education, which has been taken by a large proportion of entrants to secondary teaching at the end of their three-year degree course. This certificate has never had the status of a master's degree, but it was taken in a university department and offered a brief preparation for teaching. By 1969 there were thirty such university departments providing the one-year courses.

In an effort to shift the balance of trained non-graduate to trained graduate teachers, the DES has increased the availability of training at this level by approving one-year post-graduate courses in colleges of education and a few colleges of technology. In September 1971 there were sixty-nine colleges of education and seven technical colleges offering such courses. It has also been stipulated that new graduates entering teaching in primary schools from 1971 and in secondary schools from 1973 should have a teaching qualification. The post-graduate certificate courses have developed without the benefit of clearly defined aims or systematic critical study and research. Available courses tend to be encyclopaedic in character, with little correspondence between the course taken and the subsequent assignment of the teacher, which may be to a primary school, a secondary school, a sixth-form college, or to a college of further education. Even more striking is the lack of serious thought or practical attention that had until very recently been given to training for higher education and, in England, no teaching qualification is required for appointment to a university.

In France, the *agrégés*, who are required to undergo only four weeks of teaching practice as training for teaching, are still the élite of the secondary teachers. In increasing proportions, however, they aim at employment in higher education for which the *agrégation* remains a more important qualification than the ordinary doctorate. The major category of selective secondary teacher is the certificated graduate (*certifié*) who has worked beyond first degree level in his subject and undergone a one-year apprenticeship teaching practice under a tutor (*conseiller pédagogique*), but with scarcely any theoretical study in education. Before this system was instituted in 1952, most selective secondary teachers had no training whatsoever. The evidence is that there is something like a prejudice against the notion of training for teaching at this level of French education, since the structure exists on paper for a much more developed programme to be provided. University students wishing to become teachers can, following a competitive entry examination, enrol in an institute (*institut de préparation aux enseignements de second degré*), or an *école normale supérieure,* in which they receive a salary in return for a pledge to remain in the educational service for ten years from the date of their enrolment. The directors of the institutes may, entirely at their own discretion, require extra work or activities of their students, but this is not envisaged as training for teaching. The student teachers prepare for academic public examinations such as the theoretical part of the *certificat* or the *agrégation*. After obtaining the *licence*, whether he belongs to an institute or not, and passing the theoretical part of the *certificat*, the student-teacher continues to take courses in his discipline at the university and is attached for a year to a regional centre (*centre pédagogique régional*) at which he may follow some professionally–oriented lectures and seminars while engaged on his teaching apprenticeship. There is, however, no examination on any such work or on any aspect of pedagogical theory. The *certificat d'aptitude au professorat des enseignements de second degré* (CAPES, or CAPET with a technical bias) is awarded on the basis of both a theoretical examination in the specialist subject and a practical teaching test which is rarely failed. It should also be noted that during the mid-1960s a quarter of all the teaching staff of the *lycées* were unqualified, and the proportion rose to one-third among science teachers.[78]

In contrast there is a well-articulated and efficient system for training *Gymnasium* teachers in West Germany. The qualification for entry to training is the *Abitur* and students study for a minimum of eight semesters (four years) at a university or technical university (*Technische Hochschule*), though in practice the period is more usually six to seven years. Examinations in both the first and second phase of teacher education differ among the *Länder* but through a series of agreements of the Permanent Conference of Ministers of Education a broadly uniform framework has been introduced. Candidates usually select two academic subjects according to a list, and combinations are laid down in regulation and recommendation at *Land* and national level. All *Länder* require candidates to have passed a preliminary examination (*Philosophicum*) in philosophy and/or education, usually after the sixth semester, before presenting themselves for the *first state examination*.

In addition there is a requirement, except in Hamburg, that students will have completed some school–based experience, though this is not everywhere strictly enforced. On completing the first examination the candidate is appointed without salary, but with the status and subsistence allowance of a probationary civil servant, to a *Studien-* or *Anstaltsseminar* which is associated with a school. Here he has an opportunity to observe and teach a limited number of lessons under the supervision of members of staff, as well as undertaking regular courses and visits. At the end of this period of preparation, which has recently been reduced from two years to eighteen months, the candidate takes the *second state examination* or *pädagogische Prüfung* (educational examination) which includes both theoretical and practical tests and is assessed in a report from the Director of the *Studienseminar*. When he has passed the *second state examination* the young teacher receives a salary and later is appointed a permanent civil servant with the title of *Studienrat*. Teachers in higher education are recruited by a similar route, though they are usually able to study at university for a doctorate and, after a further period of research and work, they may present a thesis (*Habilitation*) for appointment in the first instance as a junior lecturer.

The Diversification of Teacher Education

Apart from the training of primary, intermediate and academic secondary teachers, which can be said to present a three-tier structure, there are contrasting patterns of provision for pre- and in-service training, which increasingly reflect the demands of different and more specialized roles in teaching. Public policies in the three countries have unevenly favoured these newer forms of work in accordance with perceived priorities. Moreover, apart from purely professional demands, there is an important career aspect to the efforts of teachers to improve their skills and widen their knowledge. In an occupation as diversified and stratified as teaching, many will be likely to feel that fate has placed them in the wrong category and that the acquisition of further qualifications will improve their situation. These kinds of motivation thus converge as demands for both the closer articulation of pre- and in-service training and for a diversification of provision at each level.

A description of teacher education in England must attempt to take account, however impressionistically, of a proliferation of courses in a variety of institutions. Seven of the thirty polytechnics originally established have education departments, providing in some cases overlapping provision with colleges and with departments in universities. The four technical colleges of education provide a one-year course of pre-service training which is mainly oriented to the needs of teachers in technical colleges and colleges of further education. These institutions also provide sandwich and other day-release courses for serving teachers, who are usually seconded to them by their local education authorities. [79] In 1970 there were thirteen institutions including universities, polytechnics and colleges of art where a one-year course of professional training was given to those with a graduate equivalent qualification in art and craft, and three institutions where those with a non-graduate art qualification could train professionally. Similar one-year courses of professional training are available to those with the same level of qualifications in such fields as handicraft, home economics, physical education and dance, music and business studies. Teachers working in schools for the physically and mentally handicapped require special preparation but their training is still very largely post-experience and on the job. In addition, colleges and university institutes are increasingly providing initial and in-service courses which prepare for such dual professions as teacher-counsellor, teacher-youth leader and teacher-social worker. Moreover, with the introduction of main courses in sociology and other social science areas, some colleges of education are now preparing to train for professions other than teaching. It is likely that this tendency will continue in order to help staff the new professions developing in education and the social services.

Any contemporary project to effect changes in education as a matter of public policy must at the same time be thought of as implying and requiring an evolution in the attitudes and activity of the teachers in the schools. There are many ways that teachers can become connected to the network of educational change and develop new aims and methods in their work. In-service training courses of varying lengths are offered by the universities and colleges of education, by the Department of Education and Science, by the local education authorities and by many other bodies; and degree courses provided by the Open University, including educational studies, were nationally available from January 1972. More informal professional exchange of ideas is possible at many levels, for example through local teachers' centres at which staff from different schools can meet and pursue their common interests.

Technical and vocational education are now available only from the second cycle or upper secondary level in French education. Under present arrangements, the teachers for the *collèges d'enseignement technique* (CET; short vocational courses) are trained at one of the five *écoles normales nationales d'apprentissage* for one year, the teachers for the *lycées techniques* (long technical and vocational courses) are trained at the *école normale supérieure de l'enseignement technique* for four years. The first course is thus within the category that prepares for what we have described as non-selective secondary education, while the second prepares for the selective secondary type, and in fact leads to the examination for the CAPET and to the *agrégation*. There is also a procedure at both of these levels by which teachers of needed subjects or practical experience are recruited direct from active employment in industry or elsewhere and provided with a one-year conversion course for teaching. A third of the teachers in the CETs were unqualified in 1965 and, of all those employed in the state schools, these teachers were in shortest supply.[80] A wide variety of specialized certificates can also be prepared for in the fields of art, music, physical education and other areas as in England. Training programmes are in prospect for teachers taking various responsibilities of a pastoral nature in the school system, such as school counsellors and educational psychologists, but it seems likely that the range of such services will be greatly extended as a complement to, rather than as a substitute for the development of general teacher training. They will, in other words, be developed through the post-experience training of teachers. It also seems likely that the new *unités d'enseignement et de recherche* (UERS), or departments, of educational sciences in some of the universities will contribute to establishing these new teacher roles.

Among the largest initiatives in in-service training has been the *Université Pédagogique de l'Eté*, which stems from the Catholic Institute of Paris, and which has enrolled several hundred teachers in its three-week summer sessions.[81] Overall, it is distinctively the private sector in France that affords the opportunity to teachers to develop their educational interests. With respect, however, to career-motivated in-service training, it is the public authorities who provide the *instituteurs* with the opportunity to undertake courses in the *écoles normales* to prepare their *certificats d'aptitude pédagogique*. But it is in the field of educational administration that France offers the most impressive achievement. The *Institut National d'Administration Scolaire et Universitaire* (INAS) has been offering courses for several years to headmasters and others in administrative posts in education on all aspects of their work except the pedagogical.[82] The methods used by INAS, particularly the techniques of group dynamics, appear to be finding a pedagogical application only through the efforts of academic and private organizations and associations which have virtually no equivalent in England and Germany.

The system of teacher education for those who will pursue careers in vocational and technical schools in West Germany is well established and defined. Entry to training for this segment of the teaching profession is usually built on the secondary graduation certificate (*Abitur*) and twelve months' practical work experience, and the duration is four and a half to six years at general or technological universities. As with the grammar school teachers, there are two examinations separated by a period of probationary service (*Referendariat*). In addition to this category of vocational teacher there are also teachers of practical work. These are usually trained foremen or technicians who may sometimes receive an additional one or two years of pedagogical training.

Special arrangements exist for teachers of art and music and for teachers of domestic science and PE who are usually trained at university-equivalent colleges. Qualified elementary teachers may undertake a further one to two years training at specific institutions in order to become teachers in special schools. They are usually seconded on full salary and complete their course by taking the special school teacher examination. In 1964 only just over half of the teachers in special schools had this qualification.[83]

In contrast to the first and second phases of teacher education in West Germany, in-service provision, though extending and improving, remains relatively embryonic. It recommended at the end of the Second World War on the basis of voluntary effort by teachers and teachers' associations, though particularly effective in-service provision was established from 1951 through the co-operation of teachers and the Ministry of Education in the *Hessischer Lehrerfortbildungswerk* (Hessen In-Service Work). All *Länder* now organize in-service training (*Lehrerfortbildung*) in order to help the teacher keep up to date or to provide conversion courses for teachers of special subjects in short supply. In-service training is provided by the education authorities through specialized institutions (*Institute für Lehrerfortbildung*), by the teacher organizations and by the Catholic Church. Courses are usually free and teachers can be released during school time to attend them. Some teachers may be seconded on full salary to research institutes, such as the *Deutsches Institut für Internationale Pädagogische Forschung* (German Institute for International Educational Research), but in none of these is attendance required. Only in relatively few instances does it result directly in any financial or career advantage where it may be a pre-condition to taking up a different post. In this case it is usually described as *Lehrerweiterbildung*. Provision has accelerated recently with growth of the *Hauptschule* and in particular the curricular and organizational demands of the increasing numbers of comprehensive schools, but the diffusion of innovations in German education may be complicated and inhibited by the as yet relatively underdeveloped and inadequate system of in-service provision.

There has been a correspondence between the shape of public education in the three countries and the systems by which teachers have been recruited and trained. Successive developments of the school systems towards a longer secondary education for all, a strengthened middle phase of lower secondary (as distinct from higher primary) education, the expansion of upper secondary education to accommodate a massive flow into the universities, and the development of a range of new functions for teachers in academic and pastoral roles have all induced changes in teacher training. However, in spite of a common movement towards the democratization of education, it can scarcely be said that distinctions between teachers, in terms of a dual system, or rather the three-tier structure we suggest, are disappearing. The specific objective of professional unification has been actively sought by some teachers in all the countries, but these same aspirations must be viewed in the perspective of other changes that could as well be argued to be tending in an opposite direction, towards a new differentiation of teachers on the basis of the balance of their commitment, for example, to social or academic work in the schools. This balance may well relate fairly closely to the teacher's span of responsibility with the pupil age-range.

Such potential conflicts in the teacher's role must be the starting-point for any further understanding of the evolution and reform of teacher education. The institutions of teacher education in England, France and West Germany may not have shown the same responsiveness to social change as other social institutions, such as the mass media and certain areas of government. Some undoubtedly regard this as a measure of the cultural limitations of these institutions, and therefore of the training that they can hope to offer to future teachers. But in so far as they have not adjusted to newer social pressures it could also be argued that the function of teacher training and of other educational institutions is to build a bridge between tradition and modernity by making a continuous and considered response to social change. However different the detailed prescriptions for the reform of teacher education to which these commitments have given rise, the logic of both sets of assumptions confirms the need for efficient means by which issues concerning reforms in the social process, curricula and organization of teacher education can be identified, raised and resolved.

REFERENCES

1   There appear to be two main issues, with the Government seeking to protect its investment in higher education through the University Grants Committee and, on the other hand, the challenge to the privilege of the universities from the non-university sector. See ROBINSON, E., *The New Polytechnics* (London: Cornmarket, 1968).

2   *The 1944 Education Act* (London: HMSO, 1944).

3   For details of these three reports set in historical context, see CURTIS, S. J., *History of Education in Great Britain* (London: University Tutorial Press, 1967).

4   Ministry of Education, *The New Secondary Education* (Pamphlet 9) (London: HMSO, 1947).

5   Ministry of Education, *Secondary Education in each Local Education Authority Area* (London: HMSO, 1964).

6   Secondary Schools Examination Council, *Curriculum and Examinations in Secondary Schools* (Norwood Report) (London: HMSO, 1943), p. 139.

7   In all of these schemes the technical schools were never more than a few hundred. For an overview of their development see REESE-EDWARDS, K. H. R., *The Secondary Technical School* (London: University of London Press, 1960).

8   National Foundation for Educational Research, *Procedures for the Allocation of Pupils in Secondary Education* (London: NFER, 1963), pp. 3 ff.

9   Ministry of Education, *Secondary Education for all: A New Drive* (London: HMSO, 1958).

10 Department of Education and Science, *The Organization of Secondary Education* (Circular 10/65) (London: HMSO, 1965).

11 *The 1964 Education Act* (London: HMSO, 1964).

12 Ten days after assuming office as the new Secretary of State for Education and Science Mrs Margaret Thatcher cancelled circular 10/65 and issued her own instructions. See Department of Education and Science, *The Organization of Secondary Education* (Circular 10/70) (London: HMSO, 1970).

13 BENN, C., *Comprehensive Schools in 1972: Reorganization Plans to 1975* (London: Comprehensive Schools Committee, 1972).

14 The fourteen regional Examination Boards that conduct the Certificate of Secondary Education examination employ a system of subject panels which construct syllabuses themselves or accept proposals for syllabuses direct from schools. These panels are largely composed of practising teachers. A recent Schools Council document draws an interesting distinction between teacher participation and teacher control. See Schools Council, *A Common System of Examining at 16+* (Examinations Bulletin 23) (London: Evans/Methuen, 1971), pp. 15 ff.

15 MINOT, J., *L'Administration de l'Education Nationale* (Paris: Institut Pédagogique National, 1964).

16 *Loi d'Orientation de l'Enseignement Supérieur*, Nov 7, 1968.

17 An interesting account of how these changes affected the administration of a school is provided by MALLERIN, R., 'Témoignage d'un Proviseur', *Cahiers Pédagogiques*, no. 85, Nov. 1969.

18 *Décret,* of Jan. 6, 1959.

19 *Décret,* of Aug. 3, 1963.

20 See *Cinquième Plan de Développement Economique et Social* (1966–70) (Paris: Imprimérie des Journaux Officiels, 1965), vol. 2, p. 256.

21 Among the French educationalists who have discussed this question is Majault. See MAJAULT, J., *La Révolution de l'Enseignement* (Paris: R. Laffont, 1967), pp. 160–1.

22 The Weimar Constitution envisaged a common pattern of teacher education, but the relevant articles were never given effect. For example Article 143, paragraph two declared: 'Teacher education . . . to be unified

throughout the realm on the same principles as applied generally to higher education'. Translation taken from HILKER, F., 'Organization and Structure of Teacher Education in the German Federal Republic', *Year Book of Education 1963* (London: Evans Bros., 1963).

23 One indication of this greater concern was the report presented by the Federal Government to the Bundestag in October 1967. See Bundesminister des Innern, *Bericht über den Stand der Massnahmen auf dem Gebiet der Bildungsplanung* (Deutscher Bundestag, 5 Wahlperiode, Drucksache V/2166) (Bonn: Oct. 1967).

24 Among other bodies which have encouraged the development of a broad similarity of provision are the German Committee for Education (*Deutscher Ausschuss für das Erziehungs- und Bildungswesen*) 1953–65, the Science Council (*Wissenschaftsrat*) from 1957, the German Council for Education (*Deutscher Bildungsrat*) established in 1965, and the Commission for Educational Planning (*Bund-Länder-Kommission für Bildungsplanung*) which dates from June 1970. In addition there are a number of agreements between the *Länder* on educational matters.

25 All covered in German by the generic term *Hochschule*.

26 Deutscher Bildungsrat, *Empfehlungen der Bildungskommission zur Einrichtung von Schulversuchen mit Gesamtschulen* (Bonn: 1969).

27 Deutscher Bildungsrat, *Empfehlungen der Bildungskommission – Strukturplan fur das Bildungswesen* (Bonn: 1970).

28 Der Bundesminister für Bildung und Wissenschaft, *Bildungsbericht 1970: Bericht der Bundesregierung zur Bildungspolitik* (Bonn: 1970). This Report was first published as *Bundestagsdrucksache VI/925* (Bonn-Bad Godesberg: Verlag Dr Heger, 1970).

29 Deutscher Bildungsrat, *Empfehlungen der Bildungskommission zur Neugestaltung der Abschlüsse im Sekundarschulwesen* (Bonn: 1969).

30 See LYNCH, J. 'West German Curriculum Construction', *Trends in Education*, no. 18, April 1970, pp. 18–21.

31 ANDERSON, C. A., 'Dilemmas of Talent-Centred Educational Programmes: USA, *Year Book of Education, 1962* (London: Evans Bros., 1962), pp. 445 ff.

32 See Organization for Economic Co-operation and Development, Centre for Educational Research and Innovation, *Equal Educational Opportunity: A Statement of the Problem with Regard to Recurrent Education* (Paris: OECD, CERI, 1971).

33 Although even during the war several underground groups such as the *Kreisauer Kreis* had begun the discussion of post-war educational reforms. See ROON, G. van, *Neuordnung im Widerstand* (Munich: R. Oldenbourg Verlag, 1967).

34 Board of Education, *Education after the War* (The Green Book) (London: Board of Education, 1941).

35 Commission Ministérielle d'Etude (Langevin-Wallon Commission), 'La Réforme de l'Enseignement', reprinted in *Le Plan Langevin-Wallon de Réforme de l'Enseignement* (Paris: Presses Universitaires de France, 1964).

36 TAWNEY, R. H., *Secondary Education for All* (London: Allen and Unwin, 1922).

37 In 1924 the French Minister of Public Instruction established a 'Commission de l'Ecole Unique'. For the context and sequel to this, see PROST, A., *L'Enseignement en France*: 1800–1967 (Paris: A. Colin, 1968), pp. 407 ff.

38 For an interesting chronological account of the process of integration and

differentiation in the development of German education, see SIEN-KNECHT, H., *Der Einheitsschulgedanke: geschichtliche Entwicklung und gegenwärtige Problematik* (Weinheim: Verlag Julius Beltz, 1968). At its Whit conference in 1914 the German Teachers Association had already unanimously demanded the introduction of a national comprehensive school. See TEWS, J., *Die deutsche Einheitsschule* (Leipzig: Julius Klinkhardt Verlagsbuchhandlung, 1919).

39　The 'reproduction' concept of which we have made extensive use in this study, is derived from BOURDIEU, P., and PASSERON, J. C., *La Reproduction: Eléments pour une Théorie du Système d'Enseignement* (Paris: Ed. de Minuit, 1970).

40　Organization for Economic Co-operation and Development, *Science, Growth and Society: a new Perspective* (Paris: OECD, 1971).

41　TURNER, R. H., 'Modes of Social Ascent through Education: Sponsored and Contest Mobility', *American Sociological Review*, XXV: 5, 1960, pp. 855–67.

42　A survey carried out for the French National Commission for UNESCO, although methodologically inadequate, clearly reflects the bitter discouragement of French teachers in a range of teaching situations. See MOLLO, S., *et al.* 'La Représentation de la Condition du Maître dans la Société', *Enfance*, April–Sept. 1966, pp. 1–64.

43　See, for example, LADERRIÈRE, P., 'Regional Inequalities of Opportunity in French Education and the Measures designed to reduce them', in OECD, Study Group in the Economics of Education, *Social Objectives in Educational Planning* (Paris: OECD, 1967), pp. 253 ff. and also GIRARD, A., 'Selection for Secondary Education in France', in HALSEY, A. H. FLOUD, J., and ANDERSON, C. A., *Education, Economy and Society* (New York: The Free Press, 1965), pp. 183 ff.

44　Deutscher Ausschuss für das Erziehungs– und Bildungswesens, *Rahmenplan zur Umgestaltung und Vereinheitlichung des allgemeinbildenden öffentlichen Schulwesens* (Stuttgart: Ernst Klett Verlag, 1959). The novelty of this plan may be gauged from ROBINSOHN, S. B. AND KÜHLMANN, J. C. 'Two Decades of Non-Reform in West German Education', *Comparative Education Review*, XI: Oct. 1, 1967, pp. 311–30.

45　The more important reactions to this plan were collected together and published by Karl Bungardt as *Der Bremer Plan im Streit der Meinungen* (Frankfurt/Main: Arbeitsgemeinschaft deutscher Lehrerverbände, 1962).

46　In 1968 a report on the first ten years' work of the Science Council was published, which includes a list of its recommendations. Deutscher Wissenschaftsrat, *Wissenschaftsrat 1957–1967* (Bonn: Bundesdruckerei, 1968).

47　Amongst the earliest and most influential of these was PICHT, G., *Die deutsche Bildungskatastrophe* (Freiburg: Walter Verlag, 1964).

48　A select bibliography on the theme of more recent curriculum reform can be found in der Hessische Kultusminister, 'Diskussionsentwurf zur Neuordnung der Lehrerausbildung', *Bildungspolitische Informationen*, 1A/71, pp. 84–86.

49　An overview of comprehensive schools in The Federal Republic in the academic year 1971–72 is contained in *Gesamtschulinformationen*, 4, 1971, pp. 5–12. This bulletin is published by Pädagogisches Zentrum, Berlin.

50　Schools Council, *Proposals for the Curriculum and Examinations in the Sixth Form* (A joint statement by the Standing Conference on University Entrance and the Schools Council Joint Working Party on Sixth Form

Curriculum and Examinations and the Schools Council's Second Working Party on the Sixth Form Curriculum and Examinations) (London: the Joint Working Party, 1969, mimeo.).

51 The McNair Report was a major report on teacher education in England. See Board of Education, *Teachers and Youth Leaders* (London: HMSO, 1944), p. 11.

52 Department of Education and Science (1972), *op. cit.*, chap. 5.

53 The educational problems posed by this divided nature of secondary education had long been pointed out. For example, see DURKHEIM E., *L'Evolution Pédagogique en France* (Paris: Presses Universitaires de France, 1969), p. 13 (material first given as a lecture in 1904–5).

54 LIPPERT, E., 'Geschichte der deutschen Lehrerbildung und der deutschen Einheitsschule', *die Pädagogische Provinz* (Sonderdruck), 1947, p. 30.

55 See SPRANGER, E., *Wilhelm von Humboldt und die Reform des Bildungswesens* (Berlin: 1910, reprinted Tübingen: Max Niemeyer Verlag, 1960).

56 BUNGARDT, K., *Die Odysee der Lehrerschaft: Sozialgeschichte eines Standes* (Hannover: Schroedel Verlag, 1965).

57 BECKER, C. H., *Die Pädagogische Akademie im Aufbau unseres nationalen Bildungswesens* (Leipzig: Verlag Quelle und Meyer, 1926).

58 SPRANGER, E., *Gedanken über Lehrerbildung* (Leipzig: Verlag Quelle und Meyer, 1920).

59 A full account of the rise and fall of these institutions has been provided in KITTEL, H., *Die Entwicklung der Pädagogischen Hochschulen* (Hannover: Schroedel Verlag, 1957).

60 For an overview of the differing provision of elementary teacher education in the *Länder* of the Weimar Republic, see ZIEROLD, K., and ROTH-KUGEL, P., *Die Pädagogischen Akademien: Amtliche Bestimmungen* (Berlin: Weidmannsche Buchhandlung, 1931).

61 A clear statement of this point of view was made in the Newsom Report in England. See Central Advisory Council for Education (England) *Half Our Future* (London, HMSO, 1963).

62 See RICH, R. W., *The Training of Teachers in England and Wales in the Nineteenth Century* (Cambridge: Cambridge University Press, 1933) for a historical account of the development of the English training colleges.

63 A recent general treatment of teacher education in England of an empirical sociological character can be regarded as background reading for the English elements in this study. See TAYLOR, W., *Society and the Education of Teachers* (London: Faber and Faber, 1969).

64 In October 1970, there were 10,367 staff in the colleges of education which contained 107,315 students. Department of Education and Science, *Statistics of Education 1970* (London: HMSO, 1972), vol. 4, p. 1.

65 Association of Teachers in Colleges and Departments of Education, *Higher Education and Preparation for Teaching: A Policy for Colleges of Education* (London: ATCDE, 1970).

66 Prost, *op. cit.*, p. 447.

67 *Ibid*, chap. 18: 'L'Explosion Scolaire et l'Ebranlement de la Société Enseignante'.

68 The most thorough account of the organization of teacher education in France is contained in a broader review of supply and demand factors relating to teaching personnel. See: Organization for Economic Co-operation and Development, Directorate for Scientific Affairs, *Study on Teachers: France – Ireland* (Paris: OECD, 1969).

69 Ministère de l'Education Nationale, Service Central des Statistiques et de la Conjoncture, *Statistiques des Enseignements* (Paris: Institut Pédagogique National, 1969), part 3. 1.

70 OECD (1969), *op. cit.*, p. 74.

71 A useful account of one such arrangement is given in GRANT, J. J., 'A Social Practice in the Training of Teachers', *Education for Teaching*, no. 74, pp. 19–24, Autumn 1967.

72 At the time of writing this was so in Hamburg and North Rhine-Westphalia. However the Permanent Conference of Ministers of Education had already recommended a generalization of this practice. See *Pressemitteilung aus Anlass der 140. Plenarsitzung der Ständigen Konferenz der Kultusminister der Länder in der Bundesrepublik Deutschland vom 10/11 Dezember, 1970 in Bonn*. (Press release issued Dec. 14, 1970 by the Permanent Conference of Ministers of Education.)

73 Committee on Higher Education, *Higher Education* (Robbins Report) (London: HMSO, 1963), para. 351.

74 HALLS, W. D., *Society, Schools and Progress in France* (Oxford: Pergamon Press, 1965) provides a useful general description of the French educational system, including the main features of teacher education.

75 BERGER, I., and BENJAMIN, R., *L'Univers des Instituteurs* (Paris: Editions de Minuit, 1964).

76 Prost, *op. cit.*

77 The development and organization of intermediate school teacher training in West Germany is described in DERBALOV, J. *Die Realschullehrerbildung in der Bundesrepublik* (Auswahl Reihe B., Nr. 10) (Hanover: Hermann Schroedel Verlag, 1970).

78 OECD (1969), *op. cit.*, p. 79.

79 Department of Education and Science, *Reports on Education 55: Counting School Teachers* (London: HMSO, 1969), p. 2 and Department of Education and Science (1971), *op. cit.*, p. 1.

80 OECD (1969), *op. cit.*, p. 71.

81 These sessions have been staffed by the personnel of both public and private institutions, and their programmes have been original and far-ranging.

82 The scope of the work of INAS is reflected in its quarterly bulletin *Education et Gestion*.

83 Ständige Konferenz der Kultusminister der Länder in der Bundesrepublik Deutschland, *Lehrerbestand und Lehrerbedarf: III Lehrernachwuchs* (Bonn: Sekretariat der Ständigen Konferenz, 1967), p. 101.

Chapter Two

The Analysis of Issues in Teacher Education

COMPARATIVE SOCIOLOGY OF EDUCATION

The first chapter presented an overview of teacher education as it has developed within the educational and socio-cultural contexts of England, France and West Germany. The shortcomings of such descriptions arise from the fact that observers from differing cultural standpoints will have different perceptions of the social reality of teacher education or of any other social systems. In a sense, the same social reality is open to investigation from a philosophical, historical or sociological perspective, but it is nevertheless true that the descriptive and analytical categories that we use help to select and shape the evidence we have to adduce. There is no escape from this reductionist effect when we seek to conceptualize and understand social phenomena. The compensation that we obtain in adopting a comparative sociological approach, however, is two-fold. By stating clearly at the outset that we wish to consider teacher education as a feature of the total educational system and of a broader society and culture, we can hope to develop a theoretical framework that will ensure the marshalling of compatible forms of evidence, both internally and cross-culturally. And, secondly, by defining teacher education sociologically, that is in terms of cultural values, social structures and social processes, we can aim to arrive at some measure of understanding of the dynamics of teacher-education systems in the form of both empirically and intuitively verifiable hypotheses.

Unless we believe that educational systems are socially autonomous we are obliged to search for a broadly based analytical approach rather than one that deals with established institutions and organizational procedures. In the remainder of this study we seek to go beyond the interwoven description of institutions, in which correspondences of aims and functions are assumed, and instead attempt to identify underlying cultural and structural issues. This chapter will be devoted to laying the conceptual groundwork upon which the sociological study presented in Part Two will be based. The purpose is essentially to develop a mode of analysis that is independent of any particular educational system, and which thus permits comparative study. By such means we may be led to recognize significant parallels or contrasts at a cross-cultural level between types of courses, curricula, organizations and procedures. There is, for instance, a sense in which the process of teacher socialization, if not of teacher education in a formal sense, begins in France at the secondary school level in the *école normale d'instituteurs* whereas in the other two countries the process is entirely post-secondary. It may be supposed that the French retention of the phrase *élève maître* (*pupil*-teacher) to describe these students for as long as they remain at the *école normale* implies a distinctive conception of their role. These facts, and their sociological interpretation, could lead us to expect, in the French case, contrasting patterns of recruitment and retention of primary teachers.

A balanced comparative analysis would need to approach data and issues in both sociological and historical perspectives. Even such apparently well-defined matters as the potential of teacher-aides, the demand for more effective basic training in the teaching of reading and the provision of more extensive opportunities to work with audio-visual aids pose problems of organization and priorities that blur separate discussion. The case is even more patent with socially and philosophically more abstract issues such as the formulation of professionally relevant curricula, considered across three societies or more. A comparative approach is therefore not solely concerned with resemblances in the appearance of particular educational structures or issues. The most useful characteristic of the approach may in fact lie in the way that it can help to identify idiosyncratic elements that emerge in the statement of problems, as a result of the independent aetiologies of apparently matching issues in different cultural and political contexts.

The problem is one of identifying the issues within an economical classificatory scheme which will indicate both common and distinct features in different societies. By means of such a scheme, parallel trends and configurations of characteristics could be discerned which, when considered in relation to particular problems, might help to reveal the degree of salience of the issue in a particular society, and the broader implications and repercussions that the raising of the issue involves. Many writers in the field of comparative education have pointed to the need for the development and testing of such conceptual schemes as a prerequisite to meaningful comparison.[1] However, such proposals for the utilization of models and typologies of sociological theory in cross-cultural studies of education have to be considered in the perspective of an extensive literature based upon an historical approach, at least in European writings.[2] If the complementary nature of sociological and historical approaches is to be explored, a contempory requirement is the further development and application of a comparative sociology of education.

TEACHER EDUCATION IN SOCIOLOGICAL PERSPECTIVE

Up to this point the systems of teacher education have been reviewed largely in terms of their own explicit rationales. The development of courses and institutions was taken at face value, as though ordered by a series of conscious choices. This view of teacher education has now to be placed in a sociological perspective. No sequence of social events can be fully apprehended by analysis from, as it were, the *inside*. Teacher education not only functions to produce teachers but, as a set of processes and institutions, reflects a mass of cultural and structural features both of the educational system to which it is most immediately linked and of the wider society and economy to which it owes its existence.

The relationships that can be discerned between the evolution of teacher education and the formal educational tradition and practice of society have been outlined in Chapter One and will not receive special emphasis here. It is however salutary to recognize that teacher education cannot adopt goals or methods that are contrary to those of the wider educational system. Teacher educators understand very well that their work is constantly subject to evaluation by those who control the schools and that they can do little themselves to change the schools. We shall refer later to the evidence that indicates that newly trained teachers tend to affirm their adherence to the educational values of their teacher colleagues, despite their awareness of alternative philosophies of education represented in the teachers' colleges.

More important by far, and central to our own analysis, are the relationships linking teacher education to the extra-scholastic society, even though many of these relationships are mediated by the school system. However obvious it may be, it is worth pondering that the existence of a teacher-education system and of the school system reflects the will of a political community to perpetuate itself. Even if at the individual level a teacher may question whether he is mainly concerned with transmitting a heritage of values and knowledge or with helping to create a future society that improves upon the present one, it is clear that schools operate first and foremost in the interests of established society. We cannot therefore expect to understand educational policies and their formulation unless we are taking account of the structure of the distribution of power in the wider society.

Another way of expressing the same idea is to say that teachers and educational policy-makers do not hold values or possess interpretations of society and of their own roles in society independently of the positions they themselves occupy in the social structure. A view of society can be better understood in terms of the beliefs, ideologies and values characteristic of a social group that holds this view, such as an occupational group or social class, than in terms of the social categories that the group employs. Hypotheses such as these, derived from the sociology of knowledge,[3] lead us on to questions about the aims and organization of teacher-education institutions and curricula, as well as about their procedures for selection, training, assessment and evaluation. Such features can be understood as social facts reflecting each other and dependent in turn upon broader social and economic values, structures and processes, such as economic development and social stratification, competition or conflict. But this perspective still obliges us to consider the critical operational questions as to how transformations occur between the culture and social structure of a society, and the values and institutions of its education or teacher education systems.

Some important hypotheses concerning these transformational processes are developed by Bourdieu. He understands the school to be the vehicle charged with transmitting the elements of the possessed culture to the oncoming generation.[4] This Durkheimian thesis is developed with a more acute sense of how a culture may in fact be apprehended. Durkheim's 'elementary forms' pertained essentially to religious cosmologies,[5] while for Bourdieu culture has its elementary forms which are symbiotic with a social structure and generalized through the social and intellectual routines of schooling. He focuses not upon the explicit product of ways of thought, but upon thought-processes themselves as they become internalized in a particular culture by being transmitted through the school and are enabled to reinforce the culture. In calling for comparative studies of curricula, teaching methods and of what he calls the ecological conditions of teaching, he instances how at least French schools act to reproduce the master-patterns of the culture of the society's dominant classes, while at the same time they succeed in legitimating in the value systems of virtually all pupils the high status of that culture.[6]

Before an analysis of teacher education can be pursued a sociological definition of teacher education will be needed. All the caveats entered earlier about the problem of conceptualization of complex social phenomena apply, but a deliberate conceptual scheme is still preferable to unacknowledged assumptions and unrelated assertions about the social or economic significance of one or other policy issue in teacher education. Too frequently such issues have been raised as isolated comments or criticisms whose impact has quickly been absorbed. On the other hand, the tendency to place responsibility or blame on the teachers' colleges of the three societies has led to the accumulation of a mass of unassimilated arguments. There has been an exaggerated concern for the administrative details of teacher education, as though history, culture and politics did not exist. An adequate study of teacher education must include such a societal perspective.

In the sociological approach adopted here teacher education is seen as presenting four major facets for study as follows:

(a) Teacher education is intended to bring about certain types and qualities of behaviour. Teachers, as the appliers of professional knowledge in education, either do certain things or are expected to do them. We may refer to the cultural values underlying teacher education as teacher role-expectations or, more simply, *perceptions of teaching*.

(b) The process by which these role-expectations are conveyed to teachers or student-teachers, and the progressive stages of change in attitudes and behaviour that result, whether at initial or in-service training levels, can be referred to as teacher socialization, or *the process of becoming a teacher*.

(c) The precise means by which it is intended that professional skills should develop are *the curriculum and teaching methods* employed in teacher education.

(d) The setting of the conditions, the provision of opportunities and the way in which the larger society intervenes may be called *the organization of teacher education*.

The four elements of this conceptual scheme provide a sociological definition of teacher education. This definition will be amplified in the following section of the chapter and then the analytical approach to be employed in Part Two of the study will be outlined.

Perceptions of Teaching

Teacher education is a semi-deliberate, semi-traditional activity within which a wide variety of theoretical cross-currents and experiments co-exist. The criteria for teacher education are largely intuitive distillations of common expectations within a culture about what teachers are and what they should do. It does not advance us far to say that the general purpose of teacher education is to enable teachers to develop the skills and qualities that will increase their professional effectiveness, but this does point us towards fundamental questions about the aims of the educational system. These aims are rarely explicit in any detail or, if they are, they are more likely to be prescriptive than operational principles. That is, the more specific the aims cited, the more likely it is that they represent the sectional aspirations of an ideologically committed group, rather than a national consensus.

Our starting-point is the contemporary discussion about the purpose of formal education, commenced in Chapter One, and the implications or explications of the purposes of teacher education. Stated in operational terms, the problem becomes that of accounting for perceptions of and expectations for the teacher's role, that is the tasks that are ascribed to the teacher in terms of the norms and values of the educational system and the broader culture that it serves. By means of this approach it will be possible to identify criteria for the appraisal of teacher education. The definition of these criteria remains controversial in many countries, and certainly in the three with which we are concerned, reflecting the conflicting values of such groups as the churches, political parties, professional and other organizations. In the three countries numerous educational reports and conferences have outlined the types and qualities of behaviour of teachers that have seemed, on their particular assumptions, to be desirable. And, inevitably, each of the school reforms described in Chapter One has within it the seeds of expanded or altered teacher role-expectations.

The different teacher recruitment routes which we have described lead by convention to careers in different types and levels of schools, and though it is not clear *a priori* that the profession in the three countries needs to be structured in this way, there are certain in-built assumptions as to the correspondence between traditional sets of role-expectations and particular forms of training. In all three societies the training at college of education, *école normale* or *pädagogische Hochschule* level, which contains the greatest amount of pedagogical and academic study of education, is taken as appropriate to work in primary schools and with academically less able or less motivated pupils in secondary schools. On the other hand, those who have been trained at university have been expected to be concerned with knowledge or subject-matter, often, as in France in the case of the *agrégation*, to the exclusion of any programme of pedagogical or professional preparation. They are normally thought prepared for teaching older pupils and on the first rung of the school's administrative hierarchy. This stereotype based on the *dual system*[7] may be called in question to some extent by such innovations as the B.Ed. in England or the development of the *Stufenlehrer* system in Germany.[8] Less exclusive attitudes may be fostered by the introduction of comprehensive provision at least in lower secondary education, but changes in training courses could be impeded by the rigidity of professional status categories which has existed in France and Germany, where teachers are civil servants. It could even be argued that in all three countries the degree/non-degree watershed is becoming more marked in practice as the older generation of non-graduate teachers retires and amalgamation of school-types places graduate and non-graduate teachers in competition for promotion. This competition somewhat paradoxically tends to assign the greater opportunities to the professionally less-trained categories on account of their graduate status.

Undoubtedly there is no simple solution to the conflict of role-expectations inherent in this situation. More generally we may contrast the specialization and professionalization of teaching, which follow a general trend in occupations in modern society, with the conception of teaching as a job which makes diffuse demands that tend always to amateurize the profession. Clearly there are pressures and advocates both within the profession and outside of it that would reinforce immobilist traits in the structures and conventions of teacher education. One would expect, for example, that the selective secondary school and subject specialist associations in the three countries might by and large adopt such positions. But do they effectively embody and disseminate attitudes to knowledge and to social values that constitute criteria for teacher roles? To what extent do they think in terms of bodies of knowledge that are available only to individuals with exceptional qualities of mind? Are they people who see academic training as the main aim of education? On the other hand, there will always be those in any society who, responding as Wilson has expressed it to the 'spirit of heresy',[9] will stress the view that knowledge is tentative and constantly subject to revision. They will exhibit a distrust for systems of compartmentalization in learning or for notions of social and intellectual types amongst learners. But what influence can be ascribed to these less traditional attitudes in defining the teacher's role? Recent proposals for the reform of the general educational systems in the three countries have necessarily concerned themselves either implicitly or directly with the reform of teacher education. The Plowden Report in England, in its advocacy of middle schools and in providing a major stimulus for the James Committee inquiry into teacher education, is one of many possible examples.[10] In France, the deliberations of the *Colloque d'Amiens*, though commanding less official attention, also questioned the traditional expectations that society has of its teachers. The series of reports of the German Council for Education also contain varied and direct implications for changing teachers' roles and consequently for teacher education.

It can be argued that analysis of teacher education would be facilitated if the perceptions of teaching contained in such documents were more precise and explicit. Indeed, even the statements of professional associations of teachers and teacher educators can be surprisingly opaque in the values, ideals and expectations which they claim for and urge on teacher education. This applies also to other interest-groups and not least to political parties. One might, for example, ask whether those political groups in all three countries which have for so long demanded comprehensivization, have really thought beyond an organizational unity which, in itself, could confound the educational and social aims they favoured.[11] Examples can be cited in all three countries of a reorganization that was merely nominal, from the 'grammar' streams in comprehensive schools in England,[12] to the polyvalent *collèges d'enseignement secondaire* in France and the *additive Gesamtschulen* in West Germany. Moreover, innovation tends to reveal inherent conflicts in the educational system. For example the introduction of the Certificate of Secondary Education in England, the proposals for the two-part *Abitur* in Germany and the new *baccalauréat* in France were developments that demanded specialized skills of groups of teachers whose concern was traditionally more diffuse. Conversely, the observation and guidance cycles in France and Germany and 'house systems' in comprehensive schools in England were innovations which involved diffuse demands on teachers whose previous tasks had been more exclusively academic. Teacher-education institutions need policies concerning such problems as whether to provide an increasingly specialized and differentiated profession, perhaps with some emphasis on welfare assistants and teachers' aides, or to stress the generalist, pupil-centred elements of teaching at all levels. Our concern is to attempt to understand such conflicts, their social origins and their educational implications, so that we may later examine how contrasting expectations are interpreted in teacher education in the three societies.

The Process of Becoming a Teacher

It is as important for an understanding of the social process of becoming a teacher to investigate how perceptions of teaching are successfully transmitted to would-be teachers as to ascertain the societal significance of such perceptions. This process can be thought of as the adjustment by individuals to the expectations held for them as teachers by others, whether directly or through institutionalized values. Viewed functionally, teacher education can be seen as offering members of the teaching profession or its new recruits the experience, concepts and values underlying approved models of teacher behaviour. Traditionally in the three societies, and particularly at the elementary stage, teacher education has been a relatively narrow vocational training, providing little access to other jobs, and none at a comparable social level. It consisted in following something like an apprenticeship, under an often strict regime, in institutions well and deliberately hidden from public view. The training was also characterized by being a *once and for all* experience. Relationships between teacher and taught reflected the *pupil* status of students in the training colleges, the *écoles normales* and the *Seminare*. The low job mobility of teacher-trainers, whose previous experience had usually been in the academic secondary schools only helped to reinforce a cultural cleavage from the contemporary society.

These insulated and authoritarian institutions encountered several challenges. Firstly, it became increasingly difficult to recruit appropriately motivated students for their courses and to maintain the intellectual standard of their recruits. Secondly, it has been recognized that there are a variety of occupations drawing upon the same social and academic groups as does teaching and, to some extent, requiring a similar knowledge-base. Thus it is urged that teachers, social workers and others, such as youth-workers in England or monitors for the *colonies de vacances* in France, can usefully be trained in the same institutions. The argument is pressed much further in some quarters on the grounds of the right of the student-teacher to preserve his occupational options for as long as the university student who takes a degree course. All three countries have attempted in the past few years to broaden the vocational outlook of teacher education. The introduction of social, commercial and industrial, in addition to teaching practice in colleges in Germany is possibly path-breaking in this respect. The arguments against segregating future teachers during their training have led, for example in Hamburg, to university training for all teachers or, at some English colleges of education and technical colleges, to experiments in inter-professional training.

Thirdly, a contribution of the sociological study of education has been to force institutions to question the value of training courses that afforded students little or no opportunity for learning at first hand about the society and the subcultures within which they would be teaching. The study of the social as opposed to the mainly geographical milieu in the *école normale* and the *pädagogische Hochschule*, and the growing links between training institutions and local schools and community organizations, for example in the *educational priority areas* in England,[13] have been instances of this trend. Fourthly, there is growing recognition that the teacher continues to develop his role throughout his career, and that therefore the socialization of teachers is an on-going process that can respond to the provision of opportunities over the career-span. In England there is as yet only slight development of links between initial and in-service training, while in France and Germany there is virtually none at all. Whether or not the second phase of initial training which we described in the case of Germany could provide a model for further development in the other countries is not yet clear. But suggestions for a sandwich approach have already been mooted for some English courses,[14] while in other cases it was proposed that there should actually be a second phase.[15] The recent introduction of a B.Ed. for serving teachers in England provides one example of such a development. But what further provision may be required in all three societies for the re-socialization and advanced training of personnel for newly emerging administrative and decision-making roles is already a recognizable problem for educational policy-makers.

These broad policies relating to the supply and socialization of teachers are being complemented by changing social functions within the teachers' colleges. Socialization processes depend upon the relationships that individuals have in society. Students are more likely to be changed by their peers than by the intermittent interruptions of this group life by a varied succession of outsiders and even by tutors or lecturers. No doubt in a small homogeneous institution, such as a denominational college of education, the officially sponsored socialization aims are more nearly attained.[16] However, even in 'total institutions', as Goffman has suggested, staff and clients adopt more or less polarized stances reflecting the greater or less authoritarianism of the administrative regime.[17] In England, Shipman has demonstrated some related social consequences of the expansion in size of a college of education,[18] and his work concurs in its essential conclusion with American research on attitude change in colleges.[19] Peer-group influences are strong and act to develop climates that are independent of officially declared goals. The socialization functions of particular kinds of organizations, and their implications for institution-building, cannot be neglected in a study such as this. Indeed, the way in which different cultures and educational systems may attempt to increase the compatibility of their organizational means and their socialization goals may, when considered cross-culturally, help to bring further evidence to bear on problems of this kind in the individual countries.

In the attempts that have been made to increase the supply and the quality of teachers in the three countries, new institutions for teacher education have appeared, or old ones have been expanded. As a result, it is not unusual in England to encounter colleges of education with more than a thousand students. In Germany, such expansion has been accompanied by amalgamation with universities, as in Bavaria and Hessen, or by the grouping together of similar institutions, as in North Rhine-Westphalia. The aim of this reorganization has been the improvement of academic standards and the establishing of a university-equivalent training, sometimes in the form of an educational university. In France, there is as yet only the skeleton of such development in the *instituts de préparation aux enseignements de second degré*, the *centres pédagogiques regionaux*, the *écoles normales supérieures*, and in the new training centres for intermediate and technical teachers that have already been mentioned. But common to all the countries is the question as to how such reorganization may affect the process of socialization of new recruits into the occupational role of the teacher. Little is known comparatively about the student's experience of teacher education, the divisions and groups within institutions of which he becomes a member and what these affiliations mean to him. This must be an area of concern for those who undertake the task of providing for the training of a growing mass of students including student-teachers.

The socialization of the student-teacher occurs as he sorts out his affiliations to his peer group of students, his tutors and his teacher colleagues in the schools to which he goes for practical training. On short training courses, such as the one-year post-graduate certificate courses in

England, there is no evidence that deliberate intentions on the part of the authorities to alter students' attitudes have had any success, even if it does seem probable that some homogenization of students' norms and values does occur.[20] In France, graduate teachers are trained almost exclusively on the job, and the question arises as to whether they may not therefore be particularly likely to reproduce uncritically in their teaching the practices and underlying attitudes of those who have taught them in their primary and particularly their secondary schools. If this were happening there could be serious consequences for the development of forms of school organization, teaching methods and other educational innovations which aimed to respond to the changing needs of the contemporary school population.

In Germany, in recent years, all *Länder* have introduced a stipulation that prospective graduate teachers must pass an examination in educational studies and in many *Länder* school experience during university study is also included. Many students regard these regulations as an unnecessary intrusion upon their university course, which they feel should be concerned with the study of their specialist subject. This view is often reinforced by the traditional reluctance of German universities to assume responsibility for the training of teachers, reflecting a general conviction that whilst academic theory is a pursuit worthy of universities, vocational studies and practice demean them. In the second phase, however, the student-teachers are generally attached to schools in small groups. It would be valuable to know what effects this sequential treatment of teacher preparation has on the achievement of socialization goals.

A further key element of initial teacher education that has been insufficiently studied in terms of its implications for the socialization process is the system of assessment. In the traditional institution the examination has been one of the main instruments of authority. With the widespread adoption of Piagetian psychology and Deweyan theories of education, the teachers' colleges have found their professed and practised pedagogies more and more in contradiction. New, even radical forms of assessment in teacher education have capitalized upon the psychological and sociological insights that have become widely shared, at least notionally, among teachers.[21]

In brief, it appears likely that teacher education is beginning to take account of its own *social* character. Students in the three societies are being trained for a profession which is beginning to overcome its traditionally atomized structure. Examples of staff participation in organization and policy-making in schools, integrated studies across departmental or subject boundaries and team-teaching or similar co-operative activities are becoming increasingly common.[22] Some implications of these initiatives, and the demands that they express for new modes of socialization and re-socialization for teachers, have been implicitly recognized in the changes in the form of college government in England which have involved increased student responsibilities. Similar insights have led to such experiments as the introduction of the *social practice* in Germany, the *protocol* method of teaching practice supervision in England[23] and the development of a variety of teaching methods based on group dynamics in France.

The thrust towards new forms of learning that embrace student activity and participation shows parallels in England, France and West Germany. The attempts to monitor and evaluate teacher behaviour using closed-circuit television in some of the elementary teacher-training institutions of the three countries reflects another aspect of the growth of a social approach to learning. A re-evaluation of the notion of professional preparation through both initial and in-service training and their interrelations ought to clarify which social experiences contribute to teacher education in these countries. In Chapter Four we examine the evidence which is available as to how the subjective experience of teacher education, its social environment and social relations may influence the effectiveness with which student-teachers learn the role that society prescribes for them.

Curriculum and Teaching Methods

The substantive character of teacher education is inherent in a programme or series of programmes comprising a curriculum, and indeed it could be argued that this is the most clearly identified and well-defined component of teacher education. And yet, however well-defined, the curriculum can only be understood in relation to the kinds of social constraints that the last two sections have outlined. The actual programme is often very different from the projected programme, and what is decided should occur is less important than what actually occurs or what is perceived by the learner to occur. Within the most established and familiar programmes of teacher education in the three societies, however, it can be said that a distinctive curricular epistemology has developed. This is more clearly seen in England and Germany than in France where, although pedagogy as such has its epistemology through the seminal work of historical figures such as Montaigne, Pascal, Rousseau and Durkheim, contemporary teacher education has little curricular definition. The logic of these considerations leads us to issues concerning the aims and content of different courses and the methods by which they are organized, taught, examined and evaluated. In France and to some extent in Germany the curricula and the regulations for teacher education are matters of official prescription. In England this is not the case, though the Department of Education and Science does still maintain an overview of the work of the teachers' colleges through the Inspectorate.

Traditionally the curriculum of the elementary teacher-training establishment consisted of the subjects which were taught in the elementary school and methods of teaching them. There was an element of general educational theory, often heavily historical or philosophical, and also periods of practical training at a special demonstration or model school.[24] Later as a response to the expansion of subject commitments in schools, and with the development of training courses for more academic students, there was an evolution in the range of subject offerings. More recently new subjects such as sociology and pure science have been introduced, and there has been a differentiation of the theoretical aspects of education into a variety of disciplinary approaches, as well as experiments in integrating these theoretical aspects with practice. The use of newer media in education has led to some colleges offering courses in their theory and applications. In England, the Department of Education and Science has fostered such developments by means of financial and other incentives, and similar developments had occurred in France and Germany by the mid-1960s.

A further area of concern is the specification of the disciplines which contribute to educational studies. In Germany, for example, political education is often regarded as one of the elements of the study of education. In France *l'instruction civique* is a compulsory subject in the school time-table, although it is not one for which there is formal teacher preparation. In England neither of these subjects is generally included though there have been recent explorations of the potential of political studies in schools and colleges.[25] On the other hand students in colleges of education are expected to prepare to teach religious knowledge, a subject which has no place in the *écoles normales* and is disappearing in those parts of Germany where it has hitherto been required. In many English colleges of education, and not solely denominational ones, religious education is considered to be a basic subject along with English and mathematics. Concepts within the curriculum may have varying connotations in the three countries. Words such as *theory, pedagogy, profession, programme, formation, discipline* and *subject* are to some extent culture-bound in their usage. Their strategic value has influenced organization and curricula in different ways in the three societies. The study of their usage may provide us with new light on what has been considered to comprise a worth-while programme of teacher education.[26] What effects these varying modes of formulation and control have, and how they are keyed into examinations, are rich fields for cross-cultural comparison. But the actual techniques of examination can often themselves be of secondary importance, compared with the functions that they assume as methods of teaching and evaluation. Examinations are used in varying degrees in the three countries to control entry to teaching, and the idea of an examination as a control device pre-empts the educative functions of assessment and evaluation in teacher education.

Expectations as to how far educational research should play a part in the teachers' colleges would seem to be shifting. In England and Germany it has become a matter of social prestige and educational endeavour for elementary teacher training institutions to be engaged in research. Academic freedom or *Freiheit der Lehre und Forschung* has long been the envied prerogative of universities in England and Germany. Only in recent years, and then not everywhere, has research been considered an appropriate pursuit for teacher-training institutions. Several questions arise. In what ways are educational research and research methods incorporated in the formal programme? How may their exclusion affect teachers' attitudes when they eventually join the profession? What contribution is educational research making to the development of teacher education programmes and teaching methods?

The Organization of Teacher Education

The organization of teacher education presents a more straightforward subject for study by the comparative educationist than do the three thematic areas already introduced. The administrative apparatus of this sector of education is highly visible in its regulations, staffing and policy-making procedures. Moreover there is a long tradition for the comparison, or at least the juxtaposition of these and similar features. Our task must be to review policy options as these relate both to structures from institutional to national level and to internationally recognized problems in the organization of teacher education. We shall be concerned not only with the changing configurations of responsibility which relate the three major agencies in the provision of teacher education, namely, the central government, the local or regional government and the academic institutions, but also with the various interest-groups which achieve rights to consultation or to participation up to national level in the framing of policy.[27]

There is considerable ambiguity about the status of at least some elements of teacher education in relation to the higher education system. The *écoles normales* are not part of the higher education system in France, while the English colleges are still subject to the academic control of the universities. In Germany teacher education has a similarly marginal status in higher education, in spite of the considerable changes of recent years.[28] Within the three societies, examples can be found of ways in which teacher education institutions are limited in their autonomy with respect to aims, curricula, staffing, financing and policy-making by the nature of their association with the system of higher education. The relationship could in principle vary from one of subordination to one with full rights to participation in decision-making, as for example in the proposals that have been made in recent years for a comprehensive system of higher education. One relatively unexamined area of questions here includes how personnel of teacher education are recruited, how they are prepared for their functions and what kinds of career lines they follow. Research has been undertaken in England on some of these matters,[29] but details are lacking about the patterns of professional activity of teacher educators in the three countries. There is as yet little account of the teaching work in colleges and schools undertaken by teacher-training lecturers, of the contact they have with schools and school teachers, of their own retraining and research or of their policy-making responsibilities and associational activities.

One of the most marked developments of the last decade in teacher education has been the increase in the size of training institutions. Often organizational norms have tended to get out-of-phase with this numerical expansion. Where previously the small institution was able to function with very few decision-making roles, and all matters of importance were decided by the director of the institution within fairly well-set guidelines, the need is now frequently expressed for a more representative structure for decision-making. Whether newer types of organization will facilitate developmental change in teacher education remains to be seen. A study of the institutions and of the services that support them in the wider educational system should help to identify what built-in procedures for self-appraisal may be required to ensure their ability to adapt continuously to changing needs. Modern educational systems have needed techniques and personnel whose function is to help teachers and schools to respond to demands generated by social change. The shift in function of the English Inspectorate towards that of an intelligence and advisory system is of interest here. Other examples can be cited of co-ordinating bodies and councils, and of political, syndical, economic, religious and cultural organizations in each of the three societies, which contribute to the development of the educational system and to teacher education at initial and in-service stages.

Teacher-education institutions, which had a long tradition as socially confined seminaries, based upon a narrow role-definition for the teacher, have tended to become more responsive to the wider society. By combining the training they offer with other professional and academic courses, but also by developing service-oriented activities, field-work and the study of social problems, they establish an element of dialogue with the contemporary society. The success of such innovations however will depend upon the ability of institutions to identify issues, to initiate and generalize action and to evaluate their progress.

TEACHER EDUCATION AND CULTURAL CHANGE:
THE ANALYTICAL FRAMEWORK OF THE STUDY

From a societal point of view the policy issues that have to be considered, with respect to the four thematic areas of teacher education outlined, may be posed as options to conserve or to change. In essence many of these issues are related to the growth of and further pressures towards democratization. It is inevitable in education, where the final result is a matter of individuals' thinking and action, that questions of freedom and authority are central. Education either serves to confirm the authority of established values, institutions and social groups or it favours political and philosophical growth towards a more democratic social order. The implications for teacher education are in either case direct and all-pervasive. If educational systems do function to reproduce in learners the dominant values of a culture, or to legitimate for them the status generally accorded to those values, then this function could be expected to be most clearly observable in teacher education. If it were not observable in teacher education the *reproduction* hypothesis[30] could hardly be applied to the school system at large.

Any attempt to cast a general view of teacher education in the guise of an objective study would be sociologically naïve when the atmosphere surrounding teacher education in England, France and West Germany has been one of mordant criticism. Unrepresentativeness in the portrayal of issues in this study can be ascribed both to the lack of spokesmen for the opposition to some of the severest criticisms of the present state of teacher education and to the selective perception of cultural and political phenomena by the authors. The first of these causes is of general interest and will be referred to again. The second has more immediate relevance, for a sociological study of teacher education must include the classification of goals and policy options which may appear to be quite familiar, but which can have different values and meanings for different social groups.

In a sense, the objectives urged upon teacher education are so diverse and controversial as to be unattainable. None the less, decisions have to be taken about teacher education by students, by teachers, by college and university personnel and by local, regional and national government officials, as well as by many others. To what extent is tradition the guide to decision? As knowledge about human behaviour expands, and social and other conditions change, how far are efforts at fact-finding, programme evaluation and systematic research providing an alternative and firmer basis for decisions? Does development in teacher education proceed along coherent lines rather than respond in expedient fashion to isolated problems? Such questions indicate the need to review and evaluate policy options in teacher education in terms of a coherent classificatory scheme.

Decision-making in relation to any of the four thematic areas of teacher education can be fruitfully considered in terms of the tension between *traditional* and *innovatory* functions. If we think in terms of options available in teacher education tending to one or other of these poles, each option so exercised can be seen as applying either to isolated aspects or to teacher education treated as a system. Janowitz has proposed the distinction between *specialization* and *aggregation* models in the development of urban educational systems, according to whether such development involves definitions of issues and solutions that are segmentally or, on the other hand, systemically conceived.[31] Adopting Janowitz's distinction, the combination of the two options gives the following four-cell typology (Figure 1).

FIGURE 1

Typology of Policy Options

	specialized	aggregative
traditional	cell 1	cell 2
innovatory	cell 3	cell 4

With respect to the vertical dimension of the typology, it is assumed that any relevant issue is concerned with the recognized or established role-expectations, experiences, curricula or organizational structures of teacher education, that is, with one or more of the four thematic areas, and therefore that it must involve an option to conserve or to change such elements. The dichotomy created by the second dimension of the typology is as to whether an issue is being treated at only one of the thematic levels, and in isolation from other similar decisions at its level, or whether it is being treated through the four levels and coherently with other issues in its domain. Thus classification within the typology requires judgement as to what implications any proposed policy may have for teacher education as a system. For the purpose of our sociological analysis therefore we would ask: Has the policy an underlying value-orientation to the role of the teacher that can feasibly be generalized in contemporary society? Can the results desired be achieved through formal training of teachers or other complementary experiences to produce change in people's attitudes and behaviour? What knowledge-base is available to validate the policy, and what are its implications for the totality of the curriculum? Do the organizational elements of the proposals articulate with presently existing structures, or how are requisite changes to be attained structurally and politically?

The discussion of questions of this kind must be systematically ordered if it is to reach conclusions that are relevant to sociological understanding and to educational policy-making. We have used a paradigm to guide the analysis of teacher-education policy options which have been assigned to particular cells of the typology. On the one hand we seek to understand the cultural *values* and *epistemologies* upon which teacher education is based in the different societies and on the other hand we examine the structural characteristics of its *social organization* and *control systems*.

If criticism of teacher education implies that social and cultural change can be initiated by this sector of the educational system, we are obliged in our analysis to ask where the motive force that produces this change is. Is it in the pedagogy of teacher education? It would be more plausible to suppose that pedagogy as such is neutral. Is it with the decision-makers who organize teacher education? This assumes that their decisions will be faithfully interpreted and implemented. Is it with the student-teachers? This would surely be to assume that, as a group, they are *different*, unlike their peers, and what evidence we have does not suggest this likelihood. Is it then reasonable to expect social and cultural change from teacher education? This amounts to asking whether the educational system can influence the society's choice of values, a question which is more amenable to sociological analysis than that with which we started.

The problems of the origin and transmission of values have concerned all the major contributors to the development of sociological theory. Marxist and non-Marxist sociologists alike have tended to emphasize the functions of political, religious and economic interests in the allocation of values. Even those like Durkheim who disguise the value problem with the concept of consensus do not fail to study the transmission of values as a vital function in the maintenance of society. Bourdieu[32] has gone some way towards confronting the Durkheimian notion of the reproduction function of education[33] with a hypothesis of value transmission resulting from conflict between the interests of different social classes. Bourdieu's work becomes interesting for the present analysis at the point at which he goes beyond the notion of the reproductive function of education to develop a language and a theory for apprehending the complexity of the reproductive process. He is concerned with the relations between the processes of what he terms *cultural* and *social reproduction*. Cultural reproduction is the transmission of values and patterns of behaviour referred to as cultural capital. Family life, along with its subcultural forms, its experiential variety and the educational career to which it leads the young, are the main media of cultural influence. Social reproduction, on the other hand, is the transmission of social capital, that is the social and economic characteristics of the family and its material and political standing in the wider society. Bourdieu's research indicates that cultural reproduction tends to, though it does not entirely become a special case of social reproduction, because the power of a culture to maintain exclusiveness and its dominance depends upon the simultaneous and in fact inseparable action of social and economic forces that confirm and contain the processes of cultural transmission.[34]

The present study is concerned with the hypotheses of cultural and social reproduction and of the direct relationship between these two processes. A simple paradigm is proposed for the analysis of teacher-education policy options (Figure 2).

FIGURE 2

Paradigm for the Analysis of Policy Options

Cultural Reproduction Hypothesis	⎰ Types of Values (1)
	⎱ Epistemologies (2)
Social Reproduction Hypothesis	⎰ Social Organization (3)
	⎱ Systems of Control (4)

The types of values implicit in, or held to organize the educational system and teacher education are the primary concern of any attempt to study the cultural reproduction functions of teacher education. The form these values take, and what they are accepted as meaning in social life as an epistemological projection into concepts and ideas governing teacher education, are then taken into account.[35] Correspondingly, by reviewing respectively the social organization and the systems of control of teacher education, we can focus not only upon the social reproduction hypothesis but upon the way in which cultural values and meanings are institutionalized within the social structures of the teacher-education systems.

We have now outlined an analytical framework designed to provide a sociological perspective upon the dynamics of teacher-education systems. Summarizing, teacher education will be studied in terms of four inter-related sociological themes: perceptions of teaching, the process of becoming a teacher, curriculum and teaching methods, and the organization of teacher education. A chapter will be devoted to each theme in Part Two of the study. A typology is suggested for classifying options in the development of teacher education in terms of two dimensions, one concerned with the central hypothesis of the cultural and social reproductive function of education and the other with the sociological plausibility of particular policy options. Finally, to facilitate the testing of the hypotheses of the reproductive functions of teacher education, we propose a paradigm for the ordering of the discussion of each policy option type. We have adopted a system of notation, based upon Figures 1 and 2, which indicates at the appropriate point in each of the chapters of Part Two the beginning of the discussion of each *cell* of the typology of policy options and each *level* of the analytical paradigm. Thus, for example, 4.2 would refer to the fourth, or innovatory-aggregative cell and the second, or epistemological level.

The atomized manner in which issues are defined and solutions proposed in teacher education can, especially within a cross-cultural perspective, help to account for the current sense of activity without achievement that is so widespread in the literature and professional life of the teacher-education systems. Conversely, locating and relating issues within a matrix that permits the identification and comparison of their culturally distinct aetiologies should increase understanding of the sociology of teacher education in change and of operational possibilities for its future development.

REFERENCES

1 There have been a number of explorations of methodological problems in the literature of comparative education since an early article by Anderson. See ANDERSON, C. A., 'The Utility of Societal Typologies in Comparative Education', *Comparative Education Review*, III: 1, 1959, pp. 20–22 and, as illustrative of later work: HOLMES, B., *Problems in Education: A Comparative Approach* (London: Routledge and Kegan Paul, 1965); NOAH, H. J. and ECKSTEIN, M. A., *Toward a Science of Comparative Education* (London: Collier-Macmillan, 1969).

2 KAZAMIAS, A., 'Editorial Foreword', in KING, E. J., *Education and Development in Western Europe* (Reading, Mass.: Addison-Wesley, 1969).

3 See BERGER, P. L., and LUCKMANN, T., *The Social Construction of Reality* (Harmondsworth: Penguin University Books, 1971) which advances a theory of social reality as consisting of intersubjective and negotiated meanings.

4 BOURDIEU, P., 'Systems of Education and Systems of Thought', in F. D. YOUNG, *Knowledge and Control: New Directions for the Sociology of Education* (London: Collier Macmillan, 1971).

5 DURKHEIM, E., *The Elementary Forms of the Religious Life* (Glencoe: The Free Press, 1961).

6 BOURDIEU, P. (1971), *op. cit.*

7 For some empirical examples of this polarization, see KOB, J., 'Definition of the Teacher's Role', in HALSEY, A. H., *et al.*, editors, *Education, Economy and Society* (New York: Free Press, 1961), and MUSGROVE, F. and TAYLOR, P. H., *Society and the Teacher's Role* (London: Routledge and Kegan Paul, 1969), chap. 4, 'Teachers' Role Conflicts'.

8 Der Bundesminister für Bildung und Wissenschaft, *Bildungsbericht 1970: Bericht der Bundesregierung zur Bildungspolitik* (Bonn: 1970).

9 WILSON, B., 'The Teacher's Role: A Sociological Analysis' *British Journal of Sociology*, XIII: 1, 1962, pp. 15–32.

10 Advisory Council for Education (England) (1967), *op. cit.*, vol. I, paragraph 949.

11 FORD, J., *Social Class and the Comprehensive School* (London: Routledge and Kegan Paul, 1969) is an example of an empirical study that reveals a gap between apparent intention and actual achievement in the equalization of educational opportunities.

12 BENN, C., and SIMON, B., *Half Way There* (London: McGraw-Hill, 1970) documents the extent of ability grouping in English comprehensive schools.

13 The Educational Priority Area project is a large-scale action-research undertaking that is based upon the concept of priority areas outlined in the Plowden Report, *op. cit.*, vol. I, chap. 5. For a description of how teacher education institutions have become involved in this work, see MIDWINTER, E., editor, *Teacher Education and the Educational Priority Areas* (Liverpool: EPA Project, 1970).

14 The case is probably most fully argued in England by Robinson, *op. cit.*, pp. 89–90 *et passim*. A similar American concern was evidenced in the report by Conant which emphasized the importance of a 'clinical' phase in training. See CONANT, J. B., *The Education of American Teachers* (New York: McGraw-Hill, 1963).

15 Such proposals are for example contained in a minority submission within the Plowden Report. See Advisory Council for Education (England), *op. cit.*, vol. I, pp. 493 ff.

16. This may indeed have been the reason why C. H. Becker insisted in 1926 that the *pädagogische Akademien* should be denominational. See BECKER, *op. cit.*

17 GOFFMAN, E., *Asylums* (Harmondsworth: Penguin Books Ltd, 1968), pp. 18 ff.

18 SHIPMAN, M. D., *Participation and Staff/Student Relations: a Seven Year Study of Social Change in an Expanding College of Education* (London: Society for Research into Higher Education, 1969).

19 Such conclusions emerge, for example, from the work of Newcomb and Becker. See NEWCOMB, T., *Personality and Social Change* (New York: Dryden, 1957), and BECKER, H., *et al.*, *Boys in White* (Chicago: University of Chicago Press, 1961).

20 See MCLEISH, J., *Teachers' Attitudes: a Study of National and other Differences* (Cambridge: Cambridge Institute of Education, 1969), or the more focused study: FINLAYSON, D. S. and COHEN, L., 'The Teachers' Role: A Comparative Study of the Conceptions of College of Education Students and Head Teachers', *British Journal of Educational Psychology* XXXVII: 1, 1967, pp. 22–31.

21 Some relevant experiments are reported in COLLIER, K. G., *New Dimensions in Higher Education* (London: Longmans, 1968), especially in chap. 3 on 'Syndicate Methods'.

22 FREEMAN, J., *Team-teaching in Britain* (London: Ward Lock Educational, 1969) provides a useful survey of developments.

23 One such scheme of supervision is described in CASPARI, I. E., and EGGLESTON, S. J., 'Supervision of Teaching Practice', *Education for Teaching*, no. 68, Nov. 1965, pp. 42–52.

24 SEEMANN, H. R., *Die Schulpraxis in der Lehrerbildung* (Weinheim: Verlag Julius Beltz, 1964) provides one description of the evolution of practical teaching experience in teacher training in Germany.

25 See HEATER, D. B., *The Teaching of Politics* (London: Methuen, 1969).

26 See, for example, EASON, T. W., *Colleges of Education: Academic or*

Professional? (Slough: National Foundation for Educational Research, 1970). A compelling argument concerning the power of academic concepts to homogenize and routinize the educational process is elaborated by BOURDIEU, P., and PASSERON, J. C., (1970), *op. cit.*

27 Descriptions of how these strategies are developed by teachers' organizations include: CLARK, J. M., *Teachers and Politics in France: a Pressure Group Study of the Fédération de l'Education Nationale* (Syracuse: Syracuse University Press, 1967) and MANZER, R., *Teachers and Politics* (Manchester: Manchester University Press, 1970). The latter work is a study of the National Union of Teachers and its pressure group activities over the last quarter of a century.

28 The Permanent Conference of Ministers in listing numbers in Higher Education consistently excluded those studying to become primary or intermediate teachers. See, for example, Ständige Konferenz der Kultusminister, *Kulturpolitik der Länder 1967–68* (Bonn: Deutscher Bundesverlag, 1969).

29 Reported by TAYLOR (1969), *op. cit.*, chap. 8.

30 BOURDIEU and PASSERON (1970), *op. cit.*

31 JANOWITZ, M., 'Institution-building in Urban Education', in STREET, D., *Innovation in Mass Education* (New York: Wiley, 1969).

32 A group of researchers under the direction of Pierre Bourdieu of the *Centre de Sociologie Européenne* at the *Ecole Pratique des Hautes Etudes*, Paris, has undertaken a series of research studies in the sociology of education and culture which are concerned with the 'reproduction' hypothesis in various sectors of the French educational system. See *Rapport d'Activité 1970–71*. (Paris: Centre de Sociologie Européenne, Centre de Sociologie de l'Education et de la Culture, 1971).

33 DURKHEIM, E., *Education and Sociology* (Glencoe: Free Press, 1956).

34 BOURDIEU and PASSERON (1970), *op. cit.*, pp. 202–6 *et passim*. Bourdieu has also written a briefer statement of this argument which was presented, in England, to the British Sociological Association. See BOURDIEU, P., *Cultural Reproduction and Social Reproduction*, paper given at the Annual Conference of the British Sociological Association, Durham, 1970 (mimeo). The French version of this paper was published as 'Reproduction culturelle et reproduction sociale', *Informations sur les Sciences Sociales*, X: 2, 1971, pp. 45–79.

35 See for example YOUNG, M. F. D., (1971), *op. cit.* This collection of essays develops and illustrates approaches to the study of the cultural properties of school curricula and pedagogy.

Part Two

Chapter Three

Perceptions of Teaching

Institutions of teacher education exist to give a socially approved intellectual and professional preparation to teachers. In a sense, this is to argue that teacher education cannot fully determine its own goals, or, as we expressed it in Chapter One, teacher education does not exist in a cultural vacuum. But why do such institutions command the support and resources of society? It is not because their personnel have the aims that they do. The relationship is the other way round. The wider community is sufficiently persuaded as to the importance of training teachers to provide for this by supporting colleges and their personnel. The autonomy of a teacher-training establishment in its work is relative. It depends upon the persistence of an overall public willingness to allow it to continue despite inevitable disagreement over actual policies and even underlying aims.

Preconceptions underlying education in a society are the source of expectations for teachers' roles.[1] Behind the organizational, institutional and curricular apparatus of teacher education are choices of priorities and options for education that have particular histories and cultural meanings. In Chapter Two we attempted to lay the methodological groundwork for a comparative study of the values, meanings, structures and control systems of teacher education in the three societies. The task of this chapter is to explore the basis for the teacher's role as this latter reflects elements of the particular cultures and social structures. For not only are educational systems introjections of broader social systems, but the constituent role-behaviours and values by which they are sustained are imprints of a broader culture. Whilst it would be unwarrantedly deterministic to claim that all role-behaviour of teachers can be best understood as reflecting a specific culture, it must be clear that most deliberate action and much of the actual process in teacher education responds to broader cultural influences. Thus, any discussion of teacher education must start with a consideration of the cultural values bearing upon the processes of teaching and socialization.

In traditional sociological analysis, from Durkheim to Parsons, the educational system is seen as performing an integrating function in society. Schools and schooling are used by society to transmit a way of life and to secure the commitment to its values of the new generation. Such a hypothesis logically assumes a predominantly stable society. That is, its proponents would have to be able to point to an identifiable heritage of values and mores which could plausibly be said to be in the process of transmission. But the evidence for this view has to be assessed in relation to the undoubtedly widespread conviction that, within the cultures of the modern world, the concept of change has acquired an extraordinarily commanding power. If we cannot deny change we are left with the problem of its cultural character. Is it the monolithic convergence of technology upon humanity, in the pessimistic Marcusean view?[2] Or is there room for the optimistic interpretation that human consciousness and creativity can maintain the initiative, in spite of all the deterministic influence of class, status and power in the present world community? This same problem exists at the level of the interpretation of the teacher's role. Here we will study the teacher not in a behavioural sense, but as a cultural product. This does not mean that we relieve the teacher of human individuality, but that we suggest how societies secure the teachers they need to serve socially and politically determined ends and, by this fact, largely predetermine the range of the teacher's activity by the patterns of cultural expectations generated for the educational system and for his role.

We must now therefore consider how these cultural expectations which the three societies have produced and the value systems inherent within them are transformed into cultural perceptions of the role of the teacher. These perceptions of the role of the teacher will be classified within the typology. The aim is to show that many competing or sometimes mutually supporting perceptions of teaching co-exist and interrelate in a dynamic context in different ways in the three societies. We describe each of the cells of our typology by means of a title, expressing the major role-orientations of the teacher as being subject-, system-, child-, and community-centred.

1. THE SUBJECT-CENTRED TEACHER

1.1*   In all three societies there has developed a hierarchy of teacher roles, which has grown out of systems of social stratification. The spread of national systems of education for the masses in the nineteenth century confronted policy-makers with the need to identify and integrate within a programme of teacher training role-prescriptions appropriate to society's needs. They were influenced by a hierarchical view of society and the apparent need to service and preserve that society. Traditionally teachers were regarded as responsible for passing on a culture to the next generation. It was this culturally reproductive concept of the teacher's role which historically has dominated attempts to establish teacher-education programmes.[3] Although both elementary and secondary academic teachers were involved in the transmission of values and knowledge, the former were members of the less favoured social groups who were selected and sponsored to become junior members of the educational and social establishment.[4] Through the transmission of the major values of the society they were to enable the labouring classes to service the needs of society as a whole. The first formal teacher education was thus based on the concept of the role of the teacher as the humble conserver of the cultural and social status quo in all three countries. As secondary academic teachers were already initiated into the conventions of this tradition by means of

---

* The notation system to be used throughout Part Two is explained on page 66.

their prior membership of or ascent into the middle class, and their internalization through this and university studies of the associated intellectual and social values, they were not seen as needing further training to accomplish a similar mission. Elementary teachers, on the other hand, lacking the appropriate social and intellectual qualifications, were considered to need training both to familiarize them with the values and approaches to knowledge of the dominant social classes, and to enable them to incorporate these conventions into their professional role and transmit them to the young.

Teachers in all three countries are now more often recruited from the lower-middle class[5] and in the case of England and Germany, though increasingly so in France, from those who have already completed secondary school. Teacher-education systems are thus relieved of certain tasks of cultural socialization and are enabled to concentrate on professional socialization. In addition research has seemed to indicate the social conformity of recruits to teaching,[6] and the way in which, in spite of the apparent acceptance by teachers of new forms of organization, the values and attitudes underlying traditional teacher behaviour continue to influence present practice and thus reduce the efficacy of innovation.[7] The relationship between the teachers' values and those of the dominant groups rests on the fact that teachers are the most *schooled* members of society. Clearly this public image of social conformity and teachers' own self-images have been important factors in the quantitative and qualitative development of education to this day. In England and Germany the training of teachers was delegated by society to the major religious denominations and early provision was almost entirely religious, whereas in the case of France the state retained to itself a more overtly socio-political purpose and religious values were eschewed. In each case, however, the process involved was one of the *monitorial*[8] transmission of the heritage of knowledge and conventional values: the teacher's role, whether academic secondary or elementary, rested upon a monistic rather than a pluralist system of values. Social and economic forces strengthened the knowledge-centred tendencies of the teacher and the cultural and career systems based on teaching-subjects.[9] More recently, too, Shipman has described how innovating teachers have tended to revert to these established subject stereotypes, even before support for new roles is withdrawn.[10]

1.2 Historically the prime expectation surrounding the teacher was that he would sustain the accepted view of knowledge, particularly as this has been reflected in the academic secondary schools. Within the hierarchy of knowledge systems, the teacher had his own well-prescribed place. His studies were based predominantly on teaching-subjects and his status and his own self-concept were determined by the age, sex, ability and social and academic level of the children to whom this material was to be taught.[11] The increasing impact of economic and technological advance during the nineteenth century reinforced this stratified concept of society and of knowledge and emphasized the *craft* conception of the role of the elementary teacher in particular. Indeed early student-teachers were often indentured as apprentices for a specific period of time.[12]

Such perceptions of teaching were reinforced by a socially naïve and comparatively slow-changing concept of desirable scholastic knowledge, which was further strengthened by ministerial regulation for schools and teachers' colleges,[13] by the popularity of transfer theories in psychology and by the growth of examinations. This concept of knowledge, because it has appeared so clear and susceptible to validation, has prevailed in systems of education and teacher education in all three countries. It sustains the dominance-submission relationship of the teacher towards his pupils, making more difficult the inclusion of newer types of relationship which do not rest on the assumption of the teacher's authority in knowledge, experience and culture. Pressures towards higher academic standards in all three societies have reinforced this notion, and particularly in England and Germany where the greater success of primary teachers in pursuing their social and educational objectives has resulted in a closer approximation of the subject-matter in the training of the three tiers of teachers.

At the same time however it has been observed that there is an increasing diffuseness in perceptions of the teacher's role in the primary and lower secondary school.[14] Musgrove and Taylor have described how English grammar-school teachers tend to hold a restricted view of their role and to reject social aims in their work, and they have remarked on the way in which men teachers in grammar schools particularly seem to perceive their role primarily in intellectual terms.[15] Cannon has discussed the effect this concept of teaching has on the teacher's perception of the academic dimension of his own preferred role and evidence has been assembled of the German elementary teachers' desire to cultivate an increasingly subject-specialized commitment, whilst subject teachers in grammar schools in England and the *lycées* in France show a similar tendency.[16] The specialist teacher thus becomes an important though possibly socially dysfunctional model in the view of reality that he is able to transmit to his pupils.

1.3 Until very recently in England and still predominantly in France and Germany, the concept of the teacher as a logotropic recipe-dispenser, with a specific role and arbitrary authority, has had considerable influence on the forms of knowledge seen as acceptable by the schools, and has dominated the teaching methods and grouping of pupils normally envisaged by the schools. It has often been interpreted as a dogmatic transmission or cramming of facts by the teacher, involving uncritical memorization and imitation on the part of the pupil.[17] In all three societies there has been a consequent preoccupation with the minutiae of testing and alphabetical or numerical grading. In the English elementary school the concern to establish satisfactory levels of performance was reflected in the names of the classes, viz. standards, and in France and Germany with the more contemporary problems of repeating classes (*redoublement*, *Sitzenbleiben*). Developments towards greater democratization of the educational system appear to be in direct conflict with the requirements of an intellectual tradition which envisages the teacher as having a subject-centred approach to his task and working isolated from his peers.[18] The model of the *agrégé*, and his analogues in Germany and England, the *Philologe* and the grammar-school teacher, remains the one that teachers seek to attain within a context of generally rising educational standards, as they demand universal graduate status, and it is a model which has been reinforced by post-war developments in academic subjects in English, French and German teachers' colleges.

Traditionally the acceptance of the subject-centred, custodial and instructional role of the teacher has determined not only the organization and teaching methods employed within the school, but also the status of the incumbent. Thus it has determined the structure of the teaching profession and its relationship to the wider system of social stratification. In all three countries differentials in the status of teachers have been preserved by the existence of different career routes into teaching. The circle of cultural reproduction thus formed has been further secured by numerous status-endorsing and boundary-maintaining subject associations which ensured that their subject-centred view of education, however static, was emphatically proclaimed.

In such a system the teacher is supreme; the effective autonomy of head teachers in England is the *ne plus ultra* of this tendency whereby intellectual and social submission is expected not only from the pupil but also from junior colleagues.[19] The authority of the teacher is further denoted by a high level of indifference, perhaps even antipathy towards the academically less inclined pupils and the short shrift accorded to intellectual or social non-conformity. It is against this background of a centripetal pressure of subject and job commitment, based on a pre-service training, that one can measure the prospects for successful development of newer types of role allocation which attempt to take account of the interdependence of the teacher with other professionals.

Analytically, such a definition of the role of the teacher led to vigorous selection, the concentration of preparation into a once-and-for-all initiation and, in the early institutions of elementary teacher education, a closed environment in which the student could be more effectively socialized into his professional role. Even within these latter institutions the hierarchy of teachers was being constructed as the by-product of institutionalized perceptions of the relative value of different approaches to knowledge. An example of this was in the introduction of the B.Ed. degree in England, when many colleges found difficulty in gaining acceptance by the universities of such subjects as art and physical education as being fitting areas of study for the new degree. This degree and the distinction preserved by the James Report between the B.A. and the B.A.(Ed.), along with counterpart developments in the other societies, are a further step in the selective process which divides teachers into a series of social strata.[20]

1.4 This hierarchical occupational structure has resulted in systems of control which were oriented to the preservation of traditional values and standards. The elementary teachers, as recipients of the dominant value systems, were expected to transmit to their pupils those elements of the high culture which they had received under close scrutiny during their training. At different periods in the three countries pupil-teachers were selected for training by inspectors and clergymen who required religious zeal and humility rather than intellectual powers. These qualities were then further reinforced by the strict regime and manual work of the early colleges and encouraged by financial and other incentives, when the teacher had entered the profession.

In England, for example, the teacher's work had to satisfy the chairman of the school board of governors or an inspector, and the extent of his payment depended upon their assessment. Extra emoluments were allowed for the pupils' success in certain subjects, once again directly reinforcing a hierarchical perspective and a differentiated view of knowledge. Subject inspection in the three societies served to legitimate certain areas of study in preference to others, and testing was thus as much a system of teacher control as of pupil examination. Even the growth of religious associations among teachers in Germany could play a part in the control of professional activity.[21] Curricula and reports in the three countries further testify to the close and limiting expectations which have constrained the teacher's role and depressed his social status. Overall control of teaching was assumed by the state, first of all in France but, by the end of the nineteenth century, in the other two countries where the political authorities undertook ever increasing supervisory and control functions. This led to a monotechnic approach to the training of teachers and to a heavily didactic emphasis which is still placed upon their role as conservers of the social and political status quo. Such a subject-centred, mimetic and authoritarian approach remains one of the dominant cultural reference points for the role of the teacher in all three societies.

2. THE SYSTEM-CENTRED TEACHER

2.1 The advance of industrialization and urbanization has caused educational policy decisions to centre more and more on the efficiency of the economy. The demand has grown for members of society and, correspondingly, of the teaching profession, to be sponsored more efficiently for movement up the knowledge and skill hierarchies. The teaching skills necessary for these social functions could not be acquired on the basis of a craft approach to training. Rather the need was to identify and develop the ability of the young student to internalize a system-centred view of teaching. With an increasingly organized and hierarchized education system the teacher was expected to adopt administrative as well as academic roles. The 1870 Education Act, establishing a national system in England, was matched by similar legislation in France and in parts of Germany. The structure of society and its most important social units were also changing. Musgrove has described extensively the process by which the institutions of formal education in England progressively acquired functions which had previously belonged to the family.[22] These factors and the accompanying growth of technical industries with their thirst for skilled personnel brought about a differentiation of the school system, the teaching profession and also the teacher's role. The dual system described in Chapter One has led to a situation in which two main factions in each of the societies have attempted to generalize their concept of the teacher to the whole profession. A polarity has been generated between the craft conception of the teacher's role that is described in the *first cell* and a *system*-centred role conforming to traditional academic and social norms. Schelsky has directed our attention to the way in which this encyclopaedist approach to education has declared the birth of *animal educandum* resting on the overdrawn myth of education by each institution of the whole person, which he describes as social totalitarianism.[23]

This priestlike image of the teacher was buttressed by educationists and the role was imbued with a Christian ethos that still helps to contain and prescribe desirable teacher behaviour within and outside the school. Writings in all three societies have in the past concentrated on the ideal teacher as a paragon of largely unchanging Christian virtues almost as though he were born and not made.[24] In Germany many educationists have adopted a deductive approach to the role of the teacher which has attempted to draw out, from certain classically idealistic values, implications for patterns of teacher behaviour. They have thus produced an ideal and largely philosophical picture of the teacher role which has had great influence on teacher education programmes but which has been increasingly at variance with the role performance of teachers.[25] In England, where there is a considerable descriptive and empirical literature, an abstract and often implicit approach to role-prescription still characterizes even those reports and policy documents that bear upon teacher education, while in France few writings offer a close analysis of what the main concerns of the teacher ought to be.[26]

2.2   The system-centred teacher tends to regard knowledge and knowledge-categories as given by tradition. However, the encyclopaedic expectations held for this type of teacher contrast sharply with the narrow subject-mindedness described in the *first cell*. There is here an implicit authority over a broad area of the curriculum, a curriculum which is envisaged as a means of mediating the dominant culture to a wider population. The attitude to knowledge is that of *literati* distilling and transmitting hallowed values and conclusions to the next generation, in return for which teachers are permitted a part in selecting children and allocating life-chances.[26] These encyclopaedic pretensions could enhance status only where there was undisputed scholarship, as traditionally in the case of the French *agrégé*, and other teachers have often, except in the small rural community, had a prestige which was inferior to that of their clients. It has been argued that these mediating and control functions in terms of culture, knowledge and life-chances have led in the last hundred years to the growth of a 'new despotism' of teachers over their clients.[28] For the teachers have become the guarantors of knowledge and the interpreters of the formal requirements of an examination-based process for the reproduction of socially-endorsed learning, grouped for terminal secondary examinations into conventional sets of subjects. Analytically, this is a view of knowledge which, in the hands of imitators rather than original liberal scholars, has plundered literature and replaced it with a compendium of classics and has abridged the richness of human experience while demanding an equally anthologized and scholiastic mastery from the teacher. Increasingly with the growth of demand for education such teachers are cast in the role of paraphrastic spokesmen for the dominant culture.

2.3   At the same time as teachers began to absorb a more holistic role interlocking with other elements of the educational and social systems, they began to enter into associational activities. The proto-profession of teaching began a process of politicization and differentiation which represented the early stages of a division of labour. Changes in the sex ratio in the profession, combined with such factors as initial training, qualification, salary and rank, have continued to break down its status homogeneity. The growth of professional associations has taken place in terms of different types of teacher and different areas of subject matter. These associations could only weakly influence the total occupational structure of teaching and the epistemological and behavioural assumptions underlying the teacher's role. The impact of these organizations in all three countries has been weakened by their tendency to be more concerned with the welfare of their members than the quality of the service offered,[29] and by the sectional way in which the associations have developed which has led to a kind of status war within the occupational group.

In England the first of the major national associations, the National Union of Teachers, was founded in 1871, and associational activities with similarly system-wide ambitions were being introduced or reintroduced in the other countries.[30] In France especially, teachers' organizations probably because of their sectionalism have in general had very little impact in questioning the structures within which they work.[31] Socially and intellectually, the role of the teacher was gradually being drawn towards the centre of society from the peripheral position which it occupied to begin with, and political leaders began to perceive the importance of teachers as an interest-group and in assuring ordered political development within society. The logic of this development was a demand for better training and this led in England to the establishment from 1902 of a state system of teacher training, albeit one to be dominated for many years by religious colleges. In Germany a similar recognition caused the virtual abandonment of the old *Seminar* system of training after the First World War. The workload of teachers increased and frequently extended into extra-scholastic life and activities, causing the occupational group to become socially more isolated.[32]

2.4   Apart from the control the teacher exercises over his own professional role, in his teaching activity he seeks another kind of authority. If the teacher no longer needs to coerce his pupils into enlightenment, he has none the less very powerful mechanisms of social control and approval at his command which could be equally effective in an increasingly competitive and achievement-oriented society. Indeed, his unwitting expectations may have a crucial influence on pupils' academic performance.[33] His subject-matter is not only his key to authority over parents and pupils, but a route to higher status amongst his colleagues. Equally, the successive versions of the state examinations, the General Certificate in England, the *baccalauréat* and *Abitur* in France and West Germany have been used informally to assess the competence of teachers. In all three countries examinations have had a backwash effect upon the curriculum and organization of schools that has discouraged innovation at all levels.[34] National and local inspection systems and, in France and West Germany, the system-wide prescription of curricula, have traditionally encouraged conformity rather than initiative. The academic hierarchies within teaching have allowed the more important educational selection decisions to be reserved to the more highly selected of the teachers. Thus the system has been continuously reinforced by being able to recruit to positions of status and power individuals whose achievements corresponded most closely to traditionally accepted values and understandings.

3. THE CHILD-CENTRED TEACHER

3.1 The gradual penetration of the ideal of democracy has, it would appear, at each succeeding stage led to further increments to the already diffuse and problematic role of the teacher.[35] At one remove the vying of major images of the role has led to acute conflicts of values in teacher education that have presented themselves in contrasting ways in the three societies.[36] In England a certain global concept of the teacher's role is reflected in the general certification of teachers regardless of the level and type of school to which the student aspires or is likely to be appointed. In Germany recent major national and regional reports have, with the support of the major teacher associations, advocated a *grade-teacher* approach to the training of teachers with a consequent restricted certification.[37] Such proposals however run counter to traditional French notions of the hierarchy among teachers. There is thus a difference in the three societies in this respect, for whereas the development from a subject-centred to a child- and learning-centred role orientation has seized all three societies the specificity with which this liberalization of the teacher role has been applied to plans for the structure of teacher education has differed.

The values and roles for the future teacher implicit in much of the ideological discussion surrounding education emerged only slowly in the years following the Second World War. In England the value of equality of opportunity was first legislatively enshrined in the 1944 Education Act. This Act is an appropriate example of what we have called the system-centred approach for, apart from certain democratizations of the status of the teacher and safeguards of freedom of conscience, the Act made no explicit reference to the role expected of those teachers who were to realize the ambitious reforms envisioned within it. At the same period in France the Langevin-Wallon report made clear proposals as to the principles that should govern the development of education. Democratization was to be sought not only by wider enrolment but by academic and vocational guidance, civic education and the development of the school as the centre of the community. The work of translating these often lauded principles into guidelines for the teachers' roles, however, has still not been undertaken. Post-war legislation and regulation introduced by the Allies in Germany also had a strong emphasis on equality and democratization, although this had little impact on the concept of the teacher's role envisaged in the Constitutions and School Laws of the new West German provinces.[38] Though the systems were to be democratized, traditional perceptions of the role of the teacher continued to remain unquestioned.

3.2   In the decade that followed the 1944 Education Act in England the commitment to greater parity and more equal opportunity led to ever greater pressures on the teacher and his role, but this was hardly reflected in the organization and curriculum of teacher education or in the structure of the profession. Yet the newer organizational patterns introduced as a result of the 1944 Act were making heavier demands on teachers in all types of schools. The grammar-school teachers now found themselves faced in their schools with a broader social class membership, at least during the early years of secondary education. Many of the former elementary teachers in the secondary modern schools were now having to cope with specialist teaching commitments that were new and for which they were by and large unprepared. Though there was a time-lag, these problems were analogous to those to be encountered a decade later by French and West German teachers in the CEG and the *Hauptschule*. Teachers in England saw an enlargement of their responsibility for pupils' welfare through growing contact with the statutory social, psychological and health services linked to the education system. These child-centred commitments have gradually diffused in England, but in France and Germany they have had little impact on traditional views of the teacher's role.[39] For all groups of teachers it was still their instrumental role, and the success that their pupils had in terms of the academic outcomes which would affect occupational status, that determined effectively both the status and the attitude to work and knowledge of the teachers. However in the terms of reference given to the Central Advisory Council in England in 1961 the concept of the teacher's role included 'extra-curricular activities'. A new concern for the socially disadvantaged already expressed by the Council's Report in 1963 was made much more explicit in the Plowden Report of 1967, particularly with its proposals for educational priority areas.[40] The teacher was now to be involved in a process of 'positive discrimination' which had as its aim the equalization of opportunity but still mainly through the educational system. More clearly than in any previous public document, the teacher was seen to have a concern with equality in education and in the wider community.

More recently, attempts have been made to provide empirical referents for the expectations that various groups had of the role of the teacher, to develop teacher typologies or to study teaching behaviours.[41] There has been a time-lag in reformulating the perceptions that teacher-training systems have had of the teacher and thus also delays in the reform of training. The preparatory report on initial teacher training for the *Colloque d'Amiens* in 1968 comments on the lack of any effective development from the Langevin-Wallon principles of twenty years earlier and advances some more specific ideas concerning the intellectual and social skills required for a viable teacher's role.[42] Although in the ensuing discussions and final report the need for relevant research was cited, the conclusions reached relied upon informed opinion and argument exclusively. The issue of a democratizing role for the teacher continues to be avoided in the most recent official inquiry which is concerned with the role of only one stratum of teachers.[43]

In Germany research had begun earlier with the work of such people as Gerhard Friedrich and Martin Keilhacker,[44] both of whom concentrated on the child's perception of the teacher. However this work had little influence outside Germany and was largely halted by the advent of the National Socialist regime. Later research work has attempted to investigate this changed function, and such studies as those of Schuh on the elementary school teacher, Gahlings on the female teacher, Zielinski on the vocational teacher, and Lüscher on the academic secondary school teacher, have gone some way towards a sociological definition of different categories of teachers.[45] However, at a time when the commitment to democratization of the school system has led to comprehensive forms of organization, empirical work on the role of the comprehensive-school teacher, which would be a prerequisite to many of the schemes of reform presently being discussed, is virtually unreported. The realization has developed only slowly in the three societies that a transition was taking place in the role of the teacher from being a conservative social agent to serving as a cultural bridge between social groups and between urban and rural areas.

It is inevitable, in view of the expansion of the functions of the educational systems over the past century, that the concept of a general practitioner teacher should involve the profession in intense conflict. Male, nongraduate teachers in all three societies increasingly see their career prospects as limited.[46] However other dimensions of the conflict are represented in the continuing opposition between concern for the transmission of a general culture and the social pressures within the broader society towards specialization. The external democratization of the education system proceeded without becoming integrated into the value systems of many teachers.[47] As the need arose to expand the commitment of the service even further the demands upon individual teachers were increased and diversified. In England, for example, the Government White Paper, *Secondary Education for All: A New Drive*[48] noted with satisfaction that an increasing

F

number of the *modern schools* were taking the new GCE 'O' Level examination and that the range of subjects and particularly of extra-curricular activities was increasing. The White Paper was followed the next year by the Crowther Report, the first major educational report of the post-war period, and one of the first to employ sociological methods.[49] The research-based approach that it established has been emulated by other major reports since and the information that it uncovered concerning the relationships between ability, characteristics of school and family, and scholastic achievement has undoubtedly been a significant factor in the subsequent re-evaluation of the role of the teacher. Policy-oriented research of this kind has only recently begun to be a feature of the other systems.[50]

3.3   Wider reorganizational features of the educational systems since the end of the Second World War have implications for the teacher's role. Increases in school size and the progressive raising of the school-leaving age in the three countries, the development of secondary modern schools in England, the introduction of the *classes d'éducation nouvelle* in France and the development of the *Hauptschule* as a school type with a distinct identity in West Germany, all involved an extension of commitment by teachers in curricular and social terms. Further new roles resulted from the extension of school radio and television in schools of all kinds with the less academic schools often in the vanguard with their teaching methods. Other technical developments added to the role expectations for teachers in all three societies. These included acquaintance with programming techniques and the use of associated hardware and a whole range of audio-visual aids from film and overhead projectors to video-tape recorders. All three countries were gradually expecting teachers to cultivate more active methods of presentation and pupil involvement, as in the case of the Nuffield and Schools Council materials and approaches in England, the *Rouchette* plan and *Centre de recherches et d'études pour la diffusion du français* (CREDIF) language programmes in France and similar movements in Germany including an increased participatory emphasis in civics.

These new materials and methods have demanded a more child-centred approach and the involvement of teachers in experimental programmes, though the possession of specialized subject knowledge and related qualifications have continued to be seen as the main means to professional advancement. The selection and assessment functions of the educational systems continued to evolve without losing any of their importance. The introduction of the Certificate of Secondary Education examination in England gave many secondary teachers a more significant role in the educational careers of their pupils than they had enjoyed before. With the development of unified school systems in the three societies the need for specialized provision of guidance and counselling was accentuated. In France there was an increased emphasis on a scientific underpinning for the decisions of the *conseil de classe*. In England and France courses were instituted for careers teachers and for school counsellors. Possible roles for classroom teacher assistants have been widely discussed and in England

and West Germany some limited schemes of this kind have actually been implemented. The trend towards comprehensive reorganization in all three countries, though still resting predominantly at secondary level on the selective secondary school model of the teacher role, involved greater division of labour within the schools and necessitated schemes of appointment with new specialist roles. Many of these newer positions, such as that of careers teacher, *conseiller d'orientation* or *Berufsberater*, reflected a developing concern for social objectives in the secondary schools.

This was paralleled by the introduction of more specialized teacher roles into the earlier stages of education in England, such as the middle school teachers of science, mathematics and French. Often these and other teachers were regarded as resource persons, who could assist other colleagues with a broader responsibility in the school, who might for example be working in multidisciplinary schemes with children of mixed ability or ages.[51] The introduction of responsibility allowances into the primary school in England further emphasized an approach to status based on achievement and ability in a specialist subject role, in spite of the traditional emphasis on the expressive relationship between the child and a single class-teacher. The French concept of the *bivalent* or *polyvalent* teacher represents an attempted compromise in the lower secondary school whereby the pupil will not go from a single class-teacher to a team of subject-teachers when he leaves the primary school.

West German national and regional reports have recommended the role of grade teacher, certificated for groups of classes within a unified system and strenuous efforts have been made to unify the profession and its remuneration, to respond to newer concepts of the role of the teacher and establish parity for all groups of teachers.[52] However salary reforms proposed in Hessen and Hamburg in 1971 to facilitate this development encountered the opposition of the central government. Even if socialization goals are becoming more recognized in secondary schools in the three countries, it is academic criteria that continue to govern overall school organization and the division of labour amongst teachers.

3.4   In 1962 talks on the establishment of a teachers' council similar in nature to the General Medical Council had begun in England and in 1969 a working party was set up by the DES to make recommendations on how teachers might exercise a measure of self-government.[53] Seeking greater political influence, the National Association of Schoolmasters and the National Union of Teachers affiliated to the Trades Union Congress, even though it was likely that this would compromise their achievement of professional status. The French *Fédération de l'éducation nationale* (FEN) now groups some twenty-six separate syndical organizations of teachers and, with other teachers' groups, has long accepted an industrial type of role even if pedagogical concerns are also regularly voiced.[54] In Germany five teachers' organizations have amalgamated to form the German Teachers Association (*Deutscher Lehrerverband*)[55] as a counterpart to the other main teachers' union, the Union Education and Culture (*Gewerkschaft Erziehung und Wissenschaft*). These developments embodied a wish on the part of the teachers to have a more effective voice in and influence on the aims and organization of their professional work.

In general, expectations for innovatory activity began to influence the teacher's role in spite of the continued existence of institutional restrictions such as the Ministry circular limiting pedagogical experiments in France.[56] Amongst the major inhibitory factors to educational innovation have been the salary and linked status differentials within the teaching profession. In England new salary structures introduced in 1971[57] conserved primary/secondary differentials and reinforced the stratification of the profession. In France and in West Germany there are several distinct categories of teachers with different salary structures, hours of work and other conditions, and they are subject to a corresponding hierarchy of inspectorates.

Student and teacher participation was increasing and occasionally educationists were able to envisage the potential benefits of *anticipatory socialization* in the teachers' colleges,[58] but the organizational apparatus that surrounded students in schools during their teaching practice and on entry to their profession remains far from democratic.[59] In England a few local education authorities have reformed school governing bodies to include teachers, parents and, more rarely, pupils. Comparable developments were taking place in France from 1968 in a similar pattern to that established in the early post-war years in some parts of West Germany where, in 1971, several *Länder* put forward draft proposals for securing constitutional provisions for teacher, parent and pupil participation in the government of schools. An area of particular tension in England, according to a recent comparative study, appears to be that of relations between teachers and parents.[60] What has hitherto been considered a problem of rivalry in England, and also in France, is beginning now to be looked at as an area for fruitful co-operation, as has happened long since in West Germany. Such developments as have occurred, however, have often appeared to be dominated by a concern amongst teachers to conserve professional control and autonomy.[61] The progress of innovation within the school curriculum has not been matched within teacher education, initial or in-service, so as to help teachers develop the skills necessary to manage educational institutions and their external relations, and to envisage alternative epistemological systems to those which now limit the profession's and the schools' cultural horizons.[62] In general the problem of the *cell three* policies is not their lack of plausibility but their failure to sustain adaptive change on account of the lack of coherence in their values and structures.

4. THE COMMUNITY-CENTRED TEACHER

4.1 As the diversity of social goals implicit in democratic change become more widely recognized, increased demands are made on schools and teachers. The teacher is placed in a more vulnerable position, which symbolizes dilemmas of society, by a number of developments: rising average levels of education and the appearance of a more demanding public, the fact that other agencies such as the churches and even the family, are increasingly surrendering their functions vis-à-vis the child to schools and other educational agencies. The teacher is expected at the same time both to socialize according to the traditional values of these other agencies, enlarging his social commitment in pursuit of them, and to prepare his pupils for life in a pluralist economy, society and international community. In so far as government by the people becomes a reality the teacher is called upon to play his part in a process of consultation and change which seeks to replace the very values that he has represented and to envisage the school as a pace-maker of social change.[63]

In England a series of recent publications and the developing sociological consciousness of educationists and teachers have already begun to embrace the idea of a community-centred education and to challenge the barriers dividing the social worlds of teachers and children. In France these social dimensions of the teacher's role have developed little in practice but are reflected in many contemporary writings and, for example, in the wide-spread interest in the study of group relations in certain programmes of in-service training.[64] The introduction of whole-day schooling in certain parts of West Germany has begun to alter traditional concepts of the teacher's role and of the social functions of schooling.[65] Students at all levels in the three countries are questioning the traditional passivity of the pupil upon which the elevated status of the teacher was formerly based, and are demanding a greater measure of accountability from their teachers.[66] Community leaders, whilst often lamenting modes of questioning which undermine authority, have actively encouraged the process by their pursuit of the ideals of democracy and equality of educational opportunity. Teachers and teacher educators, recognizing these contradictory expectations of society, are beginning to reject the dominance of the social values of higher education and to accept that for society to be pluralist, it must be democratic.[67] Demands are now made of the teacher as a harmonizer of the cultural diversity which constitutes the potential value system for sub-groups of the society. In England, for example, there is a growing recognition that a monistic society cannot be democratic, and that problems of cultural diversity are by no means solved with regard to indigenous sub-groups, let alone immigrant children.[68]

4.2   This new perspective has been recognized by many of the more innovative educational agencies within the countries concerned and has even been incorporated within certain programmes of study and approaches to work which emphasize the neutrality of the teacher's role as a means to cultivating the responsibility of the pupils.[69] In the professional field there is increasing involvement of teachers from different types of secondary schools in the evaluation and certification of their own pupils and those of their colleagues in the Certificate of Secondary Education in England and in the *Abitur* in West Germany. *Cell four* type policies have also led to such appointments as those in England of teachers with special responsibility for counselling, guidance and home-school relations. Implicit in these policies is the recognition of the pluralist composition of society. Schools are no longer the major source of information and learning, and demands are pressed for the de-tabooing of the street[70] and de-schooling,[71] which might result in an attenuation or even the disappearance of selection by ability and the acceptance of the ideas of recurrent education[73] and of the de-institutionalizing of teacher education itself[74] as viable policies.

The penetration and diffusion of the ideal of democracy cannot be halted at the level of academic discussion. The epistemology underlying the traditional curricular and organizational systems which have defined the role of the teacher is being subjected to scrutiny and change. The school is seen as a resource centre from which the learning and inquiry of the child, there and in the wider community, can be guided by a teacher whose commitment is to an experiential rather than to an exclusively intellectual approach to learning. This mode of learning cannot be contained within the bounds of traditional disciplines. In providing a service to his colleagues, for example in topic and other thematic work, the specialist teacher is involved in an interdisciplinary team which shares its views of knowledge to obtain an original perspective.

4.3 The validity of a teaching subject-based preparation which most teachers in all three countries have experienced in their initial training is increasingly questioned and there are proposals for broader and more relevant courses.[75] Arguments are heard for role-preparation that is concerned with such areas as curriculum development, educational technology, social education and pupil guidance.[76] In-service education, on the other hand, is increasingly addressing itself to the role of the teacher as a manager of the learning process, involving himself in flexible groupings and responding to the needs of the child, his colleagues and the community. The role of the teacher becomes gradually the role that the teacher makes for himself, a selection from a multiverse of values, qualities and activities, assembled into a specialized role that accepts the interdependence of specialists in the provision of a coherent educational service.[77]

The social context of the school and wider community is changing rapidly in all three countries. The comprehensive reorganization of education and the de-escalation of ability grouping have expanded the social and academic dimensions of the teacher's task. Appointments to particular areas within this newer organizational pattern are based on more specific roles. The insulated, multi-functional involvement of the form-teacher is being replaced by the more specialized and co-operative commitment of the house-master, counsellor or teacher-social worker, whilst further down the professional scale, technicians and assistants, both administrative and ancillary, complement the co-ordinated efforts of the staff in support roles.[78] In all three countries there are examples of representative councils linking pupils, staff and parents in collective management of the school which have been introduced voluntarily or by regulation. The school ceases to be thought of as an institution segregated from the community. Along with a community-centred function, new professional roles are envisaged and new forms of collaboration between educational workers and the personnel of other services are sought.[79] Appointments to senior positions are no longer seen as the reward exclusively of successful subject appurtenance, but rather as a financial incentive to achievement and to attract and keep *area managers* of knowledge or people and as a reward for those who can envisage knowledge in new ways or who possess relevant social or technical skills, insight and knowledge. Linking teachers effectively with para-pedagogic professions in the schools and in the local community requires the probing of the largely unexplored area of interprofessional post-experience education. The intellectual and social range of skills and ideas required is illustrated in the policies for educational compensation for social disadvantage, where society seeks to identify and aid those who are unable to take full advantage of educational opportunities. But current concern with compensatory education is only one aspect of a basic shift in the perception of the teacher's role that is now evident in many societies. The teacher is seen as an agent of the wider community, rather than merely of the school system, who must be both sensitive to the social needs of his pupils and competent to perform a linking function between the academic and social worlds.[80]

4.4   These tasks require highly skilled professionals who, through training and consequent internalization of a professional code of conduct, are able to collaborate in regulating their own and colleagues' activities, accepting the changing value and control systems that the search for a more responsive role implies within the school and community. Coding schemes for analysing teacher-pupil interaction open up new perspectives on the teacher's performance of his role.[81] Assessment of the teacher is replaced by a sharper evaluation of the curriculum and of the organization of educational institutions. Teachers, either with colleagues or researchers, participate in analysis of their own professional work.[82]

Progress with regard to the development of professional self-government may be slow at national level, but at school level and particularly in primary schools the teacher is gradually released from his subordination to the programme, the examination and the inspectorate. The appointment by teacher-education institutions of dual-professionals such as teacher-tutors, or *maîtres d'application*, or the development by teachers of competence and responsibility in initial training, means that the teacher is participating as a specialist in the control of entry to his own profession and, potentially, in actively changing perceptions of the teacher's role. This professional responsibility may be accompanied by a lowering of the protection threshhold of teachers in the form of greater accountability to the community and more centralization of policy-making in the broader aspects of organization and finance. Within the school the development of collective decision-making practices reflects the fact that the teacher is no longer a neutral and isolated actor in a pretended social vacuum. His professional status must be achieved through pursuit of the constantly evolving goals of the community and by a career-long learning of his own changing role.

REFERENCES

1 The concept of role is used here primarily in terms of a sociological approach, but for a more general treatment see BIDDLE, B. J., and THOMAS, E. J., *Role Theory: Concepts and Research* (New York: Wiley, 1966). A pioneering role-study in the educational field was GROSS, N. *et al.*, *Explorations in Role Analysis: Studies of the School Superintendency Role* (New York: Wiley, 1958), and, more recently, Eggleston has argued the utility of role identification for diagnosing changes in the work of educators. See EGGLESTON, S. J., 'The Role of the Professional Educator', in *Paedagogica Europaea 1969* (Brunswick: G. Westermann Verlag, 1970), pp. 5 ff.

2 See MARCUSE, H., *One-dimensional Man: Studies in the Ideology of Advanced Industrial Society* (London: Routledge and Kegan Paul, 1964).

3 DURKHEIM, E., *Education and Sociology* (Glencoe, Ill: Free Press, 1956). Describing the rigidity of this cultural reproduction Rich reports that masters were even forbidden to depart from the teaching methods prescribed. See RICH, R. W., *The Training of Teachers in England and Wales during the Nineteenth Century* (Cambridge: The University Press, 1933), p. 2.

4 HODGE, H., 'The Teacher Problem', *Fortnightly Review* (May 1899), quoted in TROPP, A., 'The Changing Status of the Teacher in England and Wales', in *Yearbook of Education* (London: Evans Bros., 1953), 2, chap. 3, pp. 143 ff. See also PROST, *op. cit.*, pp. 631 ff., particularly for details of the social origins of French elementary teachers. A similar recent description for Germany is COMBE, A., 'Die Soziale Herkunft der Lehrer', *Bildung und Erziehung*, XXIV: 4, 1971, pp. 241–50.

5 Undeutsch refines this point by showing that whereas grammar school teaching was considered to betoken social ascent by both working and the middle classes, elementary teaching as a career was only regarded as such by the working class. See UNDEUTSCH, U., *Motive der Abiturienten für die Wahl oder Ablehnung des Volksschullehrerberufs* (Frankfurt/Main: Max Träger Stiftung, 1964), p. 152. See also MORRISON, A., MCINTYRE, D., *Teachers and Teaching* (Harmondsworth: Penguin, 1969). In France generalization is hazardous across categories of teachers and the two sexes on available data, but women in secondary education would appear to have shown most change in the direction suggested. See a pilot-study report on a current survey: CHAPOULIE, J.-M., and MERLLIÉ, D., *Les Professeurs de l'Enseignement Secondaire* (Paris: Centre de Sociologie Européenne, 1970, mimeo.).

6 Morrison and McIntyre quoting the work of Gowan argue that teaching is a somewhat ingrown profession and hypothesize that this may be inclined to make the profession relatively impervious to outside influence. See MORRISON, A., and MCINTYRE, D. (1969), *op. cit.*, p. 50.

7 See for example BURSTALL, C., *French in the Primary School: Attitudes and Achievement* (Slough, Bucks: National Foundation for Educational Research in England and Wales, 1970).

8 The monitorial system of teaching was developed in the early years of the nineteenth century to cope with large numbers. Under it older pupils were used extensively to teach to younger pupils that which the master had first

taught them. See MORRISH, I., *Education Since 1800* (London: Allen and Unwin, 1970), pp. 7 ff.

9 A good description of the influence and tenacity of this view of knowledge is contained in STEVENS, E., *The Living Tradition: The Social and Educational Assumptions of the Grammar School* (London: Hutchinson, 1962). See also: WYKES, O., 'The Teaching Profession in France', in SELLECK, R. J. W. (Editor), *Melbourne Studies in Education 1967* (Carlton, Victoria: Melbourne University Press, 1968) and BLÄTTNER, F., *Das Gymnasium: Aufgaben der Höheren Schule in Geschichte und Gegenwart* (Heidelberg: Quelle und Meyer, 1960).

10 See SHIPMAN, M. D., *The Role of the Teacher in Selected Innovative Schools in the United Kingdom*, one of a series of papers on the changing role of the teacher prepared for the Directorate of Scientific Affairs of the Organization for Economic Co-operation and Development Experts' Meeting (Paris: OECD, 1972).

11 Kob refers to a type 'B' teacher whose professional self-concept rests on his subject specialism. See KOB, J., 'Definition of the Teacher's Role', in HALSEY, A. H., FLOUD, J., ANDERSON, C. A., *Education, Economy and Society* (New York: The Free Press, 1961), pp. 558 ff. A French research study found that teachers of different categories tended to mix very little professionally or socially, even when they were on the same school staff. See FERRY, G., and BLOUET, C., 'Les Relations entre les membres du Personnel du Premier Cycle dans un Lycée de la Région Parisienne', in Association d'Etude pour l'Expansion de la Recherche Scientifique, *Les Enseignants du Second Degré: Leur Situation dans l'Etablissement Scolaire* (Paris: Dunod, 1969).

12 TROPP, A., *The School Teachers* (London: Heinemann, 1957), p. 14, and MÖBUSS, A., *Hundert Jahre Lehrerbildung* (Lübeck: Verlag Gebrüder Borchers, 1907).

13 For the influence of ministerial regulations see for example in England the 1904 Regulations issued by the Board of Education, referred to in CURTIS, S. J., *History of Education in Great Britain* (London: University Tutorial Press, 1967), p. 323 and in Germany in the teacher training sphere the Stiehl Regulations, see FROESE, L., *Deutsche Schulgesetzgebung*: 1763– 1952 (Weinheim: Verlag Julius Beltz, 1964), pp. 76 ff. The rigours of the student's life in the *école normale* are legendary. See DUMVILLE, B., 'The French Training College System', in Board of Education, *Special Reports on Educational Subjects* (London: HMSO, 1907), vol. XVIII, pp. 174 ff.

14 See in particular, BLYTH, W. A. L., *English Primary Education: A Sociological Description* (London: Routledge and Kegan Paul, 1965), vol. I, pp. 149 ff.

15 MUSGROVE, F., and TAYLOR, P. H., 'Teachers and Parents' Conception of the Teacher's Role', *British Journal of Educational Psychology* XXXV: 2, 1965, pp. 171–9.

16 See CANNON, C., 'Some Variations on the Teacher's Role', *Education for Teaching*, no. 44, pp. 29–36; FRASER, W. R., *Reforms and Restraints in Modern French Education* (London: Routledge and Kegan Paul, 1971), especially chap. 10; and DIECKMANN, J., and LORENZ, P., *Spezialisierung im Lehrerberuf* (Heidelberg: Quelle und Meyer, 1968).

17 Tropp describes the teacher as a drill-master, who used tyrannical methods to enforce learning. See TROPP, A., 'The Changing Status of the Teacher in England and Wales', *The Year Book of Education 1953*

(London: Evans Bros. 1953), pp. 143 ff. See also CITRON, S., *L'Ecole Bloquée* (Paris: Bordas, 1971), chap. 5, and the reports on the defensive reactions sparked off by the Rouchette report. See the speech by the Minister of National Education, GUICHARD, O., 'La Réforme de l'Enseignement du Français', in *L'Education*, no. 124, Jan. 13, 1972, pp. IV–V.

18 The Langevin-Wallon Commission, *op. cit.* expressed it: 'L'école semble un milieu clos, imperméable aux expériences du monde'.

19 For a description of the evolution of the head teacher tradition in England, see BARON, G., 'Some Aspects of the Headmaster Tradition', *Researches and Studies*, June 1956, 14, pp. 7–16. The principal of a *lycée* has described how the expectations of assistant teachers can preserve an authority system that is no longer wanted. See BRECHON, R., *La Fin des Lycées* (Paris: Grasset, 1970).

20 These social strata are reinforced by the salary systems in all three countries. Recent initiatives by teacher associations in England and Germany have been concentrated on abolishing the differential between elementary and grammar teachers. A detailed account of the intricacies of salary and appointment in Germany is contained in BETTERMANN, K. A., and GOESSL, M., *Schulgliederung, Lehrerbildung und Lehrerbesoldung in der Bundesstaatlichen Ordnung* (Berlin: Duncker and Humblot, 1963). A more general discussion setting the salary issue in the context of recruitment and career considerations is contained in Organization for Economic Co-operation and Development, *Training, Recruitment and Utilization of Teachers in Primary and Secondary Education* (Paris: OECD, 1971), Part 2, chap. 3 'Teachers – Study and Recruitment'.

21 The work by Tymister describing the growth of Catholic teachers' associations in nineteenth-century Germany is unique. See TYMISTER, J., *Die Entstehung der Berufsvereine der Katholischen Lehrerschaft in Deutschland* (Bochum; Verlag Ferdinand Kamp, 1963). As late as 1908 the *Kreisschulinspektor* (district school inspector) was a member of the higher clergy. See PAULSEN, F., *Geschichte des Gelehrten Unterrichts auf den deutschen Schulen und Universitäten* (Leipzig,: Verlag von Veit und Co., 1897), vol. II.

22 A concise account of this development is to be found in MUSGROVE, F., 'The Decline of the Educative Family', *Universities Quarterly* (1960), 14, pp. 377 ff.

23 See SCHELSKY, H., *Anpassung oder Widerstand* (Heidelberg: Verlag Quelle und Meyer, 1961), p. 162.

24 For a discussion of this point, see NIPKOW, K. E., 'Beruf und Person des Lehrers: Überlegungen zu einer pädagogischen Theorie des Lehrers' in BETZEN, K. and NIPKOW, K. E., *Der Lehrer in Schule und Gesellschaft* (Munich: R. Piper and Co. Verlag, 1971), pp. 133 ff.

25 Attempts to overcome this tradition have been made amongst others by BREZINKA, W., see for example 'Die Bildung des Erziehers', in 'Beiträge zur Menschenbildung, Hermann Nohl zum 80 Geburtstag', *Erstes Beiheft der Zeitschrift fur Pädagogik* (Weinheim: Verlag Julius Beltz, 1959), and CASELMANN, CH., *Wesensformen des Lehrers: Versuch einer Typenlehre* (Stuttgart: Ernst Klett Verlag, 1964).

26 The James Report does not concern itself with the aims of teacher education, and nor does the evidence given to the James Committee by the teacher educators' association. See the Association of Teachers in Colleges

and Departments of Education, *The Professional Education of Teachers* (London: ATCDE, 1971). The situation is similar in France, where simultaneously there are proposals for the reorganization of secondary teacher education under public discussion and an official working-party inquiring into the secondary teacher's role. The teacher education problems cannot be resolved without making assumptions concerning what would be the conclusions of the working-party, but the two exercises are discrete. See Ministère de l'Education Nationale, *Le Projet de Réforme de la Formation des Maîtres: Dossier d'Information* (Paris: MEN, 1971) and the Minister's letter of Nov. 24, 1971 to M. L. Joxe, Chairman of the Commission d'Etudes sur la fonction enseignante dans le Second Degré, in *L'Education*, no. 120, Dec. 2, 1971, pp. I–II.

27 This point is suggested in BOURDIEU, P., and PASSERON, J. C., 'L'Examen d'une Illusion', *Revue Française de Sociologie*, IX (1968), pp. 227–53.

28 MUSGROVE, F., and TAYLOR, P. H., *Society and the Teacher's Role* (London: Routledge and Kegan Paul, 1969).

29 MANZER, R. A., *Teachers and Politics: The Role of the National Union of Teachers in the Making of National Education Policy in England and Wales since 1944* (Manchester: Manchester University Press, 1970).

30 The General German Teachers Association was founded on Dec. 28, 1871. See PRETZEL, C. L. A., *Geschichte des deutschen Lehrervereins in den ersten 50 Jahren seines Bestehens* (Leipzig: Julius Klinkhardt Verlagsbuchhandlung, 1921).

31 See Clark, *op. cit.*

32 KRATSCH, E. H., VATHKE, W., BERTLEIN, H., *Studien zur Soziologie des Volksschullehrers* (Weinheim: Verlag Julius Beltz, 1967).

33 The theme of the potential effects on pupils of their teachers' expectations has become a major focus of interest since the publication of an American study that involved manipulating teachers' attitudes. See ROSENTHAL, R. and JACOBSON, L., *Pygmalion in the Classroom* (New York: Holt, Rinehart and Winston, 1968).

34 One German author has argued that the examination systems in schools resemble gradings appropriate to the military world, thus indicating their origin in a pre-democratic supremacy based on the accommodation, drill, order, cleanliness and control of achievement of the 'other ranks'. He sees both spheres, the military and the scholastic as using social pressure mechanisms based on the deliberate fostering of anxiety. See GAMM, H. J., *Kritische Schule* (Munich: List Verlag, 1970), p. 183.

35 BIDDLE, B. J., 'Role Conflicts Perceived by Teachers in Four English-speaking Countries', *Comparative Education Review*, XIV: 1, 1970, pp. 30–44.

36 BANTOCK, G. H., 'Conflicts of Values in Teacher Education', in TAYLOR, W., (1969), *op. cit.*, p. 122.

37 See for example Bundesminister für Bildung und Wissenschaft, *Bildungsbericht 1970* (Bonn: 1970).

38 Indeed this aspect of democratization is almost totally ignored by them. See Arbeitsgemeinschaft deutscher Lehrerverbände, *Schulartikel in den deutschen Staats– und Länderverfassungen*, Material– und Nachrichtendienst der AGDL (1952), no. 18.

39 In a recent survey of young secondary teachers in France only two-fifths of the respondents claimed to undertake any out-of-class educational activity, such as youth work, clubs and sports. See FICHELET, R. *et al.*,

'Les Jeunes Professeurs du Second Degré: Leurs Attitudes à l'Egard de leur Formation et de Leur Pratique', in Association d'Etude pour l'Expansion de la Recherche Scientifique, *Les Enseignants du Second Degré*, p. 73. See also HUNDECK, J., and WOLFF, I., *Der Lehrer an der Höheren Schule* (Munich: Verlag Moderne Industrie, 1968), especially pp. 12 ff.

40   See Central Advisory Council for Education (England), *op. cit.*, chap. 5. Additions to pay were recommended for teachers in *educational priority areas*. See paras. 170 and 1186.

41   ALLEN, A. E., 'Professional Training of Teachers: A Review of Research', *Educational Research* V: 3, 1963, pp. 200–15. For the German scene a useful bibliography can be found in NIPKOW, K. E. (1971), *op. cit.*, in BETZEN, K., and NIPKOW, K. E. (1971), *op. cit.*

42   Association d'Etude pour l'Expansion de la Recherche Scientifique, *Pour une Ecole Nouvelle . . .*, pp. 254 ff.

43   *Commission d'Etudes sur la Fonction Enseignante dans le Second Degré.* See ref. 26.

44   A helpful yet conscise presentation of the main work conducted in Germany in this field to 1960 is contained in the introduction to ROSENSTRÄTER, H., *Lehrer und Schüler an der Berufsschule* (Essen: Verlag W. Girardet, 1961), pp. 11 ff.

45   SCHUH, E., *Der Volksschullehrer* (Hanover: Hermann Schroedel Verlag, 1962), GAHLINGS, I., and MOERING, E., *Die Volksschullehrerin* (Heidelberg, Verlag Quelle und Meyer, 1961), ZIELINSKI, J., *Der Gewerbelehrer: Bild und Wirklichkeit eines Erzieherberufes* (Ratingen: Verlag A. Henn, 1965), and the work of ROSENSTRÄTER, H. (1961), *op. cit.*, and LÜSCHER, K., *Der Beruf des Gymnasiallehrers* (Bern: Verlag Paul Haupt, 1965). The work of Eugen Lemberg in Germany is noteworthy here for the way in which he has consistently attempted to define the role of the teacher sociologically. See for example LEMBERG, E., 'Zur Soziologie des Lehrers', in *Mitteilungen und Nachrichten der Hochschule für Internationale Pädagogische Forschung*, No. 21 and 28/29, Frankfurt, 1959. A similar English study here is the work by GARDNER, D. E. M., and CASS, J. E., *The Role of the Teacher in the Infant and Nursery School* (London: Pergamon, 1965).

46   MUNGHAM, G., *The Structure of the Teaching Profession in England since 1944 with special Reference to the Secondary School Teacher.* Paper presented to a Conference of the Society for the Promotion of Educational Reform through Teacher Training, London, 1970 (mimeo.). Work has already been cited indicating the dissatisfaction with their status felt by many French primary teachers. Data on the hopes and plans of pupil-teachers, in principle preparing for primary education but hoping in considerable proportions to find posts in secondary education, is presented in RUEFF, C., 'L'Image du Maître', *Enfance* (1966), no. 2–3, pp. 65–146.

47   BARKER LUNN, J. C., *Streaming in the Primary School: A longitudinal study of children in streamed and non-streamed junior schools* (Slough, Bucks: National Foundation for Educational research in England and Wales, 1970).

48   Ministry of Education (1959), *op. cit.*

49   Central Advisory Council for Education (England) (1959), *op. cit.*

50   The official educational research functions of the French Ministry of National Education were recently reorganized into the Institut National de Recherche et Documentation Pédagogiques. This body carries out

applied research for example on the experimental CES that are attached to it. See GEMINARD, L. 'L' INRDP un an après sa Création', *L'Education*, no. 123, Jan. 6, 1972, pp. V–VI. The German Council for Education has since its inception commissioned research and writing as a basis and accompaniment to its reports and recommendations. See in particular the publications of the Council in the series *Gutachten und Studien der Bildungskommission.*

51 The experiments of this kind that have been undertaken have often been marginal within the system of education, and have suffered from a general lack of technical and logistic support as well as facilities for planning. For example, see BOISSET, C., *et al.*, 'Rénovation ou Programmes?' *Cahiers Pédagogiques*, no. 87, Jan. 1970, pp. 6–42, and Preuss-Lausitz, U., 'Bericht zur Lage von Lehrern an Gesamtschulen', *Gesamtschulen Informationsdienst*, no. 4, 1970, pp. 24 ff.

52 Similar proposals have been made in England but have found little support amongst teachers generally. See RENSHAW, P., 'A Curriculum for Teacher Education', in BURGESS, T., *Dear Lord James: A Critique of Teacher Education* (Harmondsworth: Penguin, 1971), pp. 78 ff.

53 Department of Education and Science, *A Teaching Council for England and Wales* (London; HMSO, 1970).

54 CLARK, *op. cit.*, pp. 25–30, but the largest *syndicats* have full-time officers concerned with matters of educational policy.

55 An account of this development and the organizations involved is to be found in FLUCK, B., 'Deutscher Lehrerverband gegründet', *die Höhere Schule*, XXII: 8 (1969), p. 197.

56 A Ministry circular banning unauthorized pedagogical experiments was published in the *Bulletin Officiel de l'Education Nationale* on Jan. 8., 1970.

57 Department of Education and Science, *Scales of Salaries for Teachers in Primary and Secondary Schools*, England and Wales 1971. (London: HMSO, 1971).

58 One recent article which gives an account of practices in one college based on this line of reasoning is COLLIER, K. G., 'Methods of Teaching Student Teachers', *Journal of Curriculum Studies*, vol. 3 (1971), no. 1, pp. 38–49. Few French writers appear to have given attention to institutional factors that may assist or inhibit the development of desired qualities in students, but see LALLEZ, R., 'Les changements dans le Rôle de l'Enseignant et leurs Conséquences', paper prepared for the Organization for Economic Co-operation and Development Experts' Meeting (Paris: OECD, 1972).

59 See HANNAM, C., *et al., Young Teachers and Reluctant Learners* (Harmondsworth: Penguin, 1971), chap. 1.

60 Biddle, *op. cit.*, p. 42.

61 See for example a discussion document for the National Union of Teachers Easter Conference, 1972, National Union of Teachers, *Teacher Participation: A Study Outline* (London: NUT, 1971).

62 A noteworthy exception to this in England was however an experiment in further professional study for secondary teachers organized jointly by Harlech Television and the University of Bristol Institute of Education, which included television programmes, printed background material and discussion groups. See TAYLOR, W., *Heading for Change* (Harlech Television and University of Bristol Institute of Education, 1969).

63 A number of the issues raised in the last section of this chapter are

extensively discussed in papers presented at the OECD Experts' Meeting on the Changing Role of the Teacher, held in Paris, in March 1972. See Organization for Economic Co-operation and Development, Education Committee, *The Changing Role of the Teacher and its Implications – General Report* (Paris: OECD, 1972).

64 For example, see Association pour la Recherche et l'Intervention Psycho-sociologiques, *Pédagogie et Psychologie des Groupes* (Paris: Editions de l'Epi, 1966); FILLOUX, J., 'Formation des Enseignants, Dynamique de Groupe et Changement', *Orientations*, no. 30, Apr. 1969; and FERRY, G., *La Pratique du Travail en Groupe* (Paris: Dunod, 1970).

65 Deutscher Bildungsrat, *Einrichtung von Schulversuchen mit Ganztagsschulen* (Bonn: Bundesdruckerei, 1968).

66 COCKBURN, H., and BLACKBURN, R., *Student Power: Problems, Diagnosis, Action* (Harmondsworth: Penguin, 1969).

67 Rank and File, *Democracy in Schools* (London:Rank and File, 1971).

68 The first of a planned series of reports on the *educational priority areas* project was published while this book was in press. See A. H. HALSEY (editor), *Educational Priority* (London: HMSO, 1972), vol. 1: 'EPA Problems and Policies'. On the development of policies relating to immigrant children, see TOWNSEND, H. E. R., *Immigrant Pupils in England: The LEA Response* (Slough, Bucks: NFER, 1971).

69 For an article in which the teacher is envisaged as a neutral discussion chairman, see STENHOUSE, L., 'Open-minded Teaching', *New Society*, July 24, 1969. More detailed theoretical justifications for non-directive teacher-taught relations are presented by HARGREAVES, D. H., *Interpersonal Relations and Education* (London: Routledge and Kegan Paul, 1972) and DE PERETTI, A., 'La Formation des Enseignants', *Revue Française de Pédagogie*, no. 6, Jan.–Mar. 1969, pp. 5–16.

70 GAMM, H. J. (1971), p. 225.

71 ILLICH, I., *Deschooling Society* (London: Caldar and Boyars, 1971). Illich's writings have received considerable attention in France and West Germany. See, for example, V. HENTIG, H., *Cuernavaca oder: Alternativen zur Schule?* (Stuttgart: Klett Verlag, 1971).

72 See the report that the North East London Polytechnic's students' admissions policy is in future to be based on the criterion of 'likely to benefit' rather than 'likely to succeed', in 'Polytechnic Discrimination', *Times Higher Education Supplement*, no. 15, Jan. 21, 1972.

73 OECD (Centre for Educational Research and Innovation), *Equal Educational Opportunity: A Statement of the Problem with Special Reference to Recurrent Education* (Paris: OECD, 1971).

74 OECD, Education Committee (1971), *op. cit.*

75 This is the case in the James Committee proposals for a broader curriculum for the Diploma of Higher Education (DIP. H.E.), though there is an apparent contradiction in the Committee's continuing emphasis on subject specialism elsewhere. See Department of Education and Science (1972), *op. cit.*

76 Inner London Education Authority, *Education Committee Minutes*, Wednesday May 12, 1971, Appendix, pp. 9–10. (Evidence submitted to the James Committee of Inquiry into Teacher Education.)

77 Ideas along these lines in French official circles have not been published, presumably because of their drastic implications for the whole teacher education system. This observation is based on Ministère de l'Education

Nationale, Planification Interne du Ministère, Groupe XV, 'Formation et Information des Maîtres' (Paris: MEN, 1969, mimeo).

78 Gewerkschaft Erziehung und Wissenschaft: Gesamtverband der Lehrer und Erzieher in Hessen, *Die Gesamtschule* (Frankfurt/Main: Gesamtverband der Lehrer und Erzieher in Hessen, 1971) and also der Hessische Kultusminister, *Informationen zur Gesamtschule* (Wiesbaden: Hessisches Kultusministerium, 1969 and following) (mimeo.).

79 BIRLEY, D., and DUFTON, A., *An Equal Chance: Equalities and Inequalities of Educational Opportunity* (London: Routledge and Kegan Paul, 1971).

80 The notion of such a teacher linking function was explored in a study of primary teachers in isolated areas of the Appalachian Mountains by one of the authors. See PLUNKETT, H. D., 'The Elementary School Teacher as an Interstitial Person' Unpublished PH.D. Dissertation, University of Chicago, 1967. Interest in community schools is increasingly widespread in the three countries of this study. See POSTER, C. D., *The School and the Community* (Basingstoke: MacMillan, 1971), and the report on the Centre educatif et culturel d'Yerres in TREFFEL, J., 'Des Centres Socio-culturels s'installent dans les Etablissements Scolaires', *L'Education*, no. 104, May 20, 1971. pp. II–III.

81 WRAGG, E. C., 'Interaction Analysis as a Feedback System for Student-teachers', *Education for Teaching*, no. 81, Spring, 1970, pp. 38–47.

82 For example, see HILSUM, S., and CANE, B. S., *The Teacher's Day* (Slough, Bucks: NFER, 1971). A similar study in Germany is SCHULTZE, W., and SCHLEIFFER, G., *Arbeitszeitanalyse des Volksschullehrers und Rationalisierung des Unterrichts* (Frankfurt/Main: Deutsches Institut für Internationale Pädagogische Forschung, 1965).

Chapter Four

The Process of Becoming a Teacher

We have been concerned so far in this part of the study with identifying some of the major indicators in the cultural systems of England, France and West Germany of the changing roles that teachers are expected to play, and thus which can serve to guide operational decisions in the development of teacher education. This chapter now takes up the second main theme of the study, the process of becoming a teacher, and focuses upon a number of cultural and social issues which have received only very slight attention in the three countries in discussion of post-secondary and recurrent education but which, at primary and secondary education levels, have been the central concern of educationists, both researchers and practitioners. Social learning, or socialization, was recognized classically to be the process of becoming a member of society.[1] The child had to learn to play a role in the society in terms of some generally acceptable value-orientations. The young child learns not only instrumental knowledge but also to understand and to articulate affective ideas. This process must necessarily be life-long, and yet adult socialization has been until recently a neglected area of inquiry.[2] Even though it is clear that the issues differ, this must be mainly because of the maturity and, in most practical instances of research, selected character of the population studied; however, the problem of the social and psychological realism of the objectives of any form of adult education, including teacher education, is analogous to that in other sectors of the educational system.

The process of becoming a teacher involves more than a purely professional socialization.[3] While we can start from the notion of the acquisition of values, knowledge and skills, the process has to be seen as contingent upon a whole range of psychological and social factors, of which it is the latter that directly concern us here. First, there is the set of conditions that have been grouped together for discussion in the previous chapter, that is the operational aims and role expectations held for teachers, as interpreted by the official teacher-education system. We are able to envisage this aspect of the socialization of teachers as the deliberate offering of a teacher role, which will of course vary according to the extent to which it is adequately encapsulated within institutionalized teacher education or allowed expression within its deliberately non-institutionalized or informal settings. Secondly, there are the social factors that stem from the student's accepting the role offered, that is the status and related transformations involved in becoming a teacher, including opting for or being selected into one of many possible categories of teacher. Thirdly, there is the interpretation of the social role of the teacher that is achieved by the student, depending in turn upon his social and cultural background, his social skills, social relations and other features or experiences cutting across his teacher education and not subject to institutional control. Fourthly, there is the interpretation of the professional role which the student achieves initially or as his career advances, and finally there are the age- and life-cycle factors which exert an independent influence. Undoubtedly, social, economic, religious and political experiences that are typical of different phases or generations influence social learning.

It is furthermore a plausible hypothesis that recruitment to teacher education shows social and other biases in addition to the social class bias we have already discussed. Investigations are few, and probably not reliable over time, but available studies and opinion suggest that the profile of teacher-education staff and students would already limit the objectives that the teachers' colleges can expect to entertain.[4] The youth of recruits to teacher education is criticized as inappropriate for many of the sub-roles to be learnt. The feminization of teaching in France especially must affect the aims of teacher educators or policy-makers. The relationship of the ability and qualifications of teacher-education students to those of students in other sectors of higher education, the motives of student-teachers in choosing their career amongst alternatives, whether there were alternatives, and the expectations that students have acquired for teacher education from the social image it conveys in the particular society at a particular time, are all factors that weight the scales before the institutionalized process of becoming a teacher has begun.

In this chapter, to summarize, the scene shifts from the school, for which the teacher role-expectations apply, to the teachers' college or training course through which they are expressed, in so far as they are expressed, to those individuals who are duly enrolled. Policy-makers in teacher education have to take into account whatever features they can identify in the process by which students make the transition to the role of teacher or by which teachers themselves change their roles. The study of the experiencing of teacher education, viewed not merely from the curricular or organizational point of view but also as a socializing process, is central to understanding whether and how particular perceptions of the teacher's role can be effectively and fruitfully presented to students and teachers. Such a study involves attention not only to the formal procedures of teacher education, but to a wider social and cultural context which can affect its outcomes and, no less important, to the informal structures of influence and of social behaviour within the institutions of teacher education. If we take the major orientations of the teacher's role as those outlined in Chapter Three, that is, subject-, system-, child-, and community-centred, it would be expected that a distinct social process of induction and not just a different course or curriculum would be required to reach each of the four outcomes. The question for study is whether the conditions can be obtained in which students and teachers may be expected to develop the attitudes and behaviour of the type of teacher favoured by educational, social and political policy-makers. We can therefore advance the study by projecting forward from the sets of role expectations we have suggested the types of socialization processes and policy decisions that have been pursued or will need to be considered in the three societies, if the objectives of education are to be anything other than the mere calculation of social probabilities.

1. BECOMING A SUBJECT-CENTRED TEACHER

1.1 The nineteenth century teacher, whether for elementary or for academic secondary schools, learnt his role by the supervised performance of it. The pupil-teacher system in England developed from the earlier monitorial system, and continued to co-exist with college- and later university-based teacher training until well into the twentieth century.[5] A similar apprenticeship process existed in France, where the *écoles normales* and the *écoles normales supérieures* have never had the capacity to meet the demand for the elementary and secondary teachers which they were established to train. With the passing years of the nineteenth century in Germany the system of craft apprenticeship and *Seminar* training for teaching in the elementary school was gradually supplemented, first by courses provided by individual teachers or teachers' associations and later by the introduction of separate preparatory institutions, *Präparandenanstalten*, which could service the general educational needs of the *Seminar*.[6] Academic secondary teachers, on the other hand, were educated at the *Gymnasium* and the university.[7]

The pupil-teacher systems in the three societies required the student to serve a basic apprenticeship in the teaching of his subject or subjects. The work of the teachers' colleges developed in response to a less limited public conception of education as a utilitarian solution to the needs of more advanced economies for a labour force possessing elementary skills and knowledge. The early institutions in England and Germany were religious foundations whose main declared purpose was the harnessing of education to a Christian cause. The *écoles normales* on the other hand, grew up under a centralized system concerned with implementing a nation-building programme of mass elementary education and had a more self-consciously political function.[8]

1.2 The pupil-teacher system sufficed for a large number of elementary teachers until well into the nineteenth century. But the more schooled teachers in the three countries were being prepared for a limited range of highly conventional roles through studies in teaching-subjects and practice teaching in model schools, *écoles d'application* or *Übungsschulen*. The basic stratification characterizing the school-teachers was clearly evident in the different orders of knowledge required of those in each half of the dual system. The elementary teacher never experienced secondary education for the most part in England and Germany, scarcely ever in France. He belonged from the beginning to a separate world.[9] The academic teacher experienced secondary and, increasingly, university education. Strongly committed to a subject, he none the less had little opportunity to consider its pedagogy or its place within the total curriculum. Even more than the elementary teachers, secondary teachers could be said to be acquiring a craft.

1.3   There was thus in all three societies a hierarchy of teachers and of ways of becoming a teacher. As training institutions were established, the intending teacher could go either to an elementary training college or to a university, or in France to the *école normale supérieure,* according to his academic point of departure and teaching destination. In Prussia from 1826 all selective secondary teachers had to undergo a one year probationary period and in 1890 this was extended to two years. But the effectiveness of this development was inhibited by the secondary school-teacher's traditional disdain for educational theory. The two alternative basic routes into teaching were virtually sealed off from each other, not only educationally but socially as well.

It was suggested in Chapter One that this dual system of teacher training had evolved into a contemporary *three-tier system.* In England and Germany, the training of the intermediate teacher was largely provided by the training college rather than the university,[10] and in England it has only been with the development of comprehensive secondary schools during the 1960s that the universities have trained any substantial proportion of intermediate teachers. In France, intermediate teachers are largely recruited through the *écoles normales,* but are allowed to filter through into university courses.[11] This has broken the mould of the dual system but essentially only for an élite of younger primary teachers who are permitted to change their training orientation in mid-course. For the great majority, and in all three societies, choosing to be an elementary or a secondary teacher was to all intents and purposes equivalent to choosing a different career. The institutionally-related factors contributing to maintaining this situation will be examined in Chapter Six, but its existence must be borne in mind in considering the socialization of teachers. In motivation, expectations, and in academic and social environments, the training programmes for the two major types of teacher were providing two distinct sequences of experience for two separate social groups.[12]

1.4   The traditional teachers' colleges of all three societies, which were almost entirely residential up to the early years of the twentieth century, were predominantly located in isolated rural areas and exercised a high degree of control over the lives of their trainees. The colleges were almost exclusively single-sex. In England and many parts of Germany they had a strongly religious character.[13] In England and France a pledge system operated that bound the student-teacher in return for his scholarship to a single chosen vocation.[14] Until well into the present century acceptance of elementary teacher training implied conformity to a set of social values and to a view of the world: one which was predominantly religious in England and Germany and secular in France. Students were recruited directly by the teachers' colleges, predominantly from the surrounding region.[15] This narrow form of socialization was continued after entry to teaching both through the social pressures exerted on school teachers, especially in smaller communities,[16] and because by and large the only educational contacts open to the teacher were those provided by colleagues and through professional and subject associations.

In England and Germany staff of these institutions were largely recruited from academic secondary schools and their social values were very different from those of the students. Principals of colleges were usually from universities, and often in orders, with little or no experience of teaching in schools or colleges. These teachers' colleges were authoritarian by modern standards, with their regimes of long hours of study, manual labour and confinement to the premises of the colleges except on specified occasions.[17] In France, the secondary-level element of the *école normale* exercised a preponderant influence in preserving, even to the present day, a type of rule-bound institution with an exceedingly narrow conception of its teacher-training function, in which the pupil-teacher was allowed almost no initiative.[18]

2. BECOMING A SYSTEM-CENTRED TEACHER

2.1 Social training of teachers for the task of popular education was seriously in default in the early colleges, though in England Kay-Shuttleworth believed that elementary teachers should be chosen from the working classes for the instinctive knowledge of their pupils that this would give them, and that they should not be permitted to alter their social position through their education.[19] In fact, the staffs of the English colleges were academically trained people who lacked the experience to provide a broad social education. The evidence for this lies in the restrictive format of the institutions they organized, with concentration upon bookwork, coercive methods, lecture-based instruction and students' teaching practice. The teachers' colleges in the three societies were seen from the beginning as offering aspiring students of humble social origins a chance of advancement but in fact elementary teacher training offered only a highly restricted opportunity for social mobility. Though the social experience of the future elementary teacher was severely limited, even less attention was given to the social education of future secondary teachers. There was no institutionalized training provision in England until 1890. In France the *écoles normales supérieures* for secondary teachers were two in number, and no other provision was made until the *centres pédagogiques régionaux* were established in 1952. In spite of earlier precedents, especially in Prussia, the second phase of *educational* preparation was only generalized to secondary teachers in all *Länder* of West Germany after the Second World War.[20] In short, social and professional objectives in the preparation of teachers were relatively neglected in comparison with those of an academic character.

In so far as such broader models of teacher education have been accepted in the three societies, they can be assimilated to *cell two* of the typology. A particular emphasis is encountered in some institutions upon fostering teaching vocations, and this has been the object of many of the major historical developments that have taken place within teacher education. Replacing a view of teacher education as mainly a technical matter of the supply of personnel and of skills, policies emerge in which the education of teachers is seen as the development of personalities fit for an essentially moral and indeed often religious function. Teachers' colleges in which this latter view was prevalent developed their own philosophies and traditions, and sought to perpetuate a view of teaching in which the commitment to an ethic of service was an important component. Such systems built up from the early nineteenth century, but their abiding weakness, that they existed within stratified educational systems, began to be evident with general aspirations towards educational democratization in the 1940s.

2.2   The intellectual landmarks in this approach to teacher education were not original, but derived from the traditions of university scholarship epitomized by the highly formalized use of Herbartian theories in German teachers' colleges.[21] Academic achievement provided the basis for appointment to senior staff positions in the teachers' colleges, and such appointments in turn assured the maintenance of scholarly values and epistemological structures which were then recognized and imitated by student-teachers. The enduring inferior status of the teachers' colleges in all three societies can be ascribed in large part to the fact that these institutions accepted unquestioningly the norms of academic discipleship to the wider university system and confined the professional elements of their training courses to a low status and a purely instrumental function.[22]

2.3   Far from achieving their status through training, the highest placed teachers in England and France traditionally were dispensed from training altogether. A university degree was considered sufficient prerequisite for teaching; in France the *licence d'enseignement*, which continued to exist until 1966, contained no element of professional training. In Germany, where an educational phase to the training of selective school-teachers had been generalized in Prussia in 1890, there appears to have been greater sensitivity to the need for specialist subjects and education studies, though the position of the latter remains marginal.[23] The personnel of the teachers' colleges in all three countries encountered fundamental scepticism, and even contempt for their work, and this discouraging atmosphere has constituted an undoubted blight upon the colleges' staffing and development. Beyond this basic division between the academic teachers and the rest, there were further hierarchies of subject-matter, with academic teaching-subjects having the advantage both over more practical subjects and *professional*, that is educational or pedagogical studies. Student-teachers could hardly fail to imbibe this ordering and valuing of knowledge, and their investment of effort in study, as well as their definition of their own professional role, have tended to reflect the same priorities. The most recent developments in teacher education do not appear to be countering such tendencies. For example, it seems that the English B.Ed. degree and the *Diplom-Pädagoge* qualification in Germany[24] have hardly departed from this basic epistemology, while in France there is a well-recognized practice among *normaliens* in the university towns whereby they moonlight courses in the faculties, neglecting their *école normale* studies to do so.

2.4   It was suggested in Chapter Two that students in the colleges are already exposed to two conflicting frames of reference without even considering the external pressures they encounter. On the one hand, they may work with lecturers who emphasize the virtues of theoretical understanding, while on the other they may find that the teachers in the schools where they do their practice teaching have less idealized views of teacher-pupil relations and of classroom experiences.[25] The reconciliation of this conflict cannot itself be a theoretical process. Rather, the tension for the student-teacher, stretched between the two views and trying to serve both masters, is a problem which already has a long history.[26] What policy solutions are developed, however, will depend upon a fuller analysis of the values and concepts mediated by the organization and curriculum of teacher education, within its wider academic and social context, and as these are interpreted by student-teachers to convey legitimate expectations for their present and future roles.

The early teachers' colleges assumed the character of *total institutions*, enveloping the entire existence of the student-teacher, other than during his vacations, and imposing upon him a set of values, a style of behaviour or a way of life. This can be inferred from the kinds of rules that the colleges applied, for they went far beyond any logical requirements for socialization into specific teachers' roles, and reflected the authority of social and cultural traditions and of the older generation. Up to the Second World War in English colleges autonomous student activity was extremely limited outside the recreational sphere. For some time afterwards it was not even an issue since, as Shipman reports, students could find staff concern and involvement in their corporate life gratifying.[27] There was little scope for exploration of controversial religious and social, let alone political, matters.

In the *écoles normales* discipline was little different from that of other types of secondary schools, and in fact had the added constraints associated with the residential status of almost all the students. Restricted recreation times, a curfew and time for lights-out, regulations about seeking permission to marry, and a wide range of regulations covering ideologically oriented activities continued to be enforced up to 1968. Since then they have tended to be relaxed or to become dead letters, but ministerial circulars still draw the attention of *école normale* directors to the regulations that they are responsible for maintaining.[28] Though in Germany pressure in the old *Seminare* was less direct, the regulation of the curricular and extra-curricular life of the young student was none the less stringent. Strict time-tabling and the setting of homework was continued with the founding of the *pädagogische Akademien* in the 1920s. An intensive community life was fostered within the colleges in spite of their non-residential character. Although academic teacher training in an institution of higher education *sui generis* had been conceived of as needing a strong community basis, the traditional anonymity of staff/student relationships in German universities gradually developed in the teachers' colleges as they increased in size. It was only in the mid-1960s that the almost competely separate social systems began slowly to take up contact again and by this time the development was too late to seem anything more than a liberal response to student militancy.[29] Recruitment into such institutions has involved an implicit contract to accept the prevailing system of values. As a system of socialization, the training in the teachers' colleges involved monopolistic control by the authorities. The consequences of such a one-dimensional approach are suggested in research conclusions recently reported by McLeish to the effect that the most complimentary view of colleges is taken by students who 'like the lecture system, do not value personal freedom too much, are somewhat tough-minded about education. . . .'[30]

For as long as any potential internal contradictions could be contained, it was possible to assess and modify accustomed ways. Examinations set the seal upon performance, and the whole training process was judged by very limited samples of academic or practical work. Basically teachers continue to be paid in England, France and West Germany according to their initial qualifications, and the most powerful sanction available to the authorities remains the final examination grade. The concern of examiners has become that of increasing the fairness of recognized examination procedures. Cumbersome arrangements for moderation have been evolved in all three countries, without any appreciable advance in the refinement of the criteria for assessment. In the present state of teacher education the ability to write essays about education relying upon reproducing or at best synthesizing ideas and information contained in secondary sources, and the talent for stage-managing an oral examination or a practical teaching performance in front of adult strangers, are inevitably prized.[31] The application of these narrow and artificial standards reflects the weight of academic and cultural traditions that will be balanced against reasonable reform.

Educationists have long ago recognized the educational counterproductivity of the authoritarian character of a teachers' college. A sociological understanding of teacher education, in which the student-teacher is perceived as being educated as much by his environment, its culture and its formal and informal social structure as by the curriculum or the overt intentions of the teaching staff, has only in recent years been evident in research literature.[32] Quite recently in England it was possible for a researcher to draw attention to the lack of studies seeking to relate attitude changes of student-teachers to characteristics of the social structures within which they were being trained.[33] Those studies which have now been carried out seem likely to become models for future research. If teacher education is an important experience for the student-teacher, this, from the point of view of the policy-maker, will be because it modifies the student's behaviour in desired directions; thus all factors liable to modify behaviour should receive consideration. An understanding of the developing behaviour of student-teachers must take into account the social and epistemological context that gives it meaning in terms of both social structural and experiential perspectives.

3. BECOMING A CHILD-CENTRED TEACHER

3.1 A sea-change in teacher education occurred after the Second World War when the societies of Western Europe experienced a severe break with their traditional ways of life. Families disrupted by the war, the mobility of people in search of employment, new industrial development, and associated economic, social and political aspirations, all created a different climate to which educational institutions had to respond. At first this could be seen as a requirement that educational systems should serve an intrinsic democratizing function by developing in people the knowledge that would set them free. But it began to be apparent by the late 1950s that education was still closely tied to systems of social stratification in Western Europe, and that the values to which educational systems claimed to be responding were only weakly or ineffectively supported in the societies at large.

The teachers' colleges in all three societies were late in recognizing and in coming to terms with the changing student culture with its new emphasis upon the rights of individuals and the need for social and educational reform. As the demands of dissenting groups began to be affirmed they were frequently regarded as illegitimate and provocative. Teacher education developed a counter-cyclical character, whilst the rhetorical declarations of teacher-training authorities since the war have not ceased to repeat their democratizing purposes. Gradually, however, the institutions of teacher education have been forced to recognize their responsibility for developing a critique of modern education and of modern society by calling upon the human and social sciences, if they are to recruit, train and effectively set to work a generation of democratically committed teachers. The originality of whatever contemporary achievements can be demonstrated in teacher education in the three societies should not be gauged from the frequency with which they have been demanded by educators, but from the degree of resistance to social change that has characterized teacher education for half a century.[34]

3.2 The changes that have occurred have required fresh diagnoses of educational problems and the training of specialist teachers to deal with newly identifiable tasks. Thus innovation in teacher education came to be characterized after the Second World War by the gradual addition of areas of specialism in subject-matter, and the introduction of training in new skills and by new methods. In particular there has been an emphasis upon the study of society and of the pupil rather than upon knowledge of teaching-subjects. Preliminary training courses have broadened in scope and have become longer in order to accommodate this larger purpose. In-service training has developed to assist serving teachers to revise their educational objectives and methods, through experiments with courses for probationary teachers in England and for unqualified primary teachers in France, and through the inception of a full second phase of professional education for elementary teachers and courses for the re-training of certain subject specialists in Germany.[35] With a swing back of the pendulum, these changes in training strategies have led to the development of up-dated apprenticeship systems involving master-teachers guiding the less experienced. The advisory roles being adopted by inspectors in England and France, the introduction of a *social practice* for student-teachers in West Germany,[36] the use of teacher-tutors on teaching practice and the emerging role of the local teachers' centre leader in England, are examples of experimental transformations of the authoritarian relationships within which teachers have traditionally learnt their roles.

3.3   The social organization of teacher education responded quantitatively and qualitatively to post-war needs. In England and West Germany the foundation of new institutions and the expansion of old ones began very swiftly, at first in the form of emergency training schemes. An example of the social consequences of increase of size is reported by Shipman in a longitudinal survey of Worcester College of Education.[37] In his view the personal, informal organization of the college began to break down as its numbers of students reached 500 and, despite temporary nostalgia for the community atmosphere that had disappeared, the institution was forced gradually to assume impersonal and bureaucratic characteristics and procedures, whilst separate subcultures began to form amongst staff and students. Indeed, a certain polarization of staff-student relations became evident throughout higher education in western societies by the mid-1960s, and Shipman's study reflects what has since become a well recognized social phenomenon.

   The larger college is forced to think out its purposes and to justify its operations in terms of widely acceptable goals. Practical changes can no longer be achieved by seeking to convey to students and to reinforce teacher-role models which are thought appropriate by the authorities alone. The structural conditions of the larger institution, and the cultural change in students' attitudes in modern colleges, are merely further complications in a process that was always more complex than writers about it have implied.[38] The conflict of reference groups that has been described, and the break in continuity of experience that occurs with the end of formal training, make it probable that there is considerable reversal of whatever gains are made towards the socialization objectives of teacher-education institutions at pre- or in-service levels.[39]

3.4   Various strategies appeared in efforts by institutions to combat disadvantages of expansion. In larger colleges, organization was needed to achieve communication, whether for instrumental or expressive purposes. Change engineered by authorities was at first easier, while members of institutions accepted the system of government by consensus. For example, early departmental organization and students' union activities in English colleges were, and frequently still are, subordinate to the decision-making power of the principal. Gradually however areas of autonomy, or desired autonomy, were staked out, and the ideological unity of the institutions began to disintegrate as conflicts of interest came to be acknowledged.[40] In England this first occurred at staff level, and was met by the setting up of a committee charged by the DES to examine the government of colleges of education.[41] The institution of academic boards, which was accelerated by the Weaver Report, dispersed decision-making power to some degree. However the student was still to have no part in the growth of democratic structure that the Report envisaged.

Very little has been written about the *écoles normales* in this perspective. They have grown little in size except in the largest cities, and in fact many provincial institutions have actually decreased in size as they have given up some of their pre-*baccalauréat* classes without taking in more post-secondary students. Since 1968, like all other secondary and post-secondary educational institutions, the *écoles normales* have been required to have administrative councils upon which the authorities, staff, and students are represented. It is too early to judge how far this innovation will change the authority relationships which have characterized their organization hitherto, but research on the cultural and social structural characteristics of the *écoles normales* and their effects upon teacher socialization would now be of great strategic interest for the French educational system. In Germany the social pressures of the mid–1960s ensured that student participation was in the forefront of discussions of the reform of higher education in general. Students have now achieved substantial representation in all *Länder*, in many cases holding one-third or exceptionally up to a half of the seats on committees of government, though a system of reserved items is usually built in for such matters as the election of the rector or the appointment of staff.[42] Progress in the professional institutions for training selective secondary teachers has predictably been much slower and less radical. The effectiveness of such participation is however weakened by the formalism that it has produced and the deliberate policy of certain minority left-wing radical students' organizations of seeking to control universities by the establishment of small cadres devoted to long-term revolutionary aims and rejecting traditional concepts of the freedom of research and teaching in higher education.

The aspirations of junior members of staff and of students in the three societies were frequently more concerned with life in organizations than with education, and were derived from wider currents in their societies and cultures. Within the institutions it was evidently easier for the authorities to envisage change in terms of routinization and rationalization than through the redistribution of power. With perhaps an increasing number of exceptions, institutions have resisted democratization; their innovations have been experimental, or worked out on the basis of the best opinion of the decision-makers of an experienced generation. Innovation has tended to occur within the interstices of an only very slowly evolving authority structure.

Closely relating to their ambivalent stance over authority in the institutions, assessment policies in the teachers' colleges still focus very heavily upon scheduled individual work. This system is, generally speaking, much stronger in France than in England and Germany and indeed the widespread use of the device of the *numerus clausus* in the competitive examination still marks the major transition-points in the French student's educational career. In England particularly, experiments with behaviourally defined objectives for courses aimed at reducing subjectivity and imbalances in testing, continuous assessment, the assessment of group-work, and a variety of forms of course and curriculum evaluation, are being reported within teacher education. Expertise is very scarce in this area, but the critical problems are conceptual rather than statistical. The decision to alter curricula, teaching methods and even the objectives of courses rests very often upon the degree of flexibility that can be attained in examination structures which involve many interests and institutions, and which tend to have their own powerful histories and epistemologies.[43]

4. BECOMING A COMMUNITY-CENTRED TEACHER

4.1   As the institutions of teacher education feel themselves to be increasingly a part of a changing society with a responsibility both to interpret and to influence that change, a new range of options for teacher socialization-related policies opens up. The principle of the democratization of education becomes less of an academic commonplace and more of a guideline for the education of teachers. A major *cell four* type development in a limited number of institutions is that the process of becoming a teacher is being operationally envisaged as the learning of a complex social role composed of technical tasks, moral and other affective orientations and social skills. Many of the behaviours which the student needs to learn cannot be deliberately built into a teaching programme, but must be assimilated as part of the fabric of the student's everyday experiences in both academic and social situations. The college is itself a society, and a society within a wider human community. This new perspective has become especially characteristic of the more innovatory teachers' colleges in the three societies.

Where the social dimensions of teachers' colleges are clearly recognized a constitutionally ordered pluralism of values and norms replaces an assumed cultural homogeneity. Amongst both staff and students varied points of view seek expression and the process of arguing a case and tolerating diversity of ideas becomes itself part of the experience of becoming a teacher. Even if there is a reluctance to consider the social implications of the acceptance of an inquiry-centred approach to learning, the national acceptance of this approach has become an axiom of modern higher education.[44] Further, while pre-service training programmes orient themselves increasingly to school systems in which equality of educational opportunity is the overt goal, in-service training provision must seek to change the attitudes of serving teachers, in fact to re-socialize them in terms of different social values, teaching skills, and even priorities of commitment amongst their academic and social tasks. The establishing of multilateral and comprehensive schools, and of integrated rather than subject-based curricula, cuts across the differentiated structure of traditional teacher education, with its isolated institutions giving courses to segregated strata of student-teachers with little awareness of social or occupational alternatives. Oriented by these kinds of considerations, the courses were lengthened: in the case of primary teachers from two to three years in England, in 1960, from one to two post-secondary years in France, in 1968, and progressively to three years in Germany during the 1960s. The training of the certificated teacher in England became as long as that of the degree student in the universities. The duration of professional training for graduate teachers however did not increase and in some cases was even reduced.[45] Socially the two types of experience became more similar. The staff-dominated society of the small college in England began to give way in the larger colleges to the typical students' union atmosphere of the provincial university.

4.2 Compartmentalized training courses, specialized subject studies, the recruitment of student-teachers during or immediately after their secondary schooling, and firmly crystallized curricula in schools, are all being called in question. It is becoming accepted that the knowledge, attitudes and skills appropriate to the teacher's role can be acquired through experience in practical situations and simulated exercises as well as through hearing formal expositions,[46] and this learning cuts across traditional institutional and cultural boundaries as well as epistemological categories. Many of the teachers' associations have argued for unification of their profession, simplification of its career structure and for the integration of teacher education with other forms of professional and higher education. The contradiction between the democratization of higher education that this would entail and the élitism of the basic entry qualifications usually required has not been resolved. However, pressures are building up to recast the inherited epistemology of teacher education in all three societies to reflect new socially-oriented learning theories and contemporary social priorities.[47]

4.3 Signs of the transformation of the social structure of the teachers' colleges in consistently democratizing directions can also be observed. Internally, the scope for choice and decision by students is broadened in curricular and other areas. Rules tend to be subjected to negotiation, and reformed or abolished. The life style of the college student is assimilated to that of the undergraduate. Staff-student relations shift from a vertical towards a horizontal axis. Though bureaucratization occurs to facilitate life in the larger institutions, the rights of individuals and the value of interpersonal communication in small units are upheld and pursued through the development of *open* social, academic and administrative structures.[48] Externally, the colleges reassess their relations to the community, locally and at large. Service activities, practical field-work and school experience supplement the traditional teaching practice and increase the social learning and cultural versatility of the students. The school and the community become the environment for the work rather than the terminus of the neophyte teacher. The isolation of the college gives way, within the formal course and in the personal and social life of the students, to more integrated organizational patterns.

Among current developments are the establishment of polytechnics and multi-professional colleges in England, the academic links between teachers' colleges and universities in France, as in the arrangements made for intermediate teachers to follow the first cycle of university studies, and in West Germany the assimilation of colleges of education into full university life.[49] Co-educational colleges are becoming more the norm in all three countries, if often for economic rather than for social reasons. The affiliation of students to professional associations is now tolerated, if not encouraged, in France, while professional, social and political activities have become common in many colleges in England and West Germany, with issues of local and of national concern being as closely followed by student-teachers as by students in the universities. The question of a relationship between pre- and in-service training is seriously posed in the three societies. Little consensus is discernible in the proposals that have been made to give a structure to a continuous learning and socialization process. Recent policy recommendations in the three countries include cutting short the pre-service course for some categories of teachers, lengthening it for others, imposing a probationary year course of training, permitting a second-stage qualification, or requiring in-service training for promotion, for salary increments or simply giving teachers the opportunity to update their knowledge and increase their professional efficiency.

4.4 Such new strategies for teacher education are essentially responding to the wider community in its complexity and inter-relatedness. The fact that the student-teacher's professional training is becoming increasingly related to a social context cannot be interpreted merely as a political victory for student militancy. This and other developments with a broadening cultural character reflect the commonly recognized movement in society at large away from trust in established institutions and authority; the educational system and the family are perhaps the two social institutions in which this issue has become most familiar. Far from it being a case of rigid confrontation, however, it can be argued that the holders of authority are retreating at least as fast from their positions of power as their subordinates are advancing. The collapse of philosophical, psychological and social arguments for viewing socialization as a one-dimensional process by which the young are initiated into the pre-existing society of their elders, leaves only the political, or pragmatic foundation for the maintenance of society's traditional structures. It is found, however, that this authority mutates in education as its very possessors find arguments for leaving the young to choose, to decide, to participate. The authority of the examination and selective system, so vehemently defended by the authors of the Black Papers in England,[50] is undermined by theoretical argument and empirical research, on social as well as on docimological grounds.[51]

A reaction can be noted in many teachers' colleges against the authoritarianism still extant in the schools and in relations amongst teachers at different levels of the educational hierarchy. Inspectors in England have relinquished the direct authority they held a generation or less ago, while in France they are more strongly opposed at the present time than ever before and their demeanour and roles are beginning to change. The headmaster or director of the school is under pressure to divest himself of his authority, to open up the decision-making process, to delegate his powers. In France especially, where activity was galvanized by the 1968 events, the decentralization of power in the school has to some degree been institutionalized. Reflecting these social changes, training courses in all three countries are being demanded to assist the transition to a more democratic system in curricular, pastoral and administrative areas.[52]

It has come to be assumed that student-teachers are being trained to help develop an educational system, and not merely to service it. Through rapid promotion or through processes of consultation they can expect to have influence whilst still young in such areas as curriculum development, in England and Germany, or academic selection and guidance, in France. Their training anticipates the discretion available to them in their future roles. Learning and teaching are increasingly seen as collaborative activities. The objectives of education need to be worked out by teacher and learners together and in relation to the needs of particular individuals and social groups. Practice with new media of communication, work in groups and systematic inquiries or research all constitute, in the teachers' colleges and on in-service training courses, experience of anticipatory socialization for specifiable teacher roles. Teachers' colleges are tending to concentrate less attention than formerly on the certification of individual students and more on the validation and development of particular training procedures and curricula. The criteria which are increasingly invoked are psychological, social and political objectives. The prescriptive absolutes of ministerial circulars are receding in importance in modern society, and the cultural barriers between teacher education and the wider community are seen to be removable in so far as it proves possible to overcome the ignorance involved in the scholasticism of the institutions and the formalism of their organization. These aspects of teacher education therefore provide the major themes of our next two chapters.

REFERENCES

1 DURKHEIM, E., *Education and Sociology* (New York: Free Press, 1956), pp. 71 ff.
2 See BRIM, O. G., and WHEELER, S. W., *Socialization after Childhood* (New York: Wiley, 1966).
3 For an example of a sociological study of teacher education based upon

socialization theory, see MARSLAND, D., 'An Exploration of Professional Socialization: the College of Education and the School-teacher's Role', *Research into Higher Education, 1969* (London: Society for Research into Higher Education, 1970). As will appear later, professional, or 'institutionalized' socialization forms only a part of the area of our interest in socialization in this study.

4 This field is at present little studied, but see TAYLOR, W. (1969), *op. cit.*, chap. 8: 'The Staff of the Colleges and Departments of Education' and MORTON-WILLIAMS, R., *et al.*, *Undergraduate Attitudes to Teaching as a Career* (London: Government Social Survey, 1966).

5 The final abolition of the pupil-teacher system in England was recommended in 1925. See DENT, H. C., 'An Historical Perspective', in HEWETT, S., *The Training of Teachers: A Factual Survey* (London: University of London Press, 1971), pp. 12–23.

6 The introduction of state preparatory institutions led to a rapid decline of numbers in the pupil-teacher systems. See for example GRÖNHOFF, J., *Die Berufsausbildung der Lehrer und Lehrerinnen in Schleswig-Holstein* (Kiel: Verlag Ferdinand Hirt, 1963), pp. 57 ff.

7 For a brief account of the development of the pedagogical-practical element of secondary academic teachers' training, see Ständige Konferenz der Kultusminister, *Zur Ausbildung der Lehrer an Gymnasien: Dokumentation* (Bonn: 1963, mimeo.), pp. 117 ff.

8 PROST, *op. cit.*, pp. 137 ff.

9 MINOT, *op. cit.*, p. 20.

10 Opportunities for exceptional students to attend a university after completion of their elementary teacher training were first offered in Saxony in 1865, through the influence of Ziller, a disciple of Herbart. From 1896 it was possible for students in Prussia who had completed their training in a *Seminar* to study as second-class students at a university. See BUNGARDT, K., *Der Weg der Lehrerbildung vom Seminar bis zur Universität*. (Bühl-Baden: Konkordia Verlag, 1964), pp. 8 ff.

11 The training of the French intermediate teacher (*professeur de l'enseignement général de collège*) consisted of completing the first cycle of university studies (DUEL) and following a one-year course of professional training in an *école normale* located in a university town. Students training to be *instituteurs* could transfer to the intermediate course if they were judged to be able enough, and could also take the *concours* to enter the *école normale supérieure*. See OECD (1969), *op. cit.*, pp. 190–91.

12 ANTZ, J., 'Die Seminaristische Lehrerbildung des 19. und 20. Jahrhunderts in Historischer und Kritischer Beleuchtung', *Pädagogische Rundschau*, Sonderheft, 1947, pp. 134 ff.

13 Possibly the most detailed account of the development of *Seminare* in Germany is THIELE, G., *Geschichte der Preussischen Lehrerseminare* (Berlin: Weidmannsche Verlagsbuchhandlung, 1938).

14 The English *pledge system* is described in Board of Education, *Teachers and Youth Leaders* (McNair Report) (London: HMSO, 1944), chap. 9, where it is recommended that the system of bonding students to the educational service should be discontinued. A similar system, much more rigorously enforced than was ever the case in England, still obliges French student-teacher recipients of scholarships to give ten years' service in education. See OECD (1969), *op. cit.*, p. 233.

15 This was for example the policy of the Prussian Ministry in setting up the

Pädagogische Akademien. See VAN DEN DRIESCH, J., *Die Neuordnung der Volksschullehrerbildung in Preussen* (Berlin: Weidmannsche Buchhandlung, 1925). This continues to be the policy in France where students are almost exclusively recruited to the *école normale* in their *département*. Although this regional recruitment has not been the case with the English colleges, with the recent establishment of more day colleges and the recruitment of large numbers of mature students it has been argued that the regional recruitment of students will be likely to be strengthened. See TAYLOR, W., 'Regional Origins of Students in Colleges of Education', *Education for Teaching*, no. 74, 1967, pp. 11–18.

16 These were particularly acute in the case of women teachers. See Gahlings and Moering (1961), *op. cit.*, pp. 24 ff.

17 Extensive descriptions of life in an early *Seminar* are contained in Möbuss (1907), *op. cit.*

18 BATAILLON, M., *et al.*, *Rebâtir l'Ecole* (Paris: Payot, 1967), p. 266.

19 Reported in Taylor (1969), *op. cit.*, pp. 94–95.

20 For a description of the development of academic secondary teacher training see DERBALOV, J., *Die Pädagogische Ausbildung der Lehrer an höheren Schulen durch die Universität und das Studienseminar* (Bonn: Verlag H. Bouvier and Co., 1956).

21 The development of education studies in Germany is described in GUTHMANN, J., *Über die Entwicklung des Studiums der Pädagogik* (Bühl-Baden: Konkordia Verlag, 1964).

22 It is interesting to note that, in his attempt to find a way to rehabilitate the practical learning in teacher education by proposing a clinical component, Conant argues that medical education has never suffered from a devaluing of its practical applications and the rehearsing of them in training. See CONANT, J. B., *op. cit.*

23 A useful overview of the position and content of such studies in 1968 is provided in LORENZ, G. E., 'Zum Stand und Zur Problematik der Ausbildung von Gymnasiallehrern an der Universität', *Rundgespräch*, no. 1, 1968, pp. 9–22.

24 See for example 'Diplom-Prüfungsordnung in Erziehungswissenschaft für die pädagogische Hochschule Niedersachsen', *Niedersächsisches Ministerialblatt*, no. 39, 1970, pp. 1146–49.

25 COHEN, L., 'Colleges and the Training of Teachers', *Educational Research*, XI, Nov., 1968, pp. 14–21.

26 Findings similar to Cohen's are reported in a recent survey on young teachers' opinions about their training, in which a majority of the respondents said that they experienced conflict in the expectations of their colleges and their schools with respect to the degree of formality of their teaching. See Inner London Education Authority, 'A Survey of Professional Opinion about Teacher Training' (Report of the Research and Statistics Group), in ILEA Education Committee Minutes, May 12, 1971, Appendix 2. Almost exactly the same problem was revealed in a report, cited by Jones, of the Manchester University Education Department Students' Committee on the training course in 1919. See JONES, L., *op. cit.*, p. 139.

27 SHIPMAN, M., *op. cit.*

28 Ministère de l'Education Nationale, *Circulaire no. 70–366*, Sept. 14, 1970, was a reminder from the Minister to the directors of the *Écoles Normales* as to their disciplinary duties.

29 The problem of disturbance of university life became so acute that the Federal Government was required by the *Bundestag* to report on the internal political situation in the Federal Republic and to begin negotiations for the reform of the organization of institutions of higher education. See Deutscher Bundestag, *170 Sitzung* (Bonn: May 7, 1968).

30 MCLEISH, J., *Students' Attitudes and College Environments* (Cambridge: Cambridge Institute of Education, 1970), p. 90.

31 BOURDIEU, P., and PASSERON, J. C. (1968), *op. cit.*

32 COHEN, L., *op. cit.* There is apparently no research of this kind reported in France, though the need for it is clearly recognized by LALLEZ, R., *op. cit.*, who speaks of the importance of the life-style and human relations in a teachers' college.

33 CANE, B., 'Review of recent British Research Relevant to Teacher Education', in House of Commons Select Committee on Education and Science (Session 1969–70), *Teacher Training* Minutes of Evidence Feb. 10, 1970 (London: HMSO, 1970).

34 The amount of change that has taken place should not be exaggerated. Cf. JONES, L., *op. cit.*, pp. 97–8.

35 TAYLOR, J. K., and DALE, I. R., *A Survey of Teachers in their First Year of Service* (Bristol: University of Bristol, 1971), and also Ministère de l'Education Nationale, *Circulaire no. 70353* Sept. 7, 1970, concerning the in-service training of qualified primary teachers; Ministère de l'Education Nationale, *Circulaire 70–354*, Sept. 7, 1970, dealing with similar arrangements for unqualified teachers.

36 Pädagogische Hochschule Niedersachsen, Abteilung Hildesheim, *Studienordnung* (Hildesheim, 1971, mimeo.), p. 4.

37 SHIPMAN, M., *op. cit.*

38 PIDGEON, D., 'The Implications of Teacher's Attitudes for the Reform of Teacher Training', one of a series of papers on the changing role of the teacher prepared for the Organization for Economic Co-operation and Development Experts' Meeting (Paris: OECD, 1971) argues the importance of attitude change through teacher education in increased pupil achievement. MARSLAND, D., *op. cit.*, presents an interesting model for assessing relevant change and reports success in obtaining measurements of change on ten dimensions of student-teachers' attitudes.

39 Follow-up studies of student-teachers will be needed to show whether attitude change carries over into schools. See MORRISON, A., and MCINTYRE, D., 'Changes in Opinions about Education during the First Year of Teaching', *British Journal of Social and Clinical Psychology*, VI, pp. 161–80. A study in progress in England, directed by Lacey, is concerned with the professional socialization of teachers from the beginning of their one-year post-graduate course until the end of their first year of teaching. A linked study, by one of the authors (Plunkett), is seeking to relate attitude change to structural characteristics, and former students' perceptions, of the initial training course.

40 BURGESS, T. (ed.), *Dear Lord James: a Critique of Teacher Education* (Harmondsworth: Penguin, 1971). For the French situation, see the syndical literature in particular. For example: 'Former des Maîtres', *Bulletin Mensuel du Syndicat National des Professeurs des Ecoles Normales*, no. 13, Jan. 1971 and, 'Assises Nationales pour la formation et le recrutement des Maîtres', *L'Université Syndicaliste* (periodical of the

Syndicat National de l'Enseignement Secondaire), no. 13, March 3, 1971.

41 Department of Education and Science, *Report of the Study Group on the Government of Colleges of Education* (Weaver Report) (London: HMSO, 1966).

42 On Dec. 3, 1970 the Federal Government approved an outline law for higher education as a discussion document. It was severely criticized by student representatives for its lack of clarity and precision on matters of student representation. See Westdeutsche Rektorenkonferenz, *Dokumente zur Hochschulreform 1971* (Bad Godesberg: Westdeutsche Rektorenkonferenz, 1971).

43 More recent examination regulations seem to have shown a greater sensitivity to a broader spectrum of objectives, both social and intellectual. The introduction of new regulations in North Rhine-Westphalia, permitting part of the *second state examination* for academic secondary teachers to be taken by a group of three to four candidates is an example. Letter of 17. 3. 71 from *Philologen-Verband*, North Rhine-Westphalia.

44 'Diskussionsentwurf zur Neordnung der Lehrerausbildung', *Bildungspolitische Informationen*, 1A, 1971.

45 The period of training in the second phase for academic secondary teachers has now everywhere been reduced from two years to eighteen months.

46 See KAYE, B., *Participation in Learning: a Progress Report on some Experiments in the Training of Teachers* (London: Allen and Unwin, 1970).

47 FERRY, G., *op. cit.*, chap. 1 proposes for teacher education an 'emancipation model' to take account of creative ideas and insights in the social context, defined as 'le noeud relationnel où s'enchevêtrent les composantes personnelles, inter-individuelles du drame éducatif qui est le point de convergence d'une pluralité d'approches'. See ROBINSOHN, S. B., 'Modell einer Pädagogischen Fakultät', *Bildungspolitische Informationen*, Ic, 1971, pp. 93–9. In England, though the argument was not developed, the evidence submitted by the National Union of Students to the James Committee makes a point about high status knowledge as an impediment to reform. See National Union of Students, *The Education and Training of Teachers: Perspectives for Change* (London: NUS, 1971), p. 5.

48 The West German Conference of Rectors has issued a series of documents on the reform of university administration. One of the best known is the resolution of the sixty-eighth Conference meeting in Bad Godesberg. See Westdeutsche Rektorenkonferenz, 'Empfehlungen zur Neuordnung der Universitätsorganisation' reproduced in Westdeutsche Rektorenkonferenz, *Dokumente zur Hochschulreform 1970* (Bonn-Bad Godesberg: WRK, 1970) especially para. 14.

49 An amendment to the Teacher Training Law in Bavaria of 27. 7. 1970 gave the pädagogische Hochschulen the right to give degrees, including doctorates, and laid down their incorporation into the universities by Aug. 1, 1972. Letter of Feb. 9, 1971 from Bavarian Ministry of Education and Culture. Similar provisions were introduced in Hessen in the University Law of 12. 5. 70. Letter of July 20, 1970 received from the Hessen Ministry of Culture.

50 COX, C. B., and DYSON, A. E. (eds.), *Fight for Education; The Crisis in Education; Goodbye Mr Short* (the Black Papers) (London: Critical Quarterly Society, 1969 and 1970).

51 CAPELLE, J., *Contre le Baccalauréat* (Paris: Berger-Levrault, 1968).
52 A conference was held at the beginning of 1973 by the OECD, in Paris, at which country representatives and experts from most of the member countries studied possibilities and prospects for participatory planning systems in education. The papers and a report of the Conference are to be published by the OECD, Directorate of Scientific Affairs.

Chapter Five

Curriculum and Teaching Methods

Curricula in this chapter are regarded as cultural artefacts, expressive of social intentions and of social conditions present and past. It follows that our major concern will not be with the content of curricula, that is with the syllabus, but rather with the types of knowledge that it has been expected that teachers should acquire in their professional training, and the manner in which they have been accustomed to acquire such knowledge. Bringing the knowledge-base of teacher education within the purview of a sociology of culture, in which the known and the ways of knowing are considered as relative to ways of being and perceiving, can help to check our assumptions about the objectivity of curricula while at the same time illuminating an under-studied aspect of educational systems. This approach should help to make the socio-cultural options in teacher education more explicit and consequently more available.[1]

The knowledge, skills, values and insights contained in teacher-education curricula can be assigned for descriptive purposes to the content categories of teaching-subjects, personality and culture, and the organization of knowledge systems. It will assist introductory discussion in this chapter to consider each of these categories separately. Historically teacher-education curricula in England, France and Germany have focused upon the subject-matter of teaching, that is school subjects. This emphasis gave its predominant character to the teachers' colleges in all three countries, and indeed whatever advances the colleges made academically only reinforced this tendency as they modelled their work upon the first degree courses of the universities.[2] For academic secondary school teachers in England and West Germany a subject-based professional course, essentially an abbreviated version of the college course, gave the training its main emphasis. The traditional French secondary teacher was even more dedicated to his teaching subject, particularly where, as was increasingly likely by the turn of the century, he had passed through the university and obtained the *agrégation* diploma. Later, when a training of one-year's duration was established for graduate secondary teachers, its main concern was still the development of their teaching subject specialism. Linked to the teaching subjects, for elementary and secondary academic teachers, there were elements of pedagogical and practical training for teaching.[3] Thus, whether trained or untrained, primary or secondary teachers are being considered, a strong emphasis upon the teaching subjects has prevailed in all three countries and continues to provide the main starting-point in the current debates over teacher education reform.

In Germany from the beginning of the nineteenth century until the third decade of the twentieth century, the dualism of preparation which we have encountered in the case of the other two countries was also practised. Prospective elementary teachers proceeded after an eight-year course at an elementary school and attendance at a private or state preparatory institution, to a three-year theoretical and practical training in a *Seminar*. The course was closely aligned to the culture of the elementary school and the knowledge imparted was restricted to the material to be taught in school. The second type of training followed successful graduation from the *Gymnasium* and a three- to four-year study of two or three academic subjects at the university which led to the taking of the examination *pro facultate docendi*. In the period after the Second World War, in spite of the further development of a more disciplined approach to educational studies, the emphasis on subject-matter to be taught was further intensified by a reduction of the number of subjects studied and an increase in the length of training of all prospective teachers.

To a greater or lesser extent programmes of teacher education in England have made provision for contextual studies of personality and culture and associated practical training experience, although recent growth in this aspect of the curriculum has been associated with the development of the behavioural sciences and the acceptance of their application to education. In England, the pedagogical element of teacher education remained divided between the professional or methodological studies approaches in the various teaching subjects and the educational studies which, until the 1960s, had a largely historical and descriptive character. The differentiation of education studies into complementary approaches through such disciplines as psychology and sociology, and the practical work in the field that these behavioural studies have increasingly entailed, have now become commonplace in training programmes for both non-graduates and graduates.[4]

There is little doubt that in France a major contribution to the broadening of teacher training was made by Durkheim who, while building upon a long tradition of European pedagogical writings, brought a wealth of philosophical and sociological method to bear upon education in relation to society.[5] Successive holders of Durkheim's chair of pedagogy at the Sorbonne have given impetus to these studies, and sociology was already known in the form of *l'étude du milieu* and *l'étude des faits sociaux* in the *écoles normales* in the 1920s. This early development was not followed through however since the teaching in sociological areas was left in the hands of the secondary school subject specialists who staffed the *écoles normales*, usually with a background in philosophy only. A major criticism brought against the *écoles normales* is that of their failure to develop a more scientifically-based pedagogy along with the supporting *educational sciences*. On the other hand, for their practical work students can be sent to holiday camps for poorer children and they are expected to acquaint themselves with social conditions through personal observation. At the secondary level, there is only token development of contextual studies which take the form of occasional lectures and discussions at the regional pedagogical centres, but for a minority of students and without any formal assessment.

The seminal work of such people as Herbart and Tönnies led to the early introduction in Germany of a psychological approach to education and of the concept of evolving societies in educational studies. Already in the curricula prescribed for the *pädagogische Akademien* in 1926, contextual studies were well established with defined contributions from the areas of psychology, philosophy and social studies. Such developments acquired further impetus in the 1920s following the work of Weber, and after the break of the period from 1933–45 it seemed once again to be widely accepted that knowledge of relevant psychological theory and of the relationship between education and society should have a clear place within the training of all teachers. In addition teachers' colleges in some *Länder* have initiated social and commercial practices in order that students may make personal observations of different social contexts.[7] With respect to the development of studies of personality and culture it is undeniable that in recent years a considerable discrepancy has appeared between the quality of English and German curricula and comparable French provision in teacher education.

Studies concerned with the organization of knowledge-systems have only much more recently been incorporated into the curricula of teacher education. For as long as teaching could be considered a craft concerned with the efficient transmission of knowledge there was no need for a training component that raised philosophical questions about the status of school curricula in terms of their epistemological assumptions and the social justification for the selection and classification of their content. A widespread discontent over school curricula that has for several years been evident in the English educational system has latterly made broad inroads into teacher education itself. For example, although it is not possible to speak of any general pattern, there is considerable development of a disciplined philosophical study of the school and teacher-education curricula and some relevant development of sociological studies.[8] It seems likely that in England pressure for and criticism of curriculum development is becoming built into teacher education as much as into any other sector of education, and the study of the curriculum is now developing as a part both of initial and of in-service teacher education.[9]

The study of the organization of knowledge systems has had more limited development in France, and has had little effect upon the curriculum of teacher education. It is true that recent criticisms of the conservative character of the pedagogical approach in the *école normale* have articulated the need for a renewal in the disciplines of mathematics and linguistics particularly, and that provisions have been made for these institutions to invite specialist assistance from the universities to help develop their initial teacher-education programmes. Beyond this, there are some initiatives in subject integration and an ambitious experiment in the teaching of technology in the secondary school which must raise some fundamental epistemological questions for French education. Up to the present, however, these developments appear to have been based upon separate rationales, and there is little indication of why or how they are to be generalized within the system or of any contribution that teacher education will be required to make.[10]

Whilst such pioneering work in the study of education as that of Dilthey has not been without influence on the curricula of teacher education in Germany, it has had to struggle against a long and tenacious tradition of teaching-subject specialism. Although interdisciplinary work was already popular in the schools from the 1920s attempts to devise schemata of the *elementary life forms* such as those in the work of Schleiermacher, and more recently Klafki, have tended to remain objects of study rather than instruments to facilitate questioning of the epistemological assumptions underlying teacher-education curricula.[11] For the present the advance of comprehensive forms of organization in the schools is raising some fundamental questions about the form of the curriculum and most *Länder* are in the process of changing their curriculum guidelines. More recent writings have demonstrated a sensitivity to the key position of curriculum in the reform of both general and higher educational systems in West Germany, whilst some teachers' colleges are now offering courses on curriculum theory and development.[12]

Viewing the curriculum of teacher education as historical and epistemological choices made within different cultures and institutions, we can pose in this chapter a similar set of analytical questions to those we have raised in the other chapters in a more orthodox sociological manner. Curricula and their accompanying pedagogical methods can be viewed functionally as instruments for the reproduction or modification of cultural and social patterns. The sociological perspective upon the curriculum obliges us to start by examining the relations between culture and social structure. In Chapter Two we reformulated the assumption that teacher education can change society as the sociological question of whether the educational system has the means to influence society's choice of values. We have examined the potential contributions to be made to cultural and social change through role-definitions for teachers and through the formal and informal experiences of teacher education. In this chapter we study some of the options available in curriculum and teaching methods in teacher education as representing media for the expression of any influence that the educational system may exert over the values of the broader society. It is much clearer intuitively that educational institutions may influence values through their curricula, for this is usually one of the justifications that their personnel claim for their own activity.[13] We must however face the sociological problems on the one hand that values do not simply reside in the content of what people say, or of what they claim to be saying, and on the other hand that educational systems have not provided themselves with a means of defining operationally their own aims, still less of marshalling their resources of knowledge and personnel in support of even those aims that are made explicit.[14]

We must conclude, therefore, that asking questions about the influence of teacher education upon the educational system, and thus upon the values of society, is not the same as merely asking questions about the types of values made explicit in the syllabuses, writing and speeches of teacher educators. In the examination of his 'reproduction' hypothesis, Bourdieu makes allusion to many facets of curriculum and teaching methods, including styles of thinking, criteria for judging the quality of performance and assumptions about the place of authority in teaching.[15] However, his analyses are concentrated upon structural features such as examinations and the selectivity of student recruitment into the hierarchy of higher education institutions, rather than upon the detail of curricular epistemologies. In this connection we have been unable to locate any studies that bring together the perspectives of the sociology of knowledge as it has been applied to the curriculum and the sociology of literature as the study of the products of cultures and social structures. The former approach leads to epistemological questions but seems to lack the methodology to pursue them in practical detail, while the analytical operations of the sociology of literature do not seem to have been considered by educationists. The best known exponent of the latter approach is probably Goldmann, for whom an artistic or literary product is of interest for analysis in so far as it illuminates the consciousness of its contemporary public.[16] This does not deny the value such a product may have for the connoisseur, but rather emphasizes the question: why such work at that time? In its values, structure and expression, what does the work tell us about thought and society in its historical moment? The inter-subjectivity, or shared understandings reflected in the work can be treated as a social phenomenon that extends beyond the conscious level and embraces intuitive responses to historically and socially structured experience.[17] It is in fact these wider relationships that the sociologist of literature of the Goldmann school attempts to objectify and interpret. We are not aware that Goldmann commented upon education as an object of study, but it does appear that his approach to the arts can find an application in the present inquiry, by suggesting a means by which a curriculum can be studied as both a product of culture and as a cultural microcosm. This would direct our attention both to the general features of a curriculum as a cultural artefact, that can be considered from a socio-epistemological point of view, and to the particular cultural and social conditions that can be shown or inferred to obtain in the structuring of teacher-education curricula.

Complemented by the perspectives of Bourdieu and Goldmann, the analyses of the curriculum proposed by Bernstein and by Young seem to us to be particularly compelling.[18] Some of the connections can be briefly suggested. Bernstein declares his interest in the relationship between consciousness and social control, a classical theme in the sociology of knowledge, and he sees the curriculum, or an educational paradigm linking pedagogy, curriculum and evaluation, as offering an empirical means to studying this major theme. He provides a typology of curricula according to whether they are closed (the 'collection' type) or open (the 'integrated' type) in their epistemologies and organization both internally, with respect to their component contents, and externally, in relation to the common-sense consciousness of everyday life.

The sociological interest of teacher-education curricula centres upon what they can tell us about society. What values, in other words, do their priorities and their organization reflect? If they reproduce the dominant values of the society they cannot be a source of cultural change. Only where there are divergent, minority and conflictual values finding expression through such curricula, could they have a cultural change-producing effect. Viewing teacher-education curricula in terms of the typology of options offers a way of pursuing these questions. On the typology's vertical dimension the main opposition is taken to be that between the monopolistic influence of the traditional, authority-derived curriculum and the pluralistic development of curricular innovations. The options available for teacher-education curricula upon the horizontal dimension of the typology are concerned with the degree of contextual coherence in the formulation of a curriculum. We suggest that it is possible to distinguish four types of curriculum which can be understood to correspond to the teacher role-types outlined in Chapter Three. We have called them subject-centred curriculum, encyclopaedic curriculum, learning-centred curriculum and community-centred curriculum.

1. THE SUBJECT-CENTRED CURRICULUM

1.1   In the *first cell* of the typology we would locate all those conceptions of training that saw teaching as a humble, repetitive task designed to inculcate the rudiments of simple knowledge and piety. Values of this kind were dominant with respect to teachers involved in the elementary instruction of the masses in all three countries in the nineteenth century. Whatever views teachers as individuals might have been capable of developing in other circumstances, the pupil-teacher system of apprenticeship clearly presupposed that what had to be learnt was a routine craft rather than a socially creative role. The republican spirit of the *école normale*, though not democratic by the standards of today, became firmly established in the conventional view in support of a form of education by means of which men and women of humble social origins could better their social status. A significant contrast between the cultural assumptions underlying the English and German and the French teachers' colleges lay in the prevailing attitudes to religion. In England and Germany, the Churches had taken a major part in the development of formal teacher training, while in post-revolutionary France the training of teachers was secular to the point of being laicist.

Fitting the model of the utilitarian educational systems that the three societies were developing in the nineteenth century, the type of training which was regarded as relevant for the teacher of the popular masses emphasized the validity of social hierarchies, whether of kinds of teacher, types of schools or styles of life. More fundamentally the school systems were concerned with reinforcing values and habits of thinking, so that what appears as rote-learning is also to be seen as a conditioning process, whether calculated or not, that maintains and reinforces the existing cultural and social order. In a more contemporary idiom we might say that whereas now sociological writers draw attention to the social dysfunctions of working-class children's context-boundness, and the restrictions upon choice of values, career or leisure that result from limited cultural horizons, it has been possible for educational systems to serve the interests of the dominant social groups by not only maintaining context-boundness but even making a virtue of it.[19] A clear hierarchy of values and roles in the education system, and particularly the teaching profession and in the routes into the profession represent an essential part of any strategy to build a society upon such platonic principles.

1.2   The purposes and the functions of teacher education find expression in curricula, so that if we wish to discover the cultural character of the latter we have to ask how they define knowledge and what they assume to be known or to be problematical. The different models of teacher-education curricula described at the beginning of this chapter in terms of relative emphasis given to teaching subjects, the social sciences and the study of the organization of knowledge systems, can be understood sociologically in relation to culturally and historically determined concepts of and expectations for the teacher's role. In assigning the epistemologies of teacher-education curricula to the typology we have, for purposes of emphasis, chosen to entitle the four cells by what appear to us to constitute the major defining characteristics corresponding to the cell-titles in the previous two chapters.

The particular epistemological configuration that characterizes the curriculum option of the *first cell* type emphasizes those kinds of knowledge that have traditionally been regarded as available only through practical experience. English, French and German teacher-education systems still retain something of the apprenticed craftsman model which held sway in the nineteenth century. Teaching was in terms of sets of skills which have been defined as subjects over a period of time which, in Raymond Williams' view, stretches back to the Middle Ages.[20] The subject has been, in effect, a set of codes and rites into which teachers needed to be initiated, and particularly the teachers who were to occupy the high status posts in the academic secondary schools. In fact subject loyalties were part of the mechanism by which the curricular systems were balanced in these schools. For example, the vigour of the English Modern Languages Association and of its French and German counterparts reflects the continuing strength of both an epistemological tradition and of its underlying social structural base.[21]

In the 'collection type' curricular system a number of elements are stitched together with no more explicit rationale than that they are the list of subjects studied by a particular learner. In English schools, the curriculum largely reflects the personal views of the headmaster and the vagaries of the staff skills available. In French and German schools, there is strong ministerial control of the appointment of teachers and of the syllabus but, for all teachers entering secondary schools in France training has been confined to the study of academic subjects. In Germany the problem of subject specialism is most acute in the case of the secondary academic teachers, where the various ministries even prescribe permitted combinations of subjects. The training of the primary-school teacher in the *école normale* is likewise officially confined to a time-table of subject-units with severely limited pedagogical complement.[22] All that can be said to justify such curricular systems cannot remove their character as historical vestiges, segments of knowledge and learning owing their present state more to historical accident than to educational design.

1.3 The concept of knowledge in such curricula is preserved also through the social structures that have grown up with them. The underlying values and the composition of the curricula can still only give us clues as to how they can actually be implemented. Organizational and pedagogical aspects of teacher-education programmes are further, if often less apparent indicators of the essential character of a curriculum. Corresponding to the subject-based programme there is a kind of arbitrary social superiority which takes shape in a particular pedagogy. Some French writers have referred to this form of pedagogical authority as symbolic 'violence'.[23] There seems little doubt that the traditional curricula of teacher education in the three societies have perpetrated this violence, in that they have required imitative and submissive behaviour from students. Cultural, social and pedagogical structures are found in correspondence where a fact-based and teacher-proof syllabus, widespread use of the lecture method of teaching, and an emphasis upon the *training* concept have characterized the curricula. The preservation of numerous categories of teachers by means of the selections and divisions that occur in teacher education constitute a further reinforcement of the symbols of authority in education and thus help to legitimize the dominance of teacher over taught.[24]

1.4 No less distinctive of the traditional forms of authority-based and segmented curricula in teacher education have been the forms of assessment and control they have employed. In a training system where the principal criterion of achievement was to imitate successfully what has been done before, the assessment and control procedures were logically directed to the performance of individual students. Inevitably, also, given the generality and the imprecision of the goals of the education systems, such assessment was subjective, whether directed to a student's essay or to the arbitrary choice of the ground upon which the factual learning of the student was to be tested. In this respect, the widespread use of interview selection techniques in English teacher training, of oral examinations still in West Germany and the enormous importance of both written and oral examinations at every stage of advance towards becoming a teacher in

France, constitute lynch-pins for the education systems, locking them into their respective social and cultural structures.

2. THE ENCYCLOPAEDIC CURRICULUM

2.1 Despite the prodigious development of inquiry in modern science and scholarship, man has been everywhere reluctant to surrender the idea that there might be a sense in which he could have an overview of knowledge. From Aristotle to Bacon such pretensions may not have seemed too ambitious, but the encyclopaedists, instead of condensing all knowledge into one set of volumes, actually became known for the sheer presumption they possessed. In the field with which we are concerned, the concept of the classical education as the broadest gateway to knowledge, the French idea of *la culture générale*, or the German *Allgemeinbildung* have represented the notion that a culture can be synthesized, that its values, its traditions, and the type of society that it implicitly honours can be encoded and transmitted from one generation to the next. If the elements of teacher-education curricula that we cited as belonging to the *first cell* can be seen as persisting only vestigially into contemporary educational systems, this is not the case with the values and corresponding options that we would assign to *cell two*. Not merely the value of traditional ideas, but the superior value of tradition as such, and the requirement that contemporary society and its values and institutions be brought to the bar of a cultural heritage, are characteristic of what we would for simplicity refer to as the encyclopaedic teacher-education curriculum.

Within the English tradition, the finest expression of these values is probably found in Newman,[25] and the concept of liberal education that he defines has been extremely influential in defining the role of the teacher and the desirable character and scope of his learning. Many of the teachers' colleges attached very great importance to the study and practice of religion as well as to the moral dimensions of the teaching function. There is likewise no doubt that in England this cultural tradition was instrumental in preserving the authority of the country's major social institutions and the hierarchical structure of society. For example the importance of the role played by the Church of England and the siting of many of the colleges in converted country mansions are factors in the patterning of the traditional culture of teacher education. Perhaps more important still has been the fact that simple exposure to this same culture in the universities, without any specific vocational training, has until very recently passed as the best preparation for teaching, or at the least the acceptable way of preparing for the best teaching in terms of social prestige. It is clear that in such a system inheritance is a more important principle than change, and many writers have described the conservative, socially conformist and morally committed nature of a century of English teacher education.[26]

The reproductive nature of French cultural and educational traditions is even more clearly apparent than in the case of England. After the creative thrust of the early revolutionary period, and because of the power of the institutional innovations it brought, French society settled into a cultural orthodoxy which seems to have been able to absorb every challenge.[27] If some writers have credited the educational institutions with having performed the vital transmission function that has facilitated the culturally reproductive process,[28] they are following Durkheim's conception of the functions of education in society, or the use to which society puts its educational institutions in socializing the members of its oncoming generation into its culture. Durkheim must be understood as referring to a *dominant* culture in society, and to the coalescence of social forces that maintain this culture and its dominance. Thus, the *écoles normales* serviced the whole of French society not by their often assumed function of facilitating social mobility for their students and cultural emancipation for the latter's future pupils, but by stressing the virtues of republicanism, laicism, and nationalism, while at the same time preserving the authority of the dominant culture through the hierarchy of educational institutions to which the teachers' colleges belonged. As in England, the academic secondary teacher was accepted as qualified by liberal studies and not by pedagogical training, and this education symbolized the identification of the highest prestige teacher with the dominant classes of the society.

Recent writings and reports have highlighted the reproductive functions of the West German educational system, and there is a widespread frustration with the difficulty encountered in reforming a rigidly hierarchical structure of education which has so consistently disadvantaged certain cultural and social groups.[29] The values classified in the *second cell* of the typology are secured in the case of West Germany by a tradition of academic scholarship reaching back to the Humboldt reforms at the beginning of the nineteenth century and given their fullest expression in the foundation of the University of Berlin. Gradually the concept of freedom of teaching and research introduced in Prussia at that time became identified with the interests of dominant social and political groups and successive legislation in the nineteenth century ensured for the academic secondary teachers a powerful and privileged position in the maintenance of the political and cultural status quo. Many writers have commented on the tenacity of this tradition in the face of demands for democratization.[30] The systems of social and professional stratification in the three societies have been of enormous importance in defining the roles of teachers and their general acceptance of a stratified concept of knowledge.

2.2 Looking closer at the shape of the curricula of teacher education in the three societies in the light of the values that have been suggested, we find that their societal dimensions can be apprehended in terms of the *second cell* of the typology. The segmentation of curricula as perceived in the subject-specialization and craftsmanship approaches to which we have referred are better understood and explained as elements in a larger system of cultural and social reproduction. In so far as there are curricular systems or epistemologies that have achieved coherence based on broadly accepted principles it is possible to show how these curricula follow the

logic and reinterpret the values and structure of a whole society. Encyclo-
paedism probably lasted longer in teacher education than in any other area
of formal education. The ambitions of the medieval university, reinter-
preted in the Enlightenment and finding more recent expression in forms of
liberal education, have channelled men's energies in pursuit of an authoritative system of knowledge. Traditional schemes of ideas derive their resili-
ence from the fact that they restate these older ambitions and provide the
opportunity for their legitimation within the institutional framework of
the contemporary education system, while at the same time contributing to
the legitimation of established values and hierarchies of society.

The promotion in teacher-education curricula of lecture courses aiming
to transmit the synthesized thinking of a series of acknowledged educational authorities of the past, or surveying educational provisions and
experiment, showed compulsive development in the teachers' colleges.[31] In
addition, students were expected to sample a large number of courses concerned with the pedagogy of different subjects, and to take part, in many
English and German institutions, in a closely controlled programme of
religious studies and activities. In Germany guidelines and examination
regulations are laid down by the ministries for all types of teacher education, though the interpretation of these into a programme of studies
provides some measure of freedom for staff and students.[32] The authority
and the standardization of curricula in France are both more formal and
more complete, in that the programme of studies is prescribed by the
Ministry and is binding upon the teaching institutions. Even the time-
table of the *école normale* is fixed in its essentials by ministerial decision.[33]
This is not simply a matter of the prescription of content. The idea of a
programme has built into it the symbol of authority as well as a structure of
knowledge that guarantees authority. Bourdieu argues that the function
of the school is: 'to produce individuals equipped with the system of uncon-
scious (or deeply buried) master-patterns that constitute their culture'.[34]
This attempt to show the structural similarities between systems of education and systems of thought suggests, though it does not provide, an
analysis of the curriculum as a reflection of the formal culture, as a system
of categories of perception, language, thought and appreciation that
transcend a particular social group. Thus a dominant culture is one that
succeeds in encapsulating a popular culture and giving the latter its place in
the wider cultural order.

Such an analysis could be followed through in detail using an approach
similar to Goldmann's, and searching for correspondences between elements of curriculum design and features of the society that has accommo-
dated that design. For example, curricula that stress the value of practical
activities as learning experiences have consistently failed to achieve the
prestige of more abstract courses, no matter how well adjusted the objectives of the former may have been to the pressing needs of particular social
groups. The practical course, and this has nowhere been more true than in
teacher education, assumes subordinate status to the liberal, bookish
course, though the latter may be largely concerned with retailing the

accepted learning of the past. The critical considerations are whether the curriculum in question is approved by dominant social groups and what criteria they use. Young has suggested that there are four such criteria by which the high status of elements of knowledge is determined in curricula.[35] These are abstractness, literacy of content, scope for individual performance and unrelatedness to practical everyday life. The university and secondary school courses in the three countries that offer the widest opportunities for a choice of career and secure social status fit these criteria. The arts degree from Oxford or Cambridge is probably less prestigious than a generation ago, but the French *agrégation de lettres* and the German *Promotion* and especially the *Habilitation* are still accepted as evidence of the highest distinction. Teacher education curricula can only change with difficulty while such criteria persist in the higher educational system as a whole, and this is equivalent to saying for as long as these symbols of status are institutionalized culturally and socially in the wider society.

It is less apparent how such values are in fact institutionalized in the educational system and how dominant values are preserved in continuing planning and administration by educational agencies.[36] Since authority in education is based less upon proven excellence of performance in a controlled situation than upon familiarity with complex procedures and skill in the manipulation of special codes of language and other cultural symbols, official and orthodox views in education acquire enormous influence. In terms of their potential for resisting cultural change there is little noticeable difference between the deliberations of the various French ministerial commissions, the British Universities' Council for the Education of Teachers and the Conferences of Rectors in West Germany. The proliferation of such bodies, claiming to express the views of, and to adjudicate between the large numbers of interest-groups in education, has greatly intensified in the three countries in recent years. Among those concerned with the curriculum in England the example can be given of the Schools Council which has a high proportion of teacher-members, and which has been described as being tied to the traditional categories of the curriculum in its committee-structure and in many of its projects.[37] In France the juries for competitive examinations, the corps of the inspectorate and the powerful university arts faculties all act to reinforce the subject-based curriculum system. In West Germany the regional prescription of curricula and examination guidelines, the power of the universities to manipulate such concepts as *Wissenschaftlichkeit* and the extreme conservatism of some teachers' associations have similarly served to retard much-needed curricular reform. The recent interest of the DES in the curriculum and the availability of powerful sectional groups to pursue traditional interests must be regarded as an alliance with a potential for rigidifying of curriculum decisions and development. The courses and examinations required to obtain the highest qualifications in the three countries, and indeed even to obtain higher degrees by research, are a maze of rituals with hardly less symbolic than instrumental significance. Their symbolic significance, which locates them in the *second cell*, is that the very procedures that they oblige candidates to undergo, such as following traditional curricula with limited options, adopting an approved style of responding to examination questions, using a frozen language, constructing repetitive surveys of a field of writings in painstaking detail for the opening chapters of a thesis, dressing in *subfusc* to take an examination, using honorific titles and ceremonial confrontations with the examiners, are all symbols of the subordination of the student to the authority of the academic system, and they thus set a pattern not only for teacher education but for the education system as a whole.

2.3   The principal means by which academic authority is imposed upon the effective day-to-day workings of the education system is through the hierarchies of qualifications and appointments that differentiate teachers and areas of knowledge. These have already been discussed from an epistemological standpoint but it is necessary to recognize their social structural correlates in the three countries. For example one critical issue that might be examined in this connection is the degree/non-degree watershed in teacher education which equates fairly exactly to what we have called the *dual system*. Because of the prestige of the university degree, and its convenience in demarcating a threshold between dominant and other social groups, the many practical disadvantages of the university degree course as a training for teachers of the great majority of children have continued to be tolerated. Recently there have been developments whose apparent objective was to blur the distinction between these teacher types. The bachelor of education degree in England, to which late entry is possible within the college of education, and the access to the university diploma (DUEL) for selected *école normale* students in France, have permitted individuals to move from one teacher category to another. There has long been the opportunity in Germany for assiduous elementary teachers to retrain as intermediate or exceptionally even secondary academic teachers. More recently the introduction of a new degree in education, the *Dip. Päd.*, has offered further scope for professional and interprofessional rapprochement, without in effect breaking the rigid social strata of the profession. The structure remains the same in all three countries: the certificated nongraduate teacher in England, the trained *professeur de l'enseignement général de collège* in France and the *Volksschullehrer* in West Germany, lack the standing and the occupational potentials of the teacher with a degree or its equivalent.[38] Such stratification is apparent within the occupational groups themselves, through the existence of separate associations for teachers with different qualifications. The contradiction between the values implicit in these hierarchies and the notion of a comprehensive educational system cannot be ignored in the reform of teacher education.

2.4   Perhaps the major feature of the traditional systemic approach to education in its implications for the curriculum is the credence given to the procedures by which quality or excellence is validated. The confidence of the traditional British civil service in the gifted amateur might even be justified if the qualities it assumed could clearly be shown to exist in one person and not in another.[39] Critical study of examinations in a sociological perspective would suggest the plausibility of the argument that examinations test only proxies for the qualities of examinees, and that the intervening cultural variables are so complex and numerous that there is no more socially selective device than the apparently open competitive examination. Built into the examinations systems of England, France and West Germany are assumptions about correctness, mastery in areas of knowledge, and standards of performance which only escape being recognized as subjective because they are defined by important social groups. Bourdieu proposes the comparative study of the essay type of test to show the extent to which such unnamed criteria are being employed.[40] He also cites examiners' comments on performance in the oral sections of the *agrégation* which he interprets as a process of identifying *cultural capital*. The widespread use of the oral examination in the French educational system compared with the English and the now more restricted West German practice is of special interest here, for, if Bourdieu's analysis is valid, it is here that we most plainly perceive the reproductive functioning of the educational system. The procedures by which the output of the educational system is controlled, evaluated and sanctioned may provide the clearest illustration of the action of conservative cultural forces.

3. THE LEARNING-CENTRED CURRICULUM

3.1 We have considered the social conflicts now apparent in the three societies as their educational systems are forced to adapt to change, and the incapacity of these systems to work out the implications of the democratization of education for the role of the teacher. But it is perhaps with respect to the curriculum that the least progress has been made in adapting teacher education to the needs of modern economies and societies. The direct effect of these changes is that educationists once liberated from a wide range of traditional and static values and procedural conventions, are forced to raise basic questions. Any simple adjustment moreover is made impossible by the impacting of different sets of values upon education. At a time when schools have not responded adequately to the economically biased arguments of early post-war policy-makers or to the proposals of the economists of education of the 1960s about the relative profitability of different investments both in education and between education and other sectors, it is already being concluded by authoritative commentators that 'economic growth per se is no longer a sufficient overall objective' for modern governments.[41] Notions of social equity and personal freedom are acquiring new public meanings and giving rise to plausible policies both within and outside the educational systems.

At the present time in the three societies it could be said that there is a consciousness of the reproductive functioning of education and that as a consequence much current educational innovation stems from a concern for equality of opportunity. However, the marginal status of innovators on the general educational scene is such that even those decision-makers who seek to foster democratization are in fact led to serve the requirements of a stratified social system.[42] For example, the *positive discrimination* that has been proposed for primary education in England has a negative aspect in that a section of the community is being identified and labelled, and is thus acquiring a self-image that may in fact be its greatest handicap. In the *third cell* of the typology, reserved for specialized innovatory options, we group those innovations that have this partial democratizing character in that their very existence bears testimony to the need for change, whether to make education a pace-setter for, or a follower of, wider social trends. We are immediately concerned with the kinds of democratic change which involve the absorption by the educational system of insistent external demands and the piecemeal reform of education by the isolated initiatives of innovative minorities within education. It is possible to recognize curriculum changes of this kind and they are worthy of study as regards the implications they have for teacher education, and as possible harbingers of broader social and educational change.

3.2   We have made reference already to the sense in which there was a shift over time in the curriculum of teacher education, as the subjects to be taught gave ground to studies of personality and society as well as of knowledge and knowledge-systems. The extent of the flexibility, at both conceptual and organizational levels, in the generation of new curricula provides an important indicator of the part teacher education can play in social democratization. The emergence of new disciplines in the study of man during the past century, and much more recently in teachers' colleges, has imparted a pluralistic character to the generation of knowledge. Psychology and the social sciences, linguistics and a more critical mathematics in particular have had repercussions upon teacher education both directly and through the often fruitful boundary-disputes in which they have become involved. At present teachers' college curricula in the three countries appear fragmented and uncertain in their principles. Numerous contributory factors can be cited. In the first place, subjects studied vary in their social acceptability, and researches have indicated the tendency for secondary and higher education students to select, or be selected for studies according to their family's social status,[43] and therefore for the curriculum to reveal an epistemological structure that can be harmonized with the cultural hierarchies of the society.[44] Further inquiry would be needed to show the pattern of correspondences between social status and such variables as subject choice, type of course, and career patterns of lecturing staff.

We would assign to the *third cell* of the typology all those features of teacher education curricula that appeared *prima facie* to be contributing to breaking down both traditional patterns of knowledge and relationships between these patterns and the distribution of prestige and power in society. This implies identifying those curricular developments that emphasize the concept of inquiry and the initiative of the learner. In the English teachers' colleges the study of sociology, the introduction of creative dance and drama, the fostering of inter-disciplinary work through projects and in educational studies, and training in group and team approaches to teaching, were all developments of this type that occurred in an increasing number of colleges in the 1960s. In France changes came much later, with the *écoles normales* instituting courses in such areas as linguistics, aesthetics and social anthropology following a ministerial circular in 1969,[45] and the increasing use of social relations training through group dynamics and the establishing of *educational sciences* departments in the universities. In spite of the emphasis placed in official statements on the need to provide for a conception of education as communication in France, however, there has been strong resistance to sociology and to other theoretical human science disciplines forming part of the *école normale* programmes. On the other hand human science disciplines feature strongly in the curriculum of both *pädagogische Hochschulen* and the institutions of the second phase of secondary academic teacher training in West Germany. More recent proposals have suggested the establishment of educational and sociological studies consisting of both empirical and analytical material as well as theoretical underpinnings as the core of work for all teachers.[46] There is also an upsurge of interest in group study and curriculum theory and development in some colleges.

The keynote of curricular innovation of the 1950s was probably the development of more and more specialized courses. By the end of the decade, however, the need was for greater adaptability. The strain between specialization, on the one hand, and breadth, on the other, has preoccupied curriculum developers over the intervening period, and many authorities have entered the debate with economic, social and cultural arguments. The controversy probably moved furthest in England, where the single subject degree at the top of the pyramid of higher education began to give way to broader options during the 1960s, particularly in the newer universities and in the polytechnic sector. The colleges of education have not followed this pattern, but instead have strengthened their main courses in academic subjects to the point where this work has rivalled the teacher-training function in both three-year certificate and four-year bachelor of education courses. Exceptions to this have occurred in inter-disciplinary ventures in education studies and a variety of contemporary social studies courses. The French primary teacher has not been expected to specialize in one subject in this way, but teachers increase their specialization in France progressively with the age-group of their pupils. On the other hand, subject separation remains strong in the *école normale*, and, apart from the traditional merging of history and geography, little cross-disciplinary activity has been reported. The same is true for the training of secondary teachers; little opportunity has been provided for teachers of different subjects to learn about each other's work, let alone to work together.[47] Despite the shortcomings of the English post-graduate certificate in education and the German academic secondary teachers' work in the *Studienseminar* as a professional grounding for teaching, these courses have provided students with the opportunity to study human behaviour and the organization of schools.

3.3 Along with such beginnings of a development of teacher-education curricula there have been numerous experiments in course reorganization and new teaching methods. In these areas the teachers' colleges have certainly not been as innovative as the schools, but current proposals suggest that greater reorganization and rationalization may soon occur in all three countries. The innovations that appear to us to be *cell three* type which have been occurring in the recent past include, in England, the training of graduates on a sandwich course pattern, the institution of first degrees in education, in both colleges of education and undergraduate departments of some universities and the diversification of offerings of in-service courses by teachers colleges and local education authorities. No comparable new course development has occurred in France in recent years, but a large-scale scheme for the in-service training of unqualified primary teachers has been instituted whereby such teachers can spend a term on a specially devised course at an *école normale* and obtain fully qualified teacher status.[48]

In West Germany, the introduction of the *Dip. Päd.* degree and the gaining by colleges of the right to give degrees, together with the introduction of *social practices*, have been matched at in-service level by rigorous but sporadic innovations in the provision of group study, sex education and guidance courses, the setting up of working groups of teachers and college lecturers, the establishment of many new but small in-service centres and the development of media-linked courses.[49]

In the field of teaching methods there have been many developments since the not so distant time when the lecture was the main teaching medium and, in England, the tutorial discussion was the only concession to student participation. Group methods have become widely used in England with variants such as seminar discussions, syndicate group tasks and micro-teaching.[50] In France, T-groups and sensitivity training have been extensively employed in the further training of serving teachers, though often only by specialist university and voluntary agencies. Similar isolated developments have been reported in West Germany.[51] In all three countries there has been experiment, though as yet little generalized application of closed-circuit television in teacher training especially in the area of practical teaching, but considerable extension of the use of the whole range of new media is now occurring at initial and in-service levels.[52]

3.4 Learner-centred control procedures are less apt to judge learning by how well it conforms to a predetermined model. More credit than formerly is given to personal qualities observed in the course of the work, for example through the use of continuous assessment which is now becoming widespread in English teachers' colleges, and by procedures in which the range and type of knowledge and understanding acquired is regularly sampled by the use of objective tests rather than essay discussions. There is no information available on what work of this latter kind is being done in teacher education, but the techniques are becoming known in England, and are already used in the secondary school terminal examinations, that is the

Certificate of Secondary Education and General Certificate of Education. Among other English innovations which have introduced more democratic practice to an area of education where authority had reigned supreme have been the involvement of teachers in the assessment of their own pupils in public examinations and, in teacher education, the monitoring of each other's teaching practice by students without direct supervision by their college tutors.[53] The centralized French and German systems of examination have not been amenable to developments of this kind, but perhaps a clearer indication of the impermeability of traditional authority in French education is given by the recent ministerial circular banning unauthorized experiments in education.[54] In the educational sciences departments of French universities and in the *Studienseminare* in West Germany individual and group projects may form part of final assessment, and continuous assessment is reported in several French institutions.[55]

4. THE COMMUNITY-CENTRED CURRICULUM

4.1 The education systems of the three countries have all known a period of episodic development responding to the problems of post-war population growth and social change. Curriculum innovation has come later than organizational change in the field of teacher education, and the innovations that have occurred have on the whole resulted from limited initiatives, for example in one subject, department or institution. There has only been the foreshadowing of systemic reforms. The questions about what the society expects from education and from teachers are posed in their own right; decisions about whether to preserve or change present school programmes are subordinated to broader choices of values, and the curriculum of the school ceases to be the major reference point for the education of teachers.[56] The burden of much contemporary writing about the value of existing educational organizations and programmes is that they are anachronistic, that they exhibit a serious cultural lag with respect to movements of ideas and social relations in the wider society. Education advances slowly, responding only sluggishly to major social changes.

4.2 The concept of democratization can only be applied in a notional sense in reference to contemporary educational systems, but it may be appropriate to examine the implications of a democratizing process for the epistemological and structural patterns of teacher-education curricula. For if education is in many parts of the world being turned outwards from the school towards the community, and is being thought of as the means by which young people will learn better to exercise their rights and responsibilities as citizens, then the extent to which a coherent reflection of such values can be discerned in teacher education will be an important indication of the seriousness of purpose with which the prevailing structure of society is being questioned.

Some innovative educationists are beginning to recognize that a curriculum has been inherited that rests upon finite and authoritarian assumptions about the nature and organization of society and systems of knowledge.[57] These writers provide criteria for the construction of curricula, which would extend in their objectives and content into out-of-school and after-school environments, and include experiential as well as academic learning. Applied in teacher education, this perspective demands closer study of the contemporary society, more contact with the variety of social and teaching situations that the future teacher is likely to encounter, and the critical examination of how knowledge is organized and expressed in curricula.[58]

In England a concern to relate curricula to social and educational problems, such as those of the semi-literate pupil or the ethnic minority group, found organized expression in the *educational priority areas* where colleges of education have established annexes in inner-city areas to afford their students continued close experience of the complex of social disadvantages common to large numbers of inner-city areas.[59] The traditional courses in pedagogical or educational theory are giving way in a number of colleges to more inter-related behavioural studies in education and in socially-related fields. In the teachers' colleges it will be necessary not merely to develop new courses that build upon the disciplines concerned with the study of personality and culture, but to examine the assumptions of traditional curricular organization which has divided pupils into more and less privileged strata, and to justify innovation in terms of children's and society's needs.[60] Content-oriented theories of knowledge upon which curricula have hitherto relied are now beginning to be brought under reflexive scrutiny in the form of studies in the theory of curriculum development and change.[61] While offering the opportunity to study the curriculum in terms of its underlying objectives, its assumptions, its associated pedagogy and its behavioural and affective outcomes, such work is also raising sociological questions about why and how cultural traditions express themselves through particular curricula. The issues that are central to the present study appear to be becoming more accessible to analysis, at least in English educational studies. Since the establishment of the Institute system, and particularly of the teachers' centres in England, there has been widespread development of in-service education provision. Until the last few years however the courses offered were closely related to a school epistemology rather than to any programme of educational reform effort. At the present time there is widespread experimentation in new courses in social science areas linking together concerns with personality, culture and curriculum, and even the work of non-educational social services.[62]

The Amiens meetings of 1968 brought many proposals for the development of social science-based studies in education,[63] and ideas involved in these proposals have found expression in the teaching and research of the university departments of educational sciences. These departments, however, have remained marginal to the development of teacher education, at least in terms of the provision of initial training and professional qualification.[64] Mention has already been made of the 1969 proposals from the French Ministry for programmes in social anthropology and other new disciplines, and it was understood at the time that there were much more detailed suggestions for course content prepared by the Ministry but which were never released because of official doubts about the social philosophy they reflected. Progress has thus been almost negligible in this field in the *écoles normales*, while no element of social science or pedagogical theory has a place in the initial training of French graduate teachers. Only a handful of educationists have applied themselves to the problems of curriculum theory and curriculum reform in the Anglo-Saxon sense of the phrase and this work has not yet percolated through to initial teacher training.[65] In-service education is still very undeveloped in France, but the place of permanent education is widely recognized, perhaps particularly on account of the weakness of initial teacher training. The curricula of the courses offered are however much more concerned with basic subject-teaching knowledge and skills, for example in the use of audio-visual aids and school administration, than in innovative pedagogical and educational science areas. The germ of ideas for in-service education directed to the development of new philosophies, teaching methods and social relations exists, but has almost no part yet in determining professional appointments or status.[66]

In West Germany recognition of the need for curriculum reform in the general school system dates only from the late 1960s and that in teacher education is even more recent. There has been an increased emphasis on empirical work within the field of educational studies and a new sensitivity to methodological problems associated with main subject work, manifested in a recent proposal for a centre for higher educational didactics and teacher education.[67] Attempts to improve the second phase of training for secondary academic teachers and to co-ordinate the two phases better are being made at the same time as regulations for this category of teacher training are being copied into the design of training for future primary teachers. In spite of their lack of an adequate social perspective, the proposals of the Council for Education and of the Science Council for an integrated core curriculum may well provide the basis for reform of both initial and in-service teacher education.[68] More recent proposals have envisaged an analysis of the teacher's future professional work as a starting-point for the elaboration of curriculum.[69] The writings of these educationists envisage the construction of detailed analytical and empirical studies which could elucidate bases for the construction of segments of teacher-education curricula, and enable account to be taken of innovatory roles for the teacher. However it must be said that the more widespread implementation of such proposals is hindered by the present multiplicity of courses resting upon the traditional epistemology of German teacher education, the lack of an adequate educational research tradition, which newly founded institutes are only just beginning to overcome and, until very recently, a preoccupation with organizational questions to the almost total exclusion of holistic approaches to the curriculum.

4.3   The development and organization of teacher-education curricula of the *cell four* type reflects the questioning of traditional cultural values and the appearance of new social priorities in education and overflows in its effects into the teaching process. As experimental approaches become commoner in English colleges, new types of staff team-work and student involvement in group and field-study and in research as integral parts of teacher education are being explored.[70] Ideas of inquiry-centred learning which have been acknowledged widely for a decade or more in the pedagogical theory current in these institutions are being increasingly put into practice in teacher education. Although attention has been drawn to the importance for student-teachers of the pedagogy of their own training it would be false to draw too great a distinction between the teaching methods and the curriculum content.[71] Not only the use of the seminar and syndicate methods, but the active participation of students in decisions about their own curriculum are strategies that can be observed in the exceptional institution. Similar ideas by which the learner is increasingly seen less as a recipient of knowledge and values and more as a resource for their further development can be found in parts of the *école normale* curriculum, as in the emphasis upon the *sciences de l'observation* and the *disciplines d'éveil* in ministerial circulars and the introduction of a small proportion of optional studies.[72]

In West Germany the introduction of CCTV has permitted the growth of team approaches drawing together educationists and subject specialists and the development of political education as a part of educational studies is slowly fostering a greater emphasis on experiential learning. Experiments involving teachers and college lecturers working together on curriculum reform and the establishment of a number of institutes for the study of the theory and practice of education, and drawing together university and college educationists and teachers, have been reported.[73]

4.4 A curriculum can only be considered responsive to democratic values if it is democratically established, as well as being inherently directed to democratic ends. Modern education systems have been experiencing a *malaise* in recent years as students in schools, colleges and universities have pressed for wider participation in decisions about curricula.[74] Some examples can be found of teachers' colleges where curriculum development involves co-operation between teachers, student-teachers, subject lecturers, philosophers and social scientists.[75] Such procedures necessarily imply the interdependence of teacher and taught in any programme of studies, and thus the inadequacy of assessment methods that focus solely upon performance of individual students. An important characteristic of policies that we would classify in the *fourth cell* is their concern with evaluating curricular outcomes.[76] The methodology of such evaluation is at present little developed but initiatives can be cited where curricular objectives, content and organization, as well as teaching methods and examinations are recognized in their cultural and social dimensions.[77] Indeed, this activity represents a questioning of the prevailing institutionalized controls in education, whether the initiative comes from enlightened authorities or from radical student or teacher groups. Such a recognition of convergent interests within the educational systems could become the source of a powerful boost in the energy with which teachers as a group contribute to cultural change rather than to cultural reproduction.

REFERENCES

1 This chapter owes a substantial debt for some of the principal ideas it develops to the writings of Pierre Bourdieu, in particular to BOURDIEU and PASSERON (1970), *op. cit.*

2 TAYLOR, W., *op. cit.*, p. 112. It is only very recently that any such influence has appeared in the *écoles normales*, with the provision of financial assistance to permit university teachers to give courses in mathematics and linguistics. See MEN, Circular no. 70352, Nov. 7, 1970. See also BECK-MANN, H. K., *Lehrerseminar, Akademie, Hochschule* (Weinheim: Verlag Julius Beltz, 1968), which gives an extensive account of the relationship between theory and practice in the three major phases of development of German teacher education and within this the chequered history of main subject work.

3 Requirements for the French *licence d'enseignement*, CAPES and *agrégation* did not include pedagogical theory, and the year spent by graduate student-teachers in the *centre pédagogique régional*, depending upon local initiative, might or might not offer opportunity for the study of education. In recent years this element of the year's work has been increasingly neglected.

4 TIBBLE, J. W. (ed.), *An Introduction to the Study of Education* (London: Routledge and Kegan Paul, 1966). Though concerned mainly with the theory and practice of education in the studies of future academic secondary teachers, a work by Beckmann is path-breaking in its approach to the curricular aspect of teacher education. See BECKMANN, H. K. (ed.), *Zur Reform des pädagogischen Studiums und der Lehrerausbildung, Modelle – Versuche – Erfahrungen* (Weinheim: Verlag Julius Beltz, 1968).

5 DURKHEIM, E., *L'Evolution Pédagogique en France* (Paris: Presses Universitaires de France, 1969).

6 MIALARET, G., 'La Formation des Maîtres', in Groupe Français d'Education Nouvelle, *Le Plan Langevin-Wallon de Réforme de l'Enseignement* was an early statement of a point of view that has been echoed since by large numbers of educationists.

7 See GRANT, J. J., *op. cit.*, for a brief discussion of one of the practical implications of this development. An example of the theoretical knowledge-bases referred to, is contained in 'Diplom-Prüfungsordnung in Erziehungswissenschaft für die Pädagogische Hochschule Niedersachsen', *Niedersächsisches Ministerialblatt*, no. 39, 1970, pp. 1146 ff. Similar provisions can be found in Berlin and Baden-Württemberg.

8 See RENSHAW, P., 'The Objectives and Structure of the College Curriculum', in TIBBLE, J. W. (ed.), *The Future of Teacher Education* (London: Routledge and Kegan Paul, 1971) and YOUNG, M. F. D., *op. cit.* for examples of the two approaches.

9 Arguments are developed for such studies by SKILBECK, M., 'Curriculum Development: A Task for Teachers', *Themes in Education*, no. 21, University of Exeter, Institute of Education, 1969. One such in-service course is briefly described in LYNCH, J. and PLUNKETT, H. D., 'Towards a

Comparative Sociology of the Curriculum', *Compare* III: 1, 1972, pp. 16–19.

10 A pessimistic portrait of the present structural and epistemological problems of French education is provided by CITRON, S., *L'Ecole Bloquée* (Paris: Bordas, 1971).

11 A useful account of the main trends of development of educational and didactic studies in Germany is contained in ROTH, F., and MASKUS, R., *Die Schulwirklichkeit als Studienfeld* (Frankfurt/Main: Verlag Moritz Diesterweg, 1967). See also KLAFKI, W., *Studien zur Bildungstheorie und Didaktik* (Weinheim: Verlag Julius Beltz, 1963).

12 One of the first major initiatives towards curriculum development in West Germany was ROBINSOHN, S. B., *Bildungsreform als Revision des Curriculum* (Neuwied: Luchterhand, 1967). For an example of the curriculum development studies offered to student teachers at one pädagogische Hochschule see Pädagogische Hochschule Berlin, *Personen- und Vorlesungsverzeichnis: Sommersemester 1971* (Berlin: P. H., 1971), pp. 54 ff.

13 See the emphasis placed by teachers on their moral aims in MUSGROVE and TAYLOR (1969), *op. cit.*, or the aims of *lycées* over a hundred-year period in France in ISAMBERT-JAMATI, V., *Crises de la Société, Crises de l'Enseignement* (Paris: Presses Universitaires de France, 1970).

14 See, for example, the differences between the aims of teachers and headmasters in their educational objectives in Schools Council, *Enquiry One: Young School Leavers* (London: HMSO, 1968), chap. 2.

15 BOURDIEU and PASSERON, *op. cit.* and BOURDIEU, P., and SAINT MARTIN, M. DE, 'L'Excellence Scolaire et les Valeurs du Système d'Enseignement Français' (Paris: Centre de Sociologie Européenne, 1969, mimeo.).

16 GOLDMANN, L., 'The Sociology of Literature: Status, Problems and Method', *International Social Science Journal*, XVIV: 4, 1967, pp. 493–516, but see also GOLDMANN, L., *Pour une Sociologie du Roman* (Paris: Gallimard, 1964).

17 BERGER and LUCKMANN, *op. cit.*

18 See the 'Introduction' by Young, and the first two chapters by Young and Bernstein respectively in YOUNG, M. F. D., *op. cit.*

19 BERNSTEIN, B., 'A Critique of the Concept of "Compensatory Education"', in RUBINSTEIN, D., and STONEMAN, C., *Education for Democracy* (Harmondsworth: Penguin, 1970).

20 WILLIAMS, R., *The Long Revolution* (Harmondsworth: Penguin, 1965), p. 172.

21 Recent controversies in France over time allocations to foreign language study could well be analysed in terms of the social system model of the teaching-subject proposed by MUSGROVE, F., 'The Contribution of Sociology to the Study of the Curriculum', in KERR, J. F. (ed.), *Changing the Curriculum* (London: University of London Press, 1968).

22 CAPELLE, J., *Tomorrow's Education: The French Experience* (Oxford: Pergamon, 1967).

23 BOURDIEU and PASSERON (1970), *op. cit.*, and see REPUSSEAU, J., 'Education et Violence', *Revue Française de Pédagogie*, no. 16, July–Sept. 1971, pp. 5–11.

24 Compare the experimental pedagogy of GATTEGNO, C., *What We Owe Children: the Subordination of Teaching to Learning* (London: Routledge and Kegan Paul, 1970). See also GAMM, H. J., *op. cit.*, especially pp. 82 ff.

and REBEL, K., 'Autoritätsstrukturen und Autoritätskrisen in Vergangenheit und Gegenwart' in ULSHÖFER, R., und REBEL, K., *Gymnasium und Sozialwissenschaften: Wege zur Demokratisierung der Schule* (Heidelberg: Quelle und Meyer, 1968), pp. 112–30.

25   NEWMAN, J. H., *On the Scope and Nature of University Education* (London: Dent, 1915).

26   TAYLOR, W., (1969), *op. cit.*

27   CROZIER, M., *La Société Bloquée* (Paris: Seuil, 1970), pp. 174–9.

28   BOURDIEU (1971), *op. cit.*

29   See THOMAS, H., *Innovation in Education: Germany* (Paris: OECD, CERI, 1971) and ERLINGHAGEN, K., *Katholisches Bildungsdefizit* (Freiburg: Herder, 1965). For a critique of the lack of social perspective of the *Strukturplan*, see HORNSTEIN, W., 'Bildungsplanung ohne Sozialpädagogische Perspektiven', *Zeitschift für Pädogogik*, XVII: 3 ,1971, pp. 285–314.

30   See for example LYNCH, J., 'The Birth of a Profession: German Grammar School, Teachers and New Humanism', *Comparative Education Review*, XVI: 1, 1972, pp. 87–97.

31   HOLLINS, T. B. H., *Another Look at Teacher Training* (Leeds: Leeds University Press, 1969); MAJAULT, J., *op. cit.*, p. 185.

32   After the 1848 revolution in the German provinces religion was used to impose conformity and submissiveness on teachers and student teachers. See for example the *Stiehl* regulations in FROESE, L., *Deutsche Schulgesetzgebung 1763–1952* (Weinheim: Verlag Julius Beltz, 1952) pp. 76–83. A spiritual adviser was attached to the schools in Bavaria after similar legislation (*die Normative für Lehrerbildung*). See NÜCHTER, F., 'Die geschichtliche Entwicklung der Lehrerbildung', *Schule und Gegenwart*, III: 3, pp. 53–5. The menial religious duties expected of the early teachers in Germany are referred to in FISCHER, K., *Geschichte des deutschen Volksschullehrerstandes* (Hanover: Verlag von Karl Meyer, 1892), vol, I, p. 318, and vol. II, p. 48.

33   OECD (1969), *op. cit.* p. 189 reproduces the model time-table in force at that time.

34   BOURDIEU, in Young (ed.) (1971), *op. cit.*, p. 194.

35   YOUNG, M. F. D., 'An Approach to the Study of Curricula as Socially Organized Knowledge', in Young (ed.) (1971), *op. cit.*, p. 38.

36   Some of the political aspects of this question are explored in ROBINSON (1968), *op. cit.*

37   CASTON, G., 'The Schools Council in Context', *Journal of Curriculum Studies*, III: 1, May 1971, pp. 50–64.

38   Recent proposals in England which could result in all teachers obtaining graduate qualifications have not been as democratic as might appear. They envisage two kinds of degree, the B.A. and the B.A.(Ed.), so that they preserve the stratification problem in another form. See DES, *Teacher Education and Training* (The James Report).

39   Committee on the Civil Service, *The Civil Service* (The Fulton Report) (London: HMSO, 1968), vol. I, para. 15.

40   BOURDIEU, in Young (ed.) (1971), *op. cit.*, p. 191.

41   OECD, *Science, Growth and Society: a new Perspective* (Report of the Secretary-General's *ad hoc* Group on new Concepts of Science Policy) (Paris: OECD, 1971).

42   Compare the references to the 'rehabilitation of existing structures' as a

concept of change amongst some teacher educators in RENSHAW, P., 'A Curriculum for Teacher Education', in BURGESS, T. (ed.), *op. cit.* It seems necessary to bring the stratification issue to the fore if conflicting values concerning change are to be explained, let alone resolved.

43   MILES, H. B., 'Handicaps for the Rat Race', *Times Educational Supplement*, Aug. 22, 1969, reports some results from research linking students' socioeconomic status to subject-choice in public examinations. See also SAINT MARTIN, M. DE, 'Les Facteurs de l'Elimination et de la Selection Différentielles dans les Etudes de Sciences', *Revue Française de Sociologie*, IX: 2 (1968), pp. 167–84.

44   Shipman argues that innovation in curriculum development is serving to strengthen divisions between pupils. See SHIPMAN, M., 'Curriculum for Inequality', in HOOPER, R., *The Curriculum: Context, Design and Development* (Edinburgh: Oliver and Boyd in association with The Open University Press, 1971), pp. 101–6.

45   MEN, *Circular no. IV–69–1087*, June 6, 1969, Annexe I.

46   The *Strukturplan* envisages the educational and social sciences as the core of the training of all teachers. See Deutscher Bildungsrat (1970) *op. cit.*, pp. 221 ff. Robinsohn places a similar emphasis on these studies in his proposals for an educational faculty. See ROBINSOHN, S. B., 'Vorschläge zur Ausbildung aller Lehrer an einer Pädagogischen Fakultät', in Deutscher Bildungsrat, *Materialien und Dokumente zur Lehrerbildung* (Stuttgart: Ernst Klett, 1971), pp. 31–41.

47   GIROD DE L'AIN, B., and LEGRAND, L., 'La Formation Initiale des Maîtres', in Association d'Etude pour l'Expansion de la Recherche Scientifique (1969), *op. cit.*, p. 251.

48   See chap. 4, ref. 35.

49   A mass-media linked series of courses for teachers in Bavaria is described in SCHORB, A. O., 'Das Bayerische Lehrerkolleg – Berufsfortbildung im Medienverbund', *Schulreport*, no. 4, 1971, pp. 2–3.

50   See COLLIER, K. G., 'Methods of Teaching Student Teachers', *Journal of Curriculum Studies*, III: 1, 1971, pp. 39–49.

51   FILLOUX, J., *et al.*, 'Réflexions sur Quelques Expériences de Stages de Perfectionnement d'Enseignants, de Formateurs et d'Educateurs', in Association d'Etude pour l'Expansion de la Recherche Scientifique, *Les Enseignants du Second Degré*. For a discussion of the potential use of micro-teaching in the training of academic secondary teachers in West Germany, see ZIFREUND, W., 'Micro-Teaching: Berufsbezogenes Verhaltenstraining in der Lehrerausbildung' in ULSHÖFER, R. and REBEL, K., *op. cit.*, pp. 209–29. In some cases there have been reports of teachers in training participating in discussions concerning the reform of their own preparation. See for example one such report, Initiativegruppe Giessen-Marburg, 'Überarbeiteter Entwurf zur Neuordnung der Referendarausbildung für das Lehramt an Gymnasien', *Bildungspolitische Informationen* – lc, 1971, pp. 27–33.

52   FAUQUET, M., and STRASFOGEL, S., 'Circuit Fermé de Télévision et Formation des Enseignants', *Revue de Pédagogie*, no. 10, Jan.-Mar. 1970, pp. 23–28. The first two CCTV units to be used in teacher education in West Germany were in the *pädagogische Hochschulen* in Bonn and Heidelberg. See SCHORB, A. O., *Unterrichtsmitschau: Fernsehanlagen im Dienste pädagogischer Ausbildung und Forschung* (Bad Godesberg: Verlag Dürrsche Buchhandlung, 1965) and also the information sheets of the

Erfahrungsaustauschring – *Schul-* *und* *Studienfernsehen* published in mimeo by the *pädagogische Hochschule* in Bonn from 22. 4. 1965. More recently the introduction of CCTV into in-service education has been reported in Hamburg. See LEIST, K., 'Der Beitrag der UMA für die Lehrerfortbildung' in Freie und Hansestadt Hamburg, Institut für Lehrerfortbildung, *Veranstaltungen im Sommerhalbjahr 1972* (Hamburg: 1972).

53 CASPARI, I. E., and EGGLESTON, S. J., 'Supervision of Teaching Practice', *Education for Teaching*, no. 68, 1965, pp. 42–52.

54 MEN, *Circular*, Jan 8, 1970.

55 LÉON, A., 'Les Sciences de l'Education dans les Universités Françaises', report of the Association des Enseignants de Sciences de l'Education, 1971, mimeo.

56 Compare the lines of thought in publications of the English Goldsmiths' College Curriculum Laboratory; CITRON, S., *op. cit.*, BATAILLON, M., *et al.*, *Rebâtir l'Ecole* (Paris: Payot, 1967); and HAYWARD, B., 'The Knowledge-base in Education: a Basis for Long Term Policy Planning', *Programme of Country Educational Planning* (Paris: OECD, Directorate for Scientific Affairs, 1971).

57 JAMES, C., *Young Lives at Stake: a Re-appraisal of Secondary Schools* (London: Collins, 1968). The importance of home-life in learning is suggested by the 'hidden curriculum' concept of FANTINI, M. D and WEINSTEIN, G., *The Disadvantaged: Challenge to Education* (New York: Harper and Row, 1968), and by FRIEDMANN, G., 'L'Ecole Parallèle', *Le Monde*, Jan. 7, 1966. Similar work in West Germany is contained in ROEDER, P. M., PASDZIERNY, A., WOLF, W., *Sozialstatus und Schulerfolg: Bericht über empirische Untersuchungen* (Heidelberg: Verlag Quelle und Meyer, 1965).

58 From 1972 The Open University introduced its educational studies courses, one section of which was devoted to curriculum. See for example unit 1, BELL, R., (for the course team), *Thinking About the Curriculum* (Bletchley, Bucks: The Open University Press, 1971).

59 MIDWINTER, E., *Projections: An Educational Priority Area at Work* (London: Ward Lock, 1972), especially pp. 46 ff.

60 WHITE, J., 'The Curriculum Mongers: Education in Reverse', in HOOPER, R. (ed.), *The Curriculum: Context, Design and Development* (Edinburgh: Oliver and Boyd in association with The Open University Press, 1971), pp. 273–80.

61 HIRST, P. H., and PETERS, R. S., *The Logic of the Curriculum* (London: Routledge and Kegan Paul, 1971) and ULLMO, J., *La Pensée Scientifique Moderne* (Paris: Flammarion, 1969), cited in CITRON, S., *op. cit.* See also KLAFKI, W., *Das pädagogische Problem des Elementaren und die Theorie der Kategorialen Bildung* (Weinheim: Verlag Julius Beltz, 1959) and OECD, *Curriculum Improvement and Educational Development* (Paris: OECD, c. 1966).

62 Demand for in-service training courses amongst English teachers suggests the need for broader courses dealing with areas and levels of education rather than single subjects. See DES, *Statistics of Education, Special Series no. 2: Survey of In-service Training for Teachers* (London: HMSO, 1970), p. 46.

63 *Pour une Ecole Nouvelle*, Commission D, Rapport Final.

64 LÉON, *op. cit.*

65 cf. FERRY (1970), *op. cit.*, chap. 1.

66 PÉRETTI, A. DE, 'La Formation des Enseignants', *Revue Française de Pédagogie*, no. 6, Jan.–Mar. 1969, pp. 5–16; Association pour la Recherche et l'Intervention Psycho-sociologiques, *Pédagogie et Psychologie des Groupes* (Paris: Editions de l'Epi, 1966); see also reports of the activities of the Féderation des Cercles de Recherche et d'Action Pédagogiques in their monthly journal, *Cahiers Pédagogiques*.

67 ROTH, F., 'Ein Zentrum für Lehrerausbildung und Hochschuldidaktik', *Zeitschrift für Pädagogik*, 10th Special Issue, 1971, pp. 187–96.

68 Deutscher Bildungsrat, *op. cit.*, pp. 221 ff.

69 See ROBINSOHN, S. B., 'Innovation im Erziehungswesen und ein Curriculum für Lehrerbildung', *Bildung und Erziehung*, XXV: 1, 1972, pp. 3–17 and THOMAS, H., 'Probleme der Lehrerbildung und der Forschung zur Lehrerbildung', *ibid.*, pp. 30–40. An American book which investigates similar problems is SMITH, B. O., *Research in Teacher Education: A Symposium* (Englewood Cliffs, N. J.: Prentice Hall 1971).

70 KAYE, B., *op. cit.*

71 COLLIER, K. G. (1968), *op. cit.*

72 MEN, *Circular no. IV–69–1087*, June 6, 1969 and *Circular no. IV–69–371*, Sept. 2, 1969.

73 In Aug. 1971, the province of Schleswig Holstein set up the *Landesinstitut Schleswig Holstein für Praxis und Theorie der Schule* (IPTS) which subsumed all in-service and phase two teacher education in the *Land*. The controlling council includes representatives of the university, the teachers' colleges, teachers and students. See IPTS, *Studien, Seminarberichte* no. 10, 1972 and IPTS, *Lehrerfort- und Weiterbildung in Schleswig Holstein* (Kiel: IPTS, 1971).

74 As part of the research for the present study all initial and in-service establishment of teacher education in West Germany were contacted for information on student participation. From the material which was returned it was clear that students had already achieved substantial representation on all committees in the *pädagogische Hochschulen*, including departmental areas. An example would be pädagogische Hochschule Westfalen Lippe, *Verfassung*, Sept. 22 1970 (mimeo, copy of official document IA3. 55-01 Nr 1405/70). An interesting American study on student attitudes to the curriculum is SCHWAB, J. J., *College Curriculum and Student Protest* (Chicago: University of Chicago Press, 1969).

75 See the Pilot Course Reports of the Goldsmiths' College Curriculum Laboratory, and numerous college of education syllabuses, such as the Modern World Studies course at Weymouth College, which contains a student-organized element.

76 WISEMAN, S., and PIDGEON, D., *Curriculum Evaluation* (Slough, Bucks: NFER, 1970). See also FREY, K., *Theorien des Curriculums* (Weinheim: Verlag Julius Beltz, 1971).

77 The Schools Council is undertaking a series of evaluation studies of its curriculum development projects, many of which have exposed basic problems of philosophy in their acceptability to teachers in schools. These reports are not yet published, though their potential usefulness to teachers must be beyond dispute, for the frankness with which they approach outcomes of teaching.

Chapter Six

The Organization and Control of Teacher Education

This final chapter in Part Two is built around the theme of the organizational provision by which teacher education policy-makers attempt to pursue their aims. We have been looking at how curricula correspond to culturally determined perceptions of teaching and to processes of socialization in teacher education. But in the terms of this study the values, concepts and processes of teacher education are institutionalized in a structure that is intended to facilitate the achievement of selected policies. We are however, at this point, less concerned with a single teachers' college than with seeking to clarify the various responsibilities of central and local government and other controlling agencies in teacher education. At the same time we must take account of what other financial, academic and professional interests find effective expression within this area. One set of questions, for example, must centre upon whether teachers in the three societies have been organized as participants in decision-making about teacher education. Such a study must also examine the relationship of teacher education to the general and higher education systems with regard to aims, staffing, course planning, financing and policy-making. The teacher education systems recruit, train and provide career structures for the personnel who are to carry out their aims. What patterns of training, qualification and activity characterize their personnel as distinct from responsible staff in other educational institutions? Those involved in the provision of teacher education may seek to promote their own professional self-improvement and thereby increase the efficiency of their institutions and of teacher education generally. In this latter process notions such as re-training are linked to issues of research and the diffusion of innovation both within teacher education and in its relationships, both formally and informally, to the wider educational and social systems. The balance of control in the implementation of accepted policy and in the formulation of new policy, and the relationship between teachers' colleges and inspectorates, inter-institutional co-ordinating bodies and political, syndical and religious organizations, provide further critical features of the organization of teacher education.

We have suggested in Chapter One that it is possible to analyse teacher education as a bureaucratic model. Clearly this analysis had to begin with a conventional description of the national systems of teacher education and their historical antecedents and this we have briefly attempted, relying upon an extensive literature within the field of historical, administrative and cross-cultural studies of education. Yet if we are to justify our argument for a comparative sociological study of teacher education, we must transcend a descriptive approach to organization which presupposes the coincidence of aims and functions. Some reference points for such a study can be discerned within the existing sociological and comparative literature in the theory of organizations.[1] But although the organization and control of teacher education has received far more attention from educationists and policy-makers than any of the other thematic areas we have studied, there is as yet no tradition of cross-cultural research which we can take as a starting-point for our analysis.[2] Undoubtedly, however, it is in this sense that the existence of separate teacher-education systems with their own aims, regulations and recruitment patterns is most manifest.

In attempting to identify and evaluate socially significant policy issues within this area we are faced with an underlying methodological problem. However socially sensitive our analysis of the issues, their very complexity forces on us a macro-sociological approach. We must be concerned therefore not only with the internal organization of individual institutions but, more centrally, with teacher education institution- and system-building. The comparative sociological analysis of the organization of teacher education adopts a similar methodological intent to that of the other chapters in Part Two. We draw extensively on empirical and other sources to identify and classify those organizational policy options that have been proposed or operationalized within the three societies and consider these in terms of the paradigm. The main tensions which the typology of policy options will help to classify in this chapter are those between, on the one hand, options which entail rigid or flexible structures and, on the other hand, options resulting in cellular or systemic organization.

1. THE SEGMENTAL VIEW OF TEACHER EDUCATION

1.1 The evolution of an organization for the training of teachers has been closely linked to prevailing systems of social stratification. The earliest provision of training was within schools and was regarded in most cases as a work of charity for the major religious communities in the three countries.[3] This training was intended to ensure a common basis for social and religious stability. Although in France the first institutions specifically for teacher education were politically inspired, the teachers' colleges in the three countries were expected to perpetuate prevailing social values. In England and Germany these socio-political tasks were delegated to religious bodies and, as in France, elementary teachers were recruited almost exclusively from the elementary schools. The basis of the selection procedure was the probable adequacy of candidates as purveyors of the religious or social values of the dominant culture. Colleges adopting *cell one* type policies aimed at efficient performance of this task by socializing the students in small single-sex colleges which were insulated from the outside world and ignored by other higher education institutions. The cultural remnants of this pattern of organization have shown a remarkable tenacity in France and parts of England and Germany. For example, as recently as

1939 in England,[4] of the 83 training colleges in existence, 64 had less than 150 students and 28 fewer than 100. The *écoles normales* were on a similar scale, and the Prussian *Pädagogische Akademien* were planned for about 260 students.[5] These colleges provided an opportunity for some individuals to raise themselves slightly in social status, whilst requiring them to transmit the cultural values of a stratum of society to which they might aspire but to which they could not expect to belong. In France the Napoleonic reforms abolished the control of the Church over teacher education. After the 1902 Education Act in England the churches slowly lost ground to the new local authority colleges.[6] In Germany of the fifteen *Pädagogische Akademien* founded in Prussia between 1926 and 1930, fourteen were denominational.[7] But social and ethical conformity were still the main objectives of teacher education and the social and cultural isolation of the teachers' colleges were major predisposing factors in this reproductive process. In England and France the teachers' colleges were almost entirely single-sex up to the time of the Second World War. The coercive nature of these institutions was reflected in their relationship to their clientèle and their small size permitted a strict and well-defined structure of authority, with very few effective decision-making roles, to be the channel for the presentation of relatively static and homogeneous religious and social values.[8]

1.2 In France and Germany there was a well-developed provision of training for teachers by the end of the eighteenth century, drawing financial and ideological sustenance from the churches and certain philanthropic sections of the nobility. The development was later in England, but gained its momentum from a charitable concern for the spiritual and moral welfare of the working classes. The very designation of the institutions betrayed a point of cultural significance. In France they were *écoles*; in Germany *Seminare*; in both cases they trained pupils not students. In all three societies the epistemological assumptions deriving from the social and cultural values of these institutions might be described as imitative and monotechnical. The narrow curriculum mirrored the epistemology of the schools, and their political or religious authorities, and was dominated by a traditional view of knowledge requiring little initiative of the learner. Conflicting demands for some of the academic qualities of secondary education and for relevance to the curriculum of the schools led to the development of preparatory courses in France and Germany.[9] The austere routine of the college insulated it from the surrounding community. Periods of teaching practice were carried out in specially selected or attached schools which were termed model, normal or annexed schools. The terminology, significant for its assumption of good models well practised and reproduced, is typical of the policy options of the *first cell*. Implicit in this organization was the assumption of an unchanging teacher role, imbued with high Christian ideals and discipline which found their authoritative expression in the ritual of the principal or director of the teachers' college giving his lectures on the principles of education.

K

1.3   Internally such institutions exhibited a largely undifferentiated academic commitment which rested upon what in Durkheimian terms would be described as a system of mechanical solidarity.[10] Recruitment of both staff and students was on the basis of reproductive and self-reinforcing cycles, which effectively resisted the pressures of social and educational change. While a member of a religious order was not permitted to teach in an *école normale*, in England and Germany there was usually some kind of religious test or qualification for staff appointment and the principals were often in orders.[11] As late as 1964 Taylor found that nearly 40 per cent of principals of English voluntary colleges had had no teacher training, and noted a high proportion of Oxford and Cambridge degrees among men principals.[12] From 1904, the Board of Education in England had exerted considerable control over the staffing of the training colleges, which however continued to consist, as in the nineteenth century, of two major groups: alumni of the training colleges, who on the whole favoured the traditions which the colleges represented and, with the increased demand for specialization, a growing number of academically trained lecturers, many of whom had no teaching qualification, and whose teaching experience, if any, was limited to secondary schools.[13]

Traditionally the staff of the *écoles normales* were former primary teachers who had risen to the primary inspectorate and passed a qualifying examination. This situation only evolved after the Second World War when the *baccalauréat* was introduced as a formal stage in the student-teacher's academic career to replace the older *brevet supérieur*. With the development of upper secondary work the staffing of the *écoles normales* became similar to that of the *lycée* and thus in time with the teachers' colleges of that period in the other two countries.[14]

With notable exceptions the staff that it was possible to recruit to the *Seminare* in the nineteenth century were neither well trained nor intellectually able. Poor remuneration, inadequate career opportunities and the isolated position of the establishments attracted only those predominantly young teachers who could find no position elsewhere, and who often had no experience of teaching in an elementary school.[15] Due to mass unemployment in the 1920s, on the other hand, the *Pädagogische Akademien* were particularly fortunate in being able to recruit lecturers who were both well qualified and had a sense of commitment to the ideals of the institutions. In the post-war era recruitment of staff to the *Pädagogische Hochschulen* has been mainly from the ranks of academic secondary teachers, many of whom would have preferred and later sought to move to a university position.

1.4   In spite of the aspirations of the teaching profession for higher social status and the rapidly changing social structure of the three societies in the nineteenth century, the function of the teachers' colleges was to exercise a stabilizing effect on thought and behaviour in the face of rapid social and moral change. Such was the legacy of curricular and structural reproduction that the institutions of teacher education carried with them into the first half of the twentieth century. The social claustrophobia generated by their cellular organization did little to attract or retain creative staff or students. The tradition of our *first cell* continues to exist in the subordination of colleges of education in England to the academic authority of the universities and more importantly in the widespread desire of the colleges to continue this association as the source of their own prestige.[16] Financial and academic control of the colleges in England was at first in the hands of the churches. Gradually as the state intervened the colleges acquired two masters, each applying financial and academic controls. Thereafter the Central Government enforced academic standards within the colleges until the universities began to take over this function from 1930 onwards.[17] The Government has twice rejected a system of direct grants to the colleges and financial provision for them remained in the early 1970s a divided responsibility involving the University Grants Committee, the universities, the voluntary bodies, the local education authorities and the DES.[18] *First-cell* type organizational policy options have been recently illustrated in the case of England by the piecemeal and confused implementation of the Robbins Report proposal for the introduction of a B.Ed. degree.[19]

The system of *écoles normales* was from their inception under overall central inspection and control, though the individual establishments depended materially upon the departmental authorities. As a result qualifications and appointments of staff, details of the programmes and even disciplinary arrangements were virtually standardized.[20] There were particularly stringent regulations concerning religious matters though rights of religious practice were protected. Financial control of teacher education in Germany has traditionally been exercised directly by the regional governments although from 1971 the Federal Government has participated in the financing of *pädagogische Hochschulen*. The former have set down the guidelines for teacher examinations at all levels, and have acquired added control over recruitment of staff due to the regional civil service status of teachers and the existence of qualifications which were not automatically recognized outside the *Land* of origin.[21]

2. THE SYSTEM-CENTRED VIEW OF TEACHER EDUCATION

2.1 The major features of the teacher-education systems in the three countries have derived their stability from the gradual implementation of governmental policies that sought a more centralized control and more standardized results from the different institutions involved. Policies which we would classify in *cell two* characterized the approach of both religious and political agents of development in the national consolidation of modern European states. For as long as major religious groups were prepared to accept national political and social goals, church-organized systems of education and teacher education were allowed to develop. In France, first, after the Revolution, and only in the later years of the nineteenth century in the other two countries, there began to be a serious questioning of the appropriateness of church values as the main public justification for elementary education.[22] But whether in the denominational colleges of England and Germany, or in the republican *écoles normales* in France, powerful cultural traditions were established and perpetuated by the growth of the teachers' colleges. Much influenced by the university model in the former two countries, and representing an important sector in the Napoleonic spectrum of normal and vocational schools in France, these institutions asked no more than to mirror the morally and socially approved doctrines of their day. Secondary school-teaching was from an early period in even closer conformity to the traditions of the established interests of society as interpreted through the universities or the *écoles normales supérieures*. Prestige in the secondary school rested upon mastery of inherited learning, and thus favoured the maintenance of traditional values and symbols of prestige, as well as justifying the consolidation of the cultural hierarchies depending upon church, university and the world of classical learning.

2.2　The values and symbols of what Prost has described as the 'apogée de la société enseignante' were guaranteed by the social and epistemological categories of the educational systems. Particular types and levels of educational experience or institution were graded in prestige and authority. Thus, the degrees of the older English universities, clerical orders and the study of the classics were taken as appropriate criteria for judging the social value of English teachers' college staff and courses. Professional experience was of little account in comparison with these qualifications for appointment. Although vestiges of these values remain today in the teachers' colleges, recent years have seen the development of professional expertise based upon specialist subject knowledge. A whole social system has been able to grow up in English education with this epistemological basis. Subject departments formed in the teachers' colleges and brought seniority and power to the longest-established exponents. By the same token, the university, as the source of specialized knowledge, was accorded the most prestige and justified the perpetuation of the concomitant knowledge- and people-ranking hierarchies. It is worthy of note that educational research was given little place in the teachers' colleges and universities, but that even where research on teacher education was undertaken it virtually ignored those sectors which particularly concerned the universities, such as the training of graduate teachers for academic secondary education.[23]

Equivalent hierarchies of values were institutionalized in France in the rigid cleavage between elementary education, including the *écoles normales* and the *écoles normales supérieures*, and on the other hand the world of the *lycée* and the university. The gap between these two sets of institutions was only bridged when the first teachers with university qualifications were brought in to staff the *écoles normales* after 1945. The teachers in the nineteenth century *écoles normales* had been able to develop an educational theory, asserting their interest in pedagogy as a point on which to challenge the more academic secondary sector. The strength of subject-based learning in the *lycées* and universities has been such that the unification of teacher education in France still appears to be ruled out. The implicit cultural hierarchies of subject and title, topped by the formalized academicism of the *agrégé*, retain their validity to the present day.[24]

In Germany *cell two* type policies resulted from the demand from almost all teachers' associations for an *Akademisierung* of all teacher education.[25] This was interpreted by the teachers' colleges to mean the introduction of traditional university courses separating theory and practice, and educational and subject study. The labels attached to institutions began an inflationary spiral which in some instances led to several renamings in the space of a score of years. *Akademie* was discarded in favour of *Hochschule* which was still further re-designated *wissenschaftliche Hochschule*, as institutions and their directors succeeded in gaining membership of such prestige bodies as the West German Rectors' Conference. The misgivings of the Conference concerning the elevation of institutions of teacher education to full academic parity with universities is reflected in their diffident attitude to successive demands from professional sources for the upgrading of teacher education. In its description of the *pädagogische Hochschule*, the *Deutscher Ausschuss* in 1955 argued that it was by nature of its development of the study of education that this institution could legitimately claim higher education status. A clear distinction is implied between this aspect and those which presumably are not academic, such as practical and main subject work.[26] The continued struggle for recognition of the academic standing of courses of elementary teacher training in Germany became a skirmish on many fronts during the 1950s and 1960s, and is still not resolved.

The concept of useful further learning beyond initial training levels was familiar by the early years of the twentieth century even though few resources were devoted to this work. The very terms used in the three countries, namely *refresher* courses, *recyclage* and *Lehrerfortbildungswerk* suggest an undeveloped professionalism.

2.3 System-wide policies can be said to have existed in all three countries before the end of the eighteenth century. In England, the Charity School Movement, and the later monitorial systems evolved their own provisions for teacher preparation; in France the Christian Brothers and other religious orders had developed a relatively systematic training in pre-Napoleonic France and the Pietist Movement had acted as a spur to the development of *Seminare* in many parts of Germany. Such developments in teacher preparation and certification as those which grew out of the 1846 Committee of Council on Education decisions in England improved the status of the profession, but the system of *payment by results*, which reduced the number of pupil-teachers by 5,000 in five years, further reinforced the narrow outlook of the training colleges. The *pupil-teacher centre-system*, which was particularly vigorous in the larger urban areas in the 1880s and 1890s represented the development of an aggregative policy in an attempt to deal with broader social and educational developments.[27] The Guizot Law of 1833 in France obliged each *département* to have an *école normale* for male students, and laid down regulations for their financing, organization and curriculum.[28] Whether for male or female students, however, the *écoles normales* never sufficed to provide even a majority of the teachers needed by the elementary schools, and the *écoles normales supérieures* have become increasingly exclusive institutions and have been confined to Paris. By 1800 there were already twenty-four *Seminare* in Prussia and similar developments had taken place in other provinces of Germany. The establishment of a ministry responsible for education in Prussia in 1817 laid the foundations for the control and development of teacher education, and led in 1826 to the introduction of a standardized terminal examination for students. Gradually also a pre-system was established which undertook the general educational preparation of students in *Präparandenanstalten*. By the end of the First World War, Prussia had 191 *Seminare* and 217 preparatory establishments and there was similar provision in the other German provinces.[29]

It could be argued that there was no real system of teacher education in the three countries until arrangements existed for the training of secondary-school teachers. Other than through an informal pupil-teacher system, secondary schools aimed to recruit university graduates, normally with little or no pedagogical training. The situation changed in England with the setting up of the *day-training colleges* from 1890 for students who could obtain a university degree by concurrent academic study, and then by the establishment of what is effectively the present system of *university departments of education* and their *post-graduate certificate* courses in the early years of the century. The organization of the other part of the dual system in France relied upon the *écoles normales supérieures* and the universities until after the Second World War, when the present system of *centres pédagogiques régionaux* was introduced. The lack of liaison, however, between the universities and these centres, and their extremely limited aims as training agencies, hardly entitles them to be described as a teacher-education system. Regulations for the professional preparation of secondary academic teachers were set down in Prussia as early as 1826, although a test of practical teaching had been prescribed from 1810. With the introduction of thirty-five *Studienseminare* in Prussia in 1890, a pattern of institutional commitment to secondary academic teacher preparation was established, which was generalized to the whole of West Germany after the Second World War.[30]

The period after the First World War saw the teachers' colleges in all three countries remaining socially reproductive and culturally homogeneous. By and large in the three countries it continued to be expected that teachers would defend the traditional culture, but it was becoming clearer that elementary teachers were inadequately trained for this purpose. While the *écoles normales* remained rigidly separated from secondary and higher education, first probes were made towards the university in England and Germany. It had been possible in many parts of Germany from the beginning of the century for college students to transfer to university courses and in England from the 1930s the *joint boards* were instituted and began to break down the isolation of the colleges from the developing culture of the universities. The McNair Report of 1944 succeeded ahead of the other two countries in synthesizing these developments, but in any case all three countries faced massive schemes of emergency training which had to be linked with the existing organization of teacher education at the end of the Second World War.

In England Ministry of Education Circular 112 in 1946 represented an acceptance of the principle of a federation of colleges in closer association with the universities.[31] The result was the establishment of *university institutes of education* from 1947 but, although many saw such developments as a real advance in social prestige for the colleges, the recommendations made by the McNair Report for the rationalization of resources and co-operation between institutions were given little effect until possibly in the planning of B.Ed. and post-graduate certificate courses, which were taught in the colleges from the mid-1960s. The French *académie* combined the functions of the English institute of education and the local education authority in the administration of teacher education. The English area organization was paralleled in Hessen and Bavaria from 1958 by the affiliation of the teachers' colleges to the universities and in the mid-1960s by the establishment of regional groupings of *pädagogische Hochschulen* in provinces such as Lower Saxony and North Rhine-Westphalia.

Also typical of this set of teacher-education options in England was the subsuming of in-service work under the aegis of the Ministry of Education, later the DES, the local authorities and, in a hitherto separate structure, the university institutes. Opportunities for refresher courses were offered to the mass of teachers by central providers. The resources offered by these bodies and their organizational capability led to a very great increase in such courses over the period of the 1960s. There was virtually no parallel to this development in France, where the problem of initial training was still far from solved, until the late 1960s and the establishment of substantial courses for unqualified teachers in localities under primary inspectors and in the *écoles normales*. In the case of West Germany too, the development of in-service work for teachers was severely neglected until the late 1960s. In spite of pioneer work in such post-war institutions as the *education centres* established by the Americans and the *Lehrerfortbildungswerk* set up in 1951 in Hessen, there was no generalization of this commitment until the establishment in all *Länder* of many new institutions from 1970 onwards and the expansion of in-service provision linked to further qualifications in subject areas (*Lehrerweiterbildung*).[32]

2.4 The English universities have continued to have greater financial independence than the training colleges and, though the *area training organizations* were funded, like the universities, through the University Grants Committee, the colleges have continued under direct national and local government financial control. Moreover, by its control over the financial determinants of teacher demand and supply, the DES has regulated the development of the teachers' colleges and has imposed upon them as a priority the meeting of teacher-training targets. The Conferences of Institute Directors and of Heads of University Departments of Education in England, which later coalesced into the Universities Council for the Education of Teachers, exercised a predominant influence on academic and organizational developments in teacher education, adopting an oligarchic approach, common until recently to all three countries, which resisted consultation and effectively excluded the participation of teachers and junior colleagues.[33] The directors of the *écoles normales* have their own syndical organization as well as an official annual meeting to confer with the central authorities. In Germany a similar hierarchical approach was manifested by succeeding Conferences of the *Westdeutsche Universitätspädagogen* and the *Rektorenkonferenz*.[34]

The students in the early institutions of teacher education in all three countries had been regarded as pupils, and the colleges were often in intellectual tutelage to universities and government departments which were insensitive to their needs and traditions. A system of reserved decisions existed at each stage of the organizational hierarchy and in England university senates, even where unsympathetic to broader college objectives, could exercise overall control in academic matters. Recruitment of students to teaching was controlled in the early stages by a financial or moral pledge system, and the increasingly limited negotiability of the teacher's certificate. Although the majority of the teachers' colleges in England and Germany continued to be denominational until well into the present century more direct state provision and supervision was developing, matching in many respects the powerful French *académie* and inspectorate functions.

Problems common to the three countries in the control of teacher education are illustrated in developments in England since the Second World War. From an early date the National Council on the Training and Supply of Teachers was established to give an overview on the basis of which control over the development of teacher education might be co-ordinated. This initiative failed through the ensuing disagreements on the Council which was then disbanded.[35] A period then followed of the muffling of discontent about teacher education, culminating perhaps in the excessively bland report on the subject made by the DES to the OECD in 1969.[36] Subsequently articulate criticism grew and a series of public inquiries, already mentioned in Chapter One, were undertaken. Most recently, in what has been the second major development in teacher education since the war a broad review has been provided by the James Committee on teacher education and training. The James Report recommended a streamlining of this system which would allow local and national governments, jointly with representatives of teacher-education interests, to decide on the total level and distribution of resources, through a proposed National Council for teacher Education and Training, which would set down guidelines for Regional Councils for Colleges and Departments of Education, and to make recommendations concerning the allocation of resources within their region. No machinery developed in France or West Germany for the reappraisal and reorganization of teacher education, though several public commissions and a string of fugitive reports from official and professional sources confirmed what a French writer described as, and the phrase can be applied to the two countries, its *'organisation anarchique'*.[37]

3. THE LEARNING-CENTRED VIEW OF TEACHER EDUCATION

3.1   The innovation cells of the typology trace the far-reaching changes in values and epistemological systems of the teachers' colleges which have begun to make themselves apparent in response to the twin pressures of rapid increase in size and of the widespread ideological commitment to democracy. If in England and Germany a function of increased size was the differentiation of the internal organization of the institutions of teacher education, the commitment to new concepts of authority implied that students, teachers and junior members of staff should be involved in institutional decision-making. The response to the ATCDE demand for greater organizational freedom from the control of the providing bodies, which was submitted to the Robbins Committee in England, was the setting up in 1965 of a study group to look into the government of colleges of education.[38] The fact that legislation eventually needed to be introduced in 1968 to compel some recalcitrant local education authorities to adopt the broad principles of the Weaver Report is one indication of over-bureaucratization of the college system, a phenomenon which was paralleled in the general educational systems of France and Germany by descriptions of *l'école bloquée* and by complaints of *die verwaltete Schule*.[39] In Germany new legislation concerning the constitutions of the still largely independent *pädagogische Hochschulen* had brought democratic representation for junior members of staff and students from the late 1950s.[40] In England and Germany the approach to decision-making aimed at an internal consensus which would at the same time be acceptable to the ministry or churches in Germany and to the ministry, university and providing body in England.

The colleges were beginning to accept the value of limited innovation, though the focus of this was at first external and only gradually affected work in the colleges themselves. Change seemed more acceptable and new religious and social values were having their effect upon the curricula and organization of institutions of teacher education, calling in question the paternalistic tolerance that had traditionally been exercised towards the student culture.

3.2   Acceptance of changing values in society at large implies a re-examination of the epistemological presuppositions of the organization of teacher education which, in the three societies, have been tied to the fixed point of the scholarly authority of university learning. This process logically entails the challenging of all authorities that give values and meaning to the organization of teacher education. The result of the introduction of the B.Ed. degree in England was that for the first time large numbers of staff and students in the colleges were considered fit to be involved in degree work.

The 1964 Hull Conference on the study of education, by acting as a further impetus to the development of specialized disciplines, did much to influence the way in which educational studies developed in colleges and departments and led rapidly to the foundation of various educational societies and journals.[41] The *école normale* course was lengthened to two years following the *baccalauréat* in 1968 and the pre-*baccalauréat* classes began to be suppressed so that primary teacher training in the 1970s was to become post-secondary in character. Scope was thus increased for more highly developed educational studies, but specialist staff was virtually unavailable in such areas as psychology and sociology because of rigid restrictions over the recognition for teaching purposes of the university degrees in these subjects. The original plans to provide education in pedagogical theory for secondary academic teachers in the *centres pédagogiques régionaux* were never implemented, though some courses for intermediate teachers did give more place to the social sciences.[42] The marked expansion of teachers' colleges in England and Germany also furthered work in new disciplines and altered professional commitments, bringing into focus fresh areas of study at both initial and in-service levels, and leading to the appointment of new educational specialists. Curriculum reform projects in the schools were tugging at the traditional epistemology of the school curriculum and were thereby raising issues concerning the curriculum of the colleges.[43] New disciplines were introduced along with multi-disciplinary work, and even integrated studies as main courses as well as other far-reaching innovations linking initial training for teachers and for allied professions.[44] Typical of the new options developing were those aimed at capitalizing on the resources and talents of students and requiring new approaches and methods, different forms of involvement and the creation of optional courses planned by students.[45] A greater direct interest in educational research was evidenced in the teachers' colleges, in the growth of research centres and in increasing involvement in research by practising teachers.[46]

3.3   As we have seen in Chapter Three the shift of ideological commitment within the educational system is now increasingly towards a child-centred teacher who is able to meet the aspirations of societies for social and educational democratization. These pressures have led to a large number of isolated structural innovations within teacher education which can be ascribed to the *third cell* of the typology.

The twenty university institutes of education which were set up in England after the Second World War have shown little uniformity or organization. Typical of the policies within the *third cell* was the way in which the B.Ed., degree was introduced with some universities permitting classified honours degrees to be awarded whilst others granted only ordinary degrees.[47] The way in which B.Ed. degree development has confirmed the social reproduction hypothesis is impressive, in that proportionately fewer students from infant and junior as opposed to secondary teacher-training courses have been registered for B.Ed. degrees. Such a discrepancy, if continued, could extend existing hierarchies and differentiations within the teaching profession which as in the past would be related to the age of children taught.[48]

Several new types of courses were instituted in France for the training of intermediate teachers (*professeurs d'enseignement général de collège, professeurs des classes de transition et pratique*) and the first formal pedagogical training for the *agrégés* was organized.[49] These innovations were centrally initiated and were mainly located in university towns. Apart from the facility to invite university lecturers in certain subjects to give classes in the *écoles normales*, however, there was no institutional link with universities concerning provision of initial teacher training.[50]

In West Germany by the early 1950s there were at least five major organizational structures for elementary teacher education ranging from integration into the university in Hamburg, through the autonomous *pädagogische Akademie* pattern in some north German *Länder* to the old *Seminar* tradition in south Germany. The independent college of education (*pädagogische Hochschule*) emerged as the predominant pattern by the mid-1960s although movements towards closer inter-institutional relationships were already taking place in such *Länder* as Hessen and Bavaria. In Lower Saxony all teachers' colleges were federated into a university of education and in North Rhine-Westphalia the teachers' colleges were grouped into three *pädagogische Hochschulen* consisting of four to six departments, whilst all teachers' colleges in Rhineland Palatinate were confederated in 1969 into an educational university (*erziehungswissenschaftliche Hochschule*).[51] By the early 1970s the training of intermediate teachers showed even less uniformity, with some *Länder* having completely abolished this category of teacher training altogether, whilst others retained it at university or teachers' college. Academic secondary teachers continued to press for increased status for the *Studienseminare*, where they received their professional training, at the same time as the two-phase model of their preparation began to be incorporated into the training of elementary teachers, resulting in the same conflicts between theory and practice which had been experienced by the secondary academic teacher in training.[52]

Though the institutions of teacher education were firmly established as part of the system of higher education, in England after the Robbins Report and in Germany by the early 1960s they still lacked the status of the universities in terms of staff academic standing, student recruitment and ability to grant degrees. With the introduction of three-year courses in England and Germany academic standards improved; new types of competence came to be recognized and staff were recruited on the basis of a wider range of academic qualification and experience. The large proportion of new staff with recent teaching experience favoured a number of innovations in relating the institutions to schools, while the rapid increase in size of schools and numbers of students underlined the need to find new ways of organizing school experience for a large number of students, to involve them more closely in the behavioural study of children. In England complaints of excessive demands on schools for teaching practice places and of a wide gulf between the educational approaches of schools and colleges were followed in many places by teaching practice committees, composed of representatives of teachers, local education authorities, colleges and institutes of education.[53] The search for greater efficiency in professional socialization in all three countries led to the setting up of resource centres for audio-visual aids and the use of closed circuit television in preparation for practical teaching.[54] New forms of group and social practice, joint appointments, teacher-tutor schemes and experiments involving the exchange of staff between schools and colleges were followed in England by proposals for professional training centres which were similar to the pattern of the second phase in German teacher education originally introduced for secondary teachers.[55] Few such developments occurred in France, where the introduction of a teaching practice in which the student-teacher was given control of a class has been one of the few major innovations. In fact this was regarded as a scheme which would release teachers for in-service training, and thus can hardly be considered to ensure qualitative development of the initial training of primary teachers.[56]

In England and West Germany the later 1960s were crucial years of change for both the teachers' colleges and the teacher-education system. Confederations of colleges in such provinces as North Rhine-Westphalia and Lower Saxony were designated *educational universities*, at the same time as Hessen and Bavaria began to absorb all teacher education into existing universities. Successive public inquiries into English teacher education led to proposals that envisaged a new role and status for the teachers' colleges, as *liberal arts colleges* in a closer if still subordinate relationship to the university.[57] Larger units, which brought in their wake increasingly difficult problems of professional socialization, co-educational colleges and the infusion of large numbers of day-students into the system, necessitated new and more bureaucratized patterns of social organization.[58] The DES began from 1970 to make funds available to ATOs for in-service training. Local authority interest in in-service education for teachers has been expressed over the past decade through the *teachers' centres*.[59] The continuing incoherence of provision of in-service training by very large numbers of institutions and organizations with neither national nor regional co-ordination was a matter of great concern to many of the witnesses who submitted evidence to the House of Commons Select Committee on Education and Science.[60] More exploratory in-service training activities have been developed by the universities and by a number of teachers' and academics' associations in France.[61] Apart from the *Université Pédagogique de l'Eté* mentioned in Chapter Two, there are smaller groupings in which professional development is the major aim and which organize debates, conferences and summer schools and publish newsletters and journals independent of the public authorities. The vitality evidenced in such activities must to a considerable degree be interpreted as the reaction to an over-centralized system that takes little official account of teacher-initiated developments. Though the response of the West German universites to the recommendation of the Science Council in 1966 that they should provide regular contact studies for teachers has been very limited, there has been increased activity in this area of teacher education from 1970. The KMK declaration of December 1970, and the major reports of the Federal Government and the Science and Education Councils, emphasized the need for an expansion and systematizing of in-service provision. Numerous institutes were established in all parts of West Germany; provision of courses leading to qualifications was expanded; information services for teachers were improved, and new journals published by the ministries. In some cases provision was linked to courses broadcast on radio or television, and printed study material was made available to working groups of teachers; in at least one case CCTV has been installed in an in-service institute. In-service education for teachers is also provided by the Catholic Church.[62]

3.4 Internally the major power positions within the teachers' colleges in England and Germany continued to be occupied by members of staff who had been brought to senior positions by the expansion of their institutions. The formal apparatus of representative college government has now been established in all three countries but it has generally been deficient in practice in England and Germany and closely circumscribed by official regulations in France.[63] Indeed in spite of the Weaver Report affording to the English teachers' colleges greater control over their academic affairs and greater flexibility in the management of their finances, the scope of decisions reserved to the DES, the institutes of education and the providing bodies was such that effective democratic college government seemed elusive. Successive major public reports have made proposals for the co-ordination of national policy, and the James Report endorsement of such proposals reflects a contemporary desire to balance the influence of the major interest-groups in decisions concerning teacher education.[64] The issue being fought out in France at the present time is as to whether the formal responsibility for the training of teachers conceded for the first time to the university by the *Loi d'Orientation de l'Enseignement Supérieur* of 1968 will bring teacher education under a system of democratic control similar to that of other university departments (UERs), or whether the central government interest will be pressed to the point of obtaining a special regime for the future organization of initial teacher education.[65] In West Germany new constitutions were drawn up for the teachers' colleges in all *Länder* but, although supervision by the ministries was relaxed in academic matters, the colleges continued to be directly controlled by the ministry in financial matters and in the confirmation of appointments of staff, all of whom have civil service status. In the preparation of programmes of in-service provision the views of teachers were sought and they were invited to participate in the government of some in-service institutes. In some of these developments particular institutions developed policies of participation in advance of the legislation, though in all *Länder* the *Studienseminare* were among the last institutions in implementing more democratic policies.[66]

There has been widespread discontent amongst the French and German student populations even in the traditionally less activist teachers' colleges;

demonstrations have occurred and in Germany strikes were not uncommon. In all three countries the community at large and in particular the teachers felt themselves excluded from influence over the organization of teacher education. The emphasis was still on the autonomy of educational institutions though the potentially reflexive role of research as an area of work that had not traditionally been the concern of the colleges was being increasingly recognized in England and West Germany. Policies within the *third cell* of the typology are characterized by their diversity and the spasmodic nature of their implementation. Progress in the internal democratization of the teachers' colleges was being encouraged by the wide-ranging criticism of a pluralist society, but these demands for reform, accountability and for a greater community involvement, were still far from finding a coherent response.

4. THE COMMUNITY-CENTRED VIEW OF TEACHER EDUCATION

4.1   With the failure of policy-makers in the three countries to formulate structural plans for teacher education that would fit the criteria of the *fourth cell*, a multiplicity of separate proposals overwhelms the embryonic and narrowly-based agencies presently available to process them. In this section we can only hope to identify certain democratizing features of contemporary teacher education which, if generalized, might provide the framework for more coherent and community-centred systems. Teacher education is increasingly seen as a significant area in the promotion of educational and social reform. Failure to achieve social equality through the educational system alone forces teacher education to link its organization more closely to that of other agencies in the community. Socially-oriented policies relating to internal and external democratization of all educational institutions are increasingly demanded by the logic of changing their teaching methods, knowledge and teachers' roles.[67] Issues of the rights of the child, the student and the parent can no longer be ignored.[68] Students are envisaged increasingly as maturing professionally through the exercise of individual and collective responsibility. The organization of the institution, and the means by which it relates through its staff and students to the wider community, are seen as the structural aspect of the socialization process by which the colleges are alerted to and thus enabled to prepare their staff and students for new social roles. The pluralist society produces a steady volume of criticism and of reform proposals which require to be harmonized before they can be implemented. Policies of regionalization and rationalization are proposed.[69] Such tendencies as these can be discerned in all three societies as the underlying issues become more exposed by critical analysis, and the ideals long current in systems of teacher education are translated into active proposals for reorganization.

4.2   At an epistemological level, sensitivity to the wider society suggests the need for new approaches to knowledge and new strategies for achieving explicit goals, as for example in the development of a more concentrated reflexive function through research, teacher involvement in curriculum development or the establishment of college/community links in inner-city areas. The very unpredictability of changes in society means that any normative involvement of interested parties has to be sought on the basis of a recognition of cultural pluralism that supersedes traditional psychologistic biases. The acceptance of the importance of education in preparing for cultural diversity, despite its hitherto limited role in promoting social change, has led to proposals for the development of interprofessional work in initial and in-service training.[70] The need for validation of the course aims, content and organization have led to a more widespread development of research techniques in measuring behavioural and attitude change.[71] Involvement in empirical work has acquired status and there is an appreciation of the multifarious ways in which professional socialization and re-socialization can be effected, including through sandwich courses, T-group work, field studies and the diversification of permanent education.[72] Traditional concepts of craft-type and specialized courses have begun to be questioned, and socially-oriented models of professional education integrating theoretical and practical perspectives are being counter-proposed.[73] At least in England and West Germany there is a body of public opinion favouring the comprehensivization of higher education, though prevailing government priorities and strongly embedded cultural traditions and hierarchies make swift progress towards such goals unlikely.[74]

4.3 The social structural corollaries of the acceptance of democratization as an organizational value are inevitably far-reaching. Teacher education can no longer be seen as isolated from the community and the idea that teachers should be prepared alongside the other professions with which they will need to work seems similarly irrefutable. The recognition that professional socialization is a continuous process implies decisions about the appropriate phasing of training which will need to be based upon socially valid and reliable procedures for selection and evaluation. The increasing complexity of teachers' roles has created the need in all three countries for a longer period of initial training and this is accompanied, at least in West Germany, by an increase in the professional status of the teachers' colleges.[75] In England and Germany demands for more closely planned programmes during the second, probationary phase of initial training are contained in the *second cycle* proposals of the James Report, and have resulted in the adoption by two German provinces of a second phase of training for all teachers such as the academic secondary teachers alone have enjoyed previously. In England research covering teachers' experience and their needs has noted the important work of the teachers' centres and provided useful evidence for the recommendation of permanent education and training for all teachers.[76]

The internal development of the teachers' colleges is characterized by the search for wider opportunities for staff and student involvement in academic planning and community life. Responsibility of members of staff for students is increasingly restricted in the three countries to areas of specialist competence. Students' formal lecture programmes are reduced and a greater emphasis is placed upon small group work and upon the individual's responsibility for his own learning. Advocates for the postponing of formal commitment to teaching have gained strength from the supporters of greater freedom of choice in higher education.[77] Experiments have been reported in England and Germany in which paired and group submissions form part of an examination requirement.[78] The growing complexity of the institutions has required the development of bureaucratic procedures and services, and specialist non-academic administrators have been added to the staff of many of the larger colleges. Students have obtained representation on most major internal college committees including governing bodies.[79]

In external relationships radical systemic changes have been proposed. The inclusion of institutions of teacher education within comprehensive systems of higher education, where differences would be genuine and functional rather than socially or historically determined, has been forcefully advocated by sections of the teaching profession in all three countries.[80] It is significant that these aspirations have come mainly from the teachers or from political sources rather than from any influential body of opinion within the institutions of teacher education or the universities.[81] Both the formal and the informal relationships existing between the colleges and the universities in England have impeded the democratization of higher education and have inhibited the colleges of education from espousing comprehensivization policies in higher education.

4.4   In the three societies the rapidly rising numbers of entrants to higher education confront policy-makers with numerous options. Social priorities are increasingly urged for a more equitable distribution of resources within higher and recurrent education as well as with respect to other sectors of education and of society. The similarity of organizational policy options in the three countries is the result of matching economic influences. Thus considerations of economic rationalization tend to block reform of teacher education where this implies acceptance of the need for all teacher education, initial and post-experience, to be unified and incorporated within higher education.[82] Similarly recognition is only reluctantly granted to various social, syndical and professional *consumer groups* to participate in policy-making for teacher education, since this sector might thus achieve a large measure of autonomy from the direct control of any one government or providing agency.[83] Implementation of such reforms must involve the close working together of teacher education with all other branches of higher and professional education to facilitate the national allocation of scarce resources. The growth in size and number of such institutions, and their broader professional commitment, necessitates more emphasis on democratic participation and involvement, even at the highest levels, for junior members of staff and for students. Rolling reform of the internal organization of teachers' colleges implies organizational procedures to cope with on-going change and staff training and re-training as a normal commitment of these institutions.[84] At this stage fixed appointments are dysfunctional to the colleges and particular responsibilities need to be allocated and reallocated according to individual qualities and organizational needs.

We have argued in Chapter Three that an institution can only be considered to be responsive to democratic values if these values are themselves democratically institutionalized in the organization of teacher education. This process can be said to have begun in each of the three societies, but there are inherent problems both in the extent to which this can be achieved without a formalization which destroys the very ends sought and in what democratization demands in terms of changes of attitude and skills. The self-monitoring procedures needed for evaluation of teacher-education programmes presuppose highly trained, and at the moment very scarce research personnel, sensitive to the diversifying needs of the education service and of the broader community and aware of the potential function of teacher education in more general educational reform. The question of how far it is utopian at the present time to envisage democratization in teacher education has to be assessed in relation to all four policy areas which have been reviewed in Part Two of this study. The main focus of our concluding chapter is the theme of the harmonization of policies across these four areas of teacher education in response to tidal movements of change and reaction.

REFERENCES

1 Parsons has developed a theory of social systems from which it is possible to derive a theory of organizations. One set of concepts from this general theory, the pattern variables, represents five basic dilemmas that have to be resolved as a basis for action. This conceptualization may prove useful in the further analysis of the paradigm concerned with values and epistemology, though the application of this is beyond the scope of the present study. See PARSONS, T., *The Social System* (New York: Free Press, 1951). In addition the work of Etzioni dealing with social control may be found useful at the social structural levels of the paradigm. See ETZIONI, A., *A Comparative Analysis of Complex Organizations* (New York: Free Press, 1961).

2 See, however, HOPPER, E. (ed.), *Readings in the Theory of Educational Systems* (London: Hutchinson and Co. Ltd., 1971), especially chap. 5, 'A Typology for the Classification of Educational Systems'.

3 JONES, *op. cit.*, pp. 16 ff. POINTEIL, F., *Histoire de l'Enseignement en France: 1789–1964* (Paris: Sirey, 1966), 'Préliminaire: l'Education Nationale à la Veille de 1789'. The Pietist movement in Germany was responsible for the first training institutions for teachers. See LIPPERT, E., 'Geschichte der deutschen Lehrerbildung und der deutschen Einheitsschule', *Pädagogische Provinz*, 1: 1, 1947, pp. 30 ff. See also KITTEL, *op. cit.*, pp. 176 ff. for the denominational problem in the setting-up of the *pädagogische Akademien*.

4 Board of Education, *Teachers and Youth Leaders.*

5   ZIEROLD und ROTHKUGEL, *op. cit.*

6   RICHARDSON, C. A., 'The Training of Teachers in England and Wales', in Richardson *et al.*, *The Education of Teachers in England, France and the United States* (Paris: UNESCO, 1953).

7   KITTEL, *op. cit.*

8   In terms of the Parsonian pattern variables, the relationship of the institutions to their students was affective, specific, self-oriented and particularistic, with an emphasis on academic achievement however meagre, and upon the selection function of the institution. See PARSONS (1951), *op. cit.*

9   ZIEROLD und ROTHKUGEL, *op. cit.*, p. 10.

10   DURKHEIM, E., *The Division of Labour in Society* (New York: Free Press of Glencoe, 1964).

11   By the Law of Oct. 30, 1886 the teaching personnel in primary education in French state schools was to be laicized within five years. POINTEIL, *op. cit.*, p. 290.

12   Forty per cent of men principals and nearly twenty per cent of women principals had never worked in a training college prior to becoming principal. See TAYLOR, W., 'The Training College Principal', *Sociological Review*, XII: 2, 1964, pp. 185–201. However a more recent survey by Eason seems to have recorded a change in this situation. See EASON, T. W., *Colleges of Education: Academic or Professional?* (Slough, Bucks: NFER, 1970).

13   JONES, *op. cit.*, pp. 76–7.

14   PROST, *op. cit.*, p. 448.

15   See ANTZ, *op. cit.*

16   The Principal of one college in submitting his evidence to the James Committee made reference to this desire for 'prestige by association'. See BIBBY, C., 'Memorandum of Evidence sumitted by Cyril Bibby, Principal of Kingston upon Hull College of Education to the Committee of Inquiry into Teacher Education (James Committee)' (Hull: June 1971, mimeo.). The ATCDE reflected this desire of the colleges to continue in relationship with the universities. See ATCDE, *The Professional Education of Teachers*.

17   RICH, *op. cit.*

18   See Universities Council for the Education of Teachers, *The Education of Teachers: Looking to the Future* (London: UCET, 1971) pp. 14 ff., for a discussion of some of the anomalies. New official policies were published at the end of 1972 when this book was in press. See Secretary of State for Education and Science, *Education: a Framework for Expansion* (London: HMSO, 1972). The decision to abolish the ATOS and to erect a regional administrative structure for teacher education will mean the increase of central and local government influence, except in the case of those institutions which opt to merge with the autonomous sector of higher education.

19   NUT, *The Reform of Teacher Education* (London: NUT, 1971), p. 27.

20   The first general regulations for the *écoles normales* were in the Guizot law of 1833. The situation obtaining at the beginning of the twentieth century is described in Board of Education (1907), *op. cit.* and in JONES (1924), *op. cit.*

21   See MÜHLMEYER, H., (ed.), *Jahrbuch 1970 der pädagogischen Hochschulen der Bundesrrepublik Deutschland und Berlin (West) und ihnen verwandter Einrichtungen* (Ratingen: Aloys Henn Verlag, 1970).

22   POINTEIL, *op. cit.*
23   CANE (1970), *op. cit.*
24   CAPELLE, *op. cit.*, pp. 156 ff.
25   Some eminent German educationists have however considered such demands to be inappropriate to teacher education. See SCHNEIDER, F., *Die Tragödie der Akademisierung unserer Lehrerbildung* (Donauwörth: Auer, 1957). A useful review of some of the main developments up to 1958 is given in REBLE, A., *Lehrerbildung in Deutschland* (Ratingen: Aloys Henn Verlag, 1958), pp. 11–122.
26   See 'Gutachten über die Ausbildung der Lehrer an Volksschulen', in Deutscher Ausschuss für das Erziehungs – und Bildungswesens, *Empfehlungen und Gutachten: Folge I.*, (Stuttgart: Ernst Klett Verlag, 1962), pp. 52–64.
27   JONES, *op. cit.*, p. 21.
28   PROST, *op. cit.*, p. 137.
29   ZIEROLD und ROTHKUGEL, *op. cit.*, p. 10.
30   DERBALOV, *op. cit.*
31   Ministry of Education, *Circular 112* (London: HMSO, 1946).
32   All *Länder* reported an increase in the provision of in-service opportunities, including courses leading to named qualifications, in the biennial report of the KMK. See Ständige Konferenz der Kultusminister, *Kulturpolitik der Länder 1969 und 1970* (Bonn: Deutscher Bundes-Verlag, 1971). Extensive programmes of in-service work were also advertised by all *Länder* during 1972, in some cases linked to newly-founded institutes such as the one at Dillingen in Bavaria. See Bayerisches Staatsministerium für Unterricht und Kultus, *Lehrerfortbildung in Bayern, 1972, 1* (Munich, 1972). Not all provision is by the regional government. The *Institut für Lehrerfortbildung* in Essen-Werden is supported by the five dioceses of North Rhine-Westphalia. See Institut für Lehrerfortbildung, *Veranstaltungen 1972: I.* (Essen: Dec., 1971).
33   Universities Council for the Education of Teachers, *Bulletin*, No. 1, 1969.
34   A concise account of the development of the WRK is FISCHER, J., *Westdeutsche Rektorenkonferenz – Geschichte, Aufgaben, Gliederung* (Bad Godesberg: WRK, 1966).
35   The exact history of events leading to the suspension of the National Advisory Council's activities does not appear to have been documented, but see BURGESS, T., 'Teacher Training within Higher Education', in Burgess (ed.) (1971), *op. cit.*
36   OECD, *Study on Teachers: Germany, Belgique, United Kingdom* (Paris: OECD, 1969), pp. 179 ff.
37   MIALARET, *op. cit.*, p. 26.
38   DES, *The Weaver Report.*
39   CITRON, *op. cit.*, and PÖGGELER, F., *Der Pädagogische Fortschritt und die Verwaltete Schule* (Freiburg, Herder Verlag, 1960).
40   Constitutions for the teachers' colleges in West Germany are laid down by the *Land* government and within this by the individual institution or department. See for example *Gesetz- und Verordnungsblatt für das Land Nordrhein-Westfalen*, no. 35, Apr. 16, 1970, 'Gesetz über die wissenschaftlichen Hochschulen des Landes Nordrhein-Westfalen vom Apr. 7, 1970', and the accompanying constitution of the pädagogische Hochschule Westfalen-Lippe, 'Verfassung der Pädagogischen Hochschule Westfalen-Lippe'.

41 A book which synthesized these developments was TIBBLE, J. W. (ed.) (1966), *op. cit.*

42 MEN, *Circular*, June 12, 1952 on the organization and functioning of the *centres pédagogiques régionaux*. For the main lines of contemporary criticisms of these centres, see GIBIAT, J. P., 'Formation des Maîtres: une Perspective raisonnable', *L'Education*, no. 120, Dec. 2 1971, pp. 11–14.

43 One significant new development has been the setting-up of courses in sociology and in social studies as teaching-subjects for schools. See MCCREADY, D. (ed.), *Guide to Social Science Courses in Departments and Colleges for Teacher Training* (ATCDE Sociology Section, 1972).

44 CRAFT, M., 'Teaching, Social Work and Interprofessional Training', in BULMAN, I., CRAFT, M., MILSON, F. (eds.), *Youth Service and Interprofessional Studies* (Oxford: Pergamon Press, 1969).

45 WEBSTER, H., 'Module Practice', *Times Educational Supplement*, Feb. 26, 1971, gives an account of a participative initial training course for teachers at Trent Polytechnic.

46 CANE, B., and SCHROEDER, C., *The Teacher and Educational Research* (Slough, Bucks: NFER, 1969).

47 See NUT, *The Reform of Teacher Education* (London: NUT, 1971), pp. 27 ff.

48 ATCDE, *Newssheet*, no. 70, 1970, pp. 2–4.

49 Recent official proposals for the reform of teacher education in France have all taken the present structure of the teaching profession as their point of departure. The primary teacher training in the *écoles normales* has been lengthened and the programmes changed. Courses for intermediate teachers have been separately organized. Currently proposals are under discussion for a reform of secondary teacher education to replace the *centres pédagogiques régionaux* by *centres de formation professionnelle des maîtres*, one in each university, and providing a theoretical training in education along with teaching-subject studies. Articulation between the different types of teacher training would be possible by following consecutively the course for the *instituteur*, the *professeur de l'enseignement général de collège* and *professeur certifié*. It is however clear that, for those who do not obtain internal promotion, the hierarchy of teachers remains as it is, with the *agregés* in no way even affected by the reforms. See MEN, *Le Projet de Réforme de la Formation des Maîtres: Dossier d'Information* (Paris: MEN, 1971, mimeo.).

50 MEN, *Circular no. 70–352*, Sept. 7, 1970, established the conditions under which university lecturers in mathematics and linguistics could give courses in the *écoles normales*. In comparison with the college-university collaboration made possible in England through the setting up of the *institute* system, the difficulties in the French case may be judged from the fact that this circular instructed the directors of the *écoles normales* to send copies of their budget proposals for any such assistance sought to three separate Ministry directorates.

51 The debate surrounding elementary teacher education has been documented by Kittel. See KITTEL, H., *Selbstbehauptung der Lehrerbildung* (Heidelberg: Comenius Institut, 1965) and 'Selbstbehauptung der Lehrerbildung II', *Zeitschift für Pädagogik*, XIII: 4, 1967, pp. 363–80.

52 An account of the development of the *Studienseminar* is contained in Ständige Konferenz (1963), *op. cit.* The present situation and some of the

problems are discussed in FACKINER, K., 'Situation und Probleme der Gymnasiallehrerbildung aus der Sicht der zweiten Phase', *Zeitschrift für Pädagogik*, Tenth Special Issue, 1971, pp. 9–14. For an interesting discussion of some of the problems of the first phase and its co-ordination with the second phase of academic secondary-school teacher education, see LORENZ G. E., 'Zum Stand und zur Problematik der Ausbildung von Gymnasiallehrern an der Universität', *Rundgespräch*, no. 1, 1968, pp. 9–22.

53 See NUT, *Teacher Education: The Way Ahead* (London: NUT, 1970), pp. 20 ff.

54 PORCHER, L., 'Audiovisuel et Formation des Enseignants', *Revue Française de Pédagogie*, no. 10, Jan.–Mar., 1970, pp. 16–22. SCHORB, A. O. (1965), *op. cit.* See also SCHORB, A. O., 'Technologie in der Lehrerbildung', in deutscher Bildungsrat, *Materialien und Dokumente zur Lehrerbildung*.

55 DES, *The Education and Training of Teachers*.

56 A three-month teaching-practice was instituted for the second year of professional training of *école normale* students by MEN, *Circular no. I V–69–1087*, June 6, 1969, to be known as the 'stage en situation' and in which the student would have responsibility for a class. This has also been planned as a means of affording primary teachers an opportunity to attend in-service training.

57 ATCDE, *Higher Education and Preparation for Teaching* (London: ATCDE, 1970).

58 SHIPMAN (1969), *op. cit.*

59 STEVENS, A., 'Centres for Action', *Times Educational Supplement*, Dec. 17, 1971, describes the present situation with 520 teachers' centres in operation throughout the country.

60 WILEY, F. T., and MADDISON, R. E., *An Enquiry into Teacher Training* (London: University of London Press, 1971).

61 For details of official in-service training activities in France, see UNESCO, International Bureau of Education, *International Yearbook of Education*, XXXI (1969), pp. 56–57.

62 Expansion of in-service provision has been impressive since the beginning of 1971, with the establishment of many new institutes and the development of new courses and approaches and the growth of co-operative enterprises. For one example of the latter see Studiengruppe Lehrer-Dozenten, pädagogische Hochschule Heidelberg, *Informationsschriften* 1, 2 and 3, (1971–72). Mention should also be made of the Quadriga radio courses in education and mathematics organized by the *Länder* Baden-Württemberg, Hessen, Rhineland Palatinate and the Saarland in conjunction with the *Deutsches Institut für Fernstudien an der Universität Tübingen*.

63 LOCKETT, T. A., 'The Government of Colleges of Education' in BURGESS, T., *Dear Lord James: A Critique of Teacher Education* (Harmondsworth: Penguin, 1971).

64 Association of Education Committees, *Memorandum of Evidence to the Teacher Training Enquiry*, Extract from the Executive Minutes, ref. no. 314, March 25, 1971.

65 For details of the rejection of the current Government reform proposals by the presidents of the universities, VÉLIS, J. P., 'Formation des Maîtres', *L'Education*, no. 130, Feb. 24, 1972, pp. 6–7.

66 Some of the Institutes of In-Service Education in West Germany have

facilities for correspondence courses. See Landesinstitut für Schulpäda-gogische Bildung, Nordrhein-Westfalen, *Lehrerfortbildung* 1, 1972.

67 OECD, *Training, Recruitment and Utilization of Teachers in Primary in Primary and Secondary Education* (Paris: OECD, 1973), Part 3.

68 ADAMS, P. *et al.*, *Children's Rights: Towards the Liberation of the Child* (London: Elek, 1971).

69 The *Loi d'Orientation de l'Enseignement Supérieur* of 1968 in fact states that the universities 'forment les maîtres de l'Education nationale' and this has become a point of controversy in the further planning of teacher education.

70 CRAFT, *op. cit.*

71 WISEMAN and PIDGEON, *op. cit.*; the Schools Council studies referred to in chap. 5, ref. 76; and, for a French appraisal of evaluation work, see LALLEZ, *op. cit.*

72 Several articles on the aims and organization of school-based experience in the second phase of academic secondary teacher training are included in BECKMANN, H. K. (1968), *op. cit.*, pp. 205–301. Problems of co-ordinating the two phases are discussed in ZIMMERMANN, W., 'Zur wissenschaftlichen und didaktischen Ausbildung der Gymnasiallehrer', *Das Studienseminar*, XIII: 2, 1968, pp. 88–98. The proposals of the student-teachers (*Assessoren und Referendare*) are contained in SCHATZ, F. H., 'Bundesrahmenplan zum Vorbereitungsdienst für das Lehramt an Gymnasien', *die Höhere Schule*, XXII: 8, 1969, pp. 202–5.

73 Inner London Education Authority Research and Statistics Group, *op. cit.* and cf. CALTHROP, K. and OWENS, G. (eds.), *Teachers for Tomorrow: Diverse and Radical Views about Teacher Education* (London: Heinemann, 1971); KEMBLE, B. (ed.), *Fit to Teach* (London: Hutchinson, 1971); GIROD DE L'AIN and LEGRAND, *op. cit.*

74 The attitude of British dons to mass higher education and the expansion of the teaching of their own subject are dealt with in HALSEY, A. H. and TROW, M., *The British Academics* (London: Faber and Faber, 1971). Considerable work has been done on élites in German society. See ZAPF, W., *Wandlungen der deutschen Elite: Ein Zirkulationsmodell deutscher Führungsgruppen, 1919–1961* (Munich: R. Piper and Co. Verlag, 1965).

75 Current unpublished working-papers in the French Ministry of National Education accept the notion of a three-year minimum for initial teacher training, but the Government is not yet ready to face the financial implications of this expansion.

76 CHAPUIS, R., 'La Formation Permanente des Maîtres' in *Pour une Ecole Nouvelle*. An account of a new structure for courses in the Bristol ATO area is described in TAYLOR, W., 'Unit Shape and Bristol Fashion', *The Times Higher Education Supplement*, I: 29, 1972. p. 14. See also the Bristol Survey of Teachers in their first year of teaching. DES, *Reports on Education*, no. 68, January 1971. A description of a co-operative research group, composed of members of teachers' colleges and a university, is to be found in STONES, E., 'Co-operative Research in Teacher Education: Progress and Prospects', Society for Research into Higher Education, Sixth Annual Conference (London: SRHE, 1971).

77 See for example CRAFT, M., 'A Broader Role for Colleges of Education', in TIBBLE, J. W., *The Future of Teacher Education* (London: Routledge and Kegan Paul, 1971). Increasingly non-degree teachers in France are

being permitted to undertake university studies, though the geographical locations of the departmental *écoles normales* makes this impossible on a concurrent basis for most primary teachers.

78 As part of their examination for the Certificate in Education in the Southampton ATO it is possible for students to present a joint piece of work. See also new regulations for the second state examination for academic secondary teachers in North Rhine-Westphalia. Letter from Philologenverband Nordrhein-Westfalen, 17. 3. 71.

79 One example of this is the University Law for North Rhine-Westphalia which prescribes participation of students in all committees. See 'Gesetz über die wissenschaftlichen Hochschulen des Landes Nordrhein-Westfalen', *op. cit.*

80 Both the NUT and its German equivalent the GEW have advocated a comprehensive pattern of higher education. See NUT, *The Reform of Teacher Education* and 'Kongress Erziehung und Wissenschaft 1971', *Allgemeine Deutsche Lehrerzeitung*, XXIII: 7, 1971, pp. 3–12. Proposals for the amalgamation of all teacher training within the university, in *university institutes of pedagogy*, allowing access to a variety of courses, have been made by the Syndicat Général de l'Education Nationale. See *Syndicalisme Universitaire*, no. 548, Mar. 4, 1971, 'Débat sur la Formation des Maîtres'.

81 PEDLEY, R., *The Comprehensive University* (Exeter: The University, 1969). A discussion of this concept is to be found in FIELDING, T., 'Dr Pedley's Comprehensive University', *The Red Paper* (Edinburgh: Islander Publications, 1970) pp. 20–22. See also Select Committee on Education and Science, Session 1969–70, *Teacher Training* (Minutes of Evidence Thursday Mar. 19th, 1970, University of Exeter Institute of Education) (London: HMSO, 1970). For the German scene, in addition to material already referred to see 'Zwischen Szylla und Charybdis: eine Dokumentation zu den Gesamthochschulplänen', *Wirtschaft und Wissenschaft*, XVIII: 1, 1970, pp. 8–14, and EVERS, C. H. and RAU, J., *Oberstufenreform und Gesamthochschule* (Frankfurt/Main: Verlag Moritz Diesterweg, 1970).

82 Differentials in salary between grades of teacher in France are great enough virtually to rule out serious discussion of the unification of teacher education. The main advocate of such a development is the Syndicat National d'Instituteurs, which would have the most to gain materially. See the motions voted by the Congress of the Fédération de l'Education Nationale, in which the SNI wields a majority of votes, in *L'Enseignement Public*, no. Jan. 5, 1970, p. 22.

83 MANZER, *op. cit.* and CLARK, *op. cit.*

84 No attention was given to this matter in the English James Report. However, the Association of Teachers in Colleges and Departments of Education, through its various subject *sections*, does serve an in-service training function for teacher educators, for example, in the series of annual courses organized jointly by the DES and the ATCDE Sociology Section. Beginning in 1971, there has been an in-service training course for *école normale* staff at the Ecole Normale Supérieure de St Cloud. This course lasts four months and is to recruit persons with teaching experience who are joining an *école normale* as well as those already holding appointments in teacher education.

Part Three

Chapter Seven

Teacher Education and Cultural Change

THE PROBLEMATIC OF TEACHER EDUCATION

We have described and illustrated how, independently of its particular setting, teacher education is the disputed territory of conflicting tendencies: on the one hand, there is the tendency to maintain and to reproduce the patterns of traditional ways of valuing, thinking and organizing; on the other, there is the tendency to promote innovation and reform. The importance of this conflict is that it is a reflection of broad and deep cultural differences, here focused upon the conception, selection and transmission of the values that inform a vital sector of social functioning and the very crucible of educational values, namely, the education of teachers. Our intention has been to study teacher education, within contrasting national contexts, as a set of values and institutions and as a struggle over the form these are to have. This systemic concept of teacher education has depended upon the recognition of alternative value systems and their different modes of expression in the societies, the plural social groupings espousing these values, and the differential access to policy-making positions by the interest-groups involved. Although our analysis is too limited for firm conclusions, we can identify some of the main evolutionary trends within the teacher-education systems of England, France and West Germany, and our final chapter is concerned with their elucidation both substantively and methodologically.

We have adopted a comparative sociological approach, viewing teacher education as cohering in socio-political systems which are developing, to a greater or lesser extent, in response to particular sets of policy-orientations. The source of these policy-orientations is to be found both in the cybernetic functioning of the general educational systems and in the cultural and structural characteristics of the wider societies. There are few studies of teacher education which could be called comparative, and thus a comparative sociological approach can help to screen out the endemic ethnocentrism of the perspectives in which teacher education is usually viewed. At the same time, some basis would be provided for formulating hypotheses and judgements relevant to teacher education and sensitive to key cultural and social factors.

Several comparative sociologists have proposed the construction of typologies of educational systems as the starting-point for broader social analysis through the generating and testing of correlational and causal hypotheses. In our view comparative education is not a discipline, nor even a methodology in its own right, but is simply the field of application of theories and methods properly belonging to the human sciences. We do not accept a view of comparative education that separates it either from the applied human science disciplines or from concern with educational policies and development. The present work is basically a study of the formulation of policies relating to significant issues in teacher education. The choice of the subject-matter reflects not merely a social analytical viewpoint, for almost any institution or practice could be taken as a paradigm or microcosm of the educational system, but also the instinct to locate the sensitive point at which the health of the educational system could be gauged and deliberately influenced. Part of the cost of this concentration is the loss of the richness of an historical-descriptive approach to the study of education. Some readers may find the approach taken here too structured, perhaps even desiccated. Our last chapter takes more account of such points of view but, whatever the limitations of the methodological apparatus that we are using, we see it as essential to our task and as building upon a growing body of comparative sociological studies in education.

Our intentions in the next two sections of the chapter are exploratory, but we would argue that most studies in comparative education stop at the very point at which they should attempt to evaluate broader hypotheses. Having accepted in Part Two the limitations of a sparse research and information base for our study, we intend in concluding to use our judgement more assertively, for the number of facets to the subject of study which it seems important to discuss is far in excess of those for which there is adequate analysis in the literature, let alone detailed empirical investigation. In seeking to portray teacher education sociologically in terms of four themes, and by treating these themes in four chapters, we may have tended to overemphasize their separateness. In reality the four aspects are interrelated, and policies affecting one theme have implications for the others: problems of aims and experience must be seen as interlocking with problems of curriculum and organization.

Similarly the typology of policy options applies sociological criteria to the development of teacher education. Its first dimension dichotomizes traditional and innovatory policies but does not take account of the person-centred as opposed to institution-centred values which we have suggested are gaining ground in education. The second dimension, dichotomizing segmental and systemic policies, is more concerned with the coherence of educational systems than with their creativity. It is the combination of the two dimensions, leading to the identification of *cell four* type options, that can represent the balance of freedom and sharing, in which education is seen as personal growth through a new political and philosophical contract. It is the elements classified in *cell four* in each of the preceding chapters that provide the starting-point for our concluding discussion. We must however go beyond the point reached in Part Two, not only in dealing with policies for which there is as yet little empirical referent, but also in attempting to see policies in the four thematic areas relating to each other. That is, we must attempt to present a holistic view of teacher education. Taking account of earlier analysis, we introduce as a further criterion of the adequacy of particular policies the degree to which they can plausibly be harmonized, that is, are sociologically compatible with other proposals in their same cell or with options classified in *cell four* for each of the other themes. It is evident that we do not have any final set of criteria, and that our assessments are to a large extent judgemental, but we are enabled to raise questions about systems of teacher education or the appropriateness and viability of teacher-education policies in societal perspective. In this sense we hope to have provided a useful instrument for analysis of teacher-education policies which is capable of more general application in decision-making within increasingly decentralized, and even de-institutionalized socio-educational systems.

TEACHER EDUCATION POLICIES AND THE REPRODUCTION HYPOTHESIS

The policy options available to the general educational systems of the three societies were categorized in Chapter One with respect to issues of efficiency, equity and freedom of choice. Given that teacher education draws for its values on broader social and intellectual principles current within society as well as influencing the latter, we propose to discuss the culture and structure of teacher education in terms of these three categories. Attempts to express aims for teacher education have usually been diffuse and inconclusive and discussion has most often turned to consideration of organizational issues. But organizational policies are subject to the influence of broader cultural philosophies and meanings which even where they emphasize the rationalization of educational provision, or its function in promoting greater equity or in facilitating enhanced freedom of choice, can favour either prevailing or countervailing tendencies in society. It is thus apparent that the aims of teacher education are problematic, in so far as the society and the role on which they are focused themselves reflect contradictory tendencies to change or to conserve, to democratize or to accept the authority of tradition. The following sections preserve the cultural and social reproduction paradigm, which has been used throughout as the ordering framework for discussion, to illustrate the dilemmas with which teacher education policy-makers will have to come to terms if they are to provide more articulate statements of aims. Many of the policy options that we propose to highlight in this way may not yet have been elaborated with sufficient coherence to fully justify their inclusion as *cell four* type policy options, but it has seemed to us important not to ignore what may be some of the emergent features of teacher education reform.

THE CULTURE OF TEACHER EDUCATION

Aims and Assumptions

The major influence in the early post-war years in determining the development of teacher education in the three societies has been a concern with economic efficiency. In many sectors of education the concept of investment in human capital was highly influential throughout the 1960s. Policymakers in teacher education were mainly concerned with how to cope as efficiently as possible with the expansion of the school system and they took as their principal *modus operandi* the preservation of the monotechnic approach to the education of teachers and the subordination of the teachers' colleges to governmental manpower plans. Gradually it became evident that, where the division of labour was at an advanced stage, rationalization of teacher education could more effectively be achieved through greater specialization and differentiation in the commitment of institutions and personnel. Expansion in England and West Germany permitted the colleges to specialize in their recruitment of staff, and this policy in turn favoured the development of higher academic standards, the establishment of new social science-based and other courses, and fostering of links with other specialized institutions and the first research developments in the teachers' colleges. In Chapter One reference has been made to the way in which the aims or values inherent in the educational systems of the three West European countries have gone beyond the logic of economics or of arguments based upon productivity. Equality of educational opportunity came to be seen by many in the late 1960s as a desirable social investment, even if not economically justifiable. This was after some considerable period of years when the value of such equality had been voiced by political and educational leaders without any of the massive action that would be needed to make it a reality being purposefully undertaken. If the reality of educational democracy is to be judged solely by its fruits then the evidence for it is still slight, but it has at least become one of the guiding principles of educational policy. The notion of education being a universal right has in these countries been transmuted into the axiom of equal educational opportunity, and discussion now centres on how to invest this axiom with practical and verifiable meaning. Effectively it can still be asked whether democratization in other than a figurative sense is conceivable in education. Can everyone really have, in the sense of actually exercising it, an equal right to knowledge, to skill development or to training?

Modern industrial societies are said to be meritocratic as a result of the democratization of their educational systems. This thesis is highly dubious as an interpretation of the manner in which power, prestige and profit come to depend upon mastery of the special knowledge and conventions of contemporary formal education. In so far as educational systems are entrusted with the granting of the credentials with which increasing proportions of the population seek their economic livelihood, education threatens to become its own end, and to speak of the democratization of education without reference to the wider society is to indulge in illusion. The kind of democratization that can be expected from a rationally ordered society is itself technocratic; it is productive of a society in which people are persuaded to accept from others definitions of their own interests. It is hard to escape the conclusion that there is a flaw in the notion of a rationally-ordered democracy, which would be one that was well-organized, coherent and impelled towards the implantation of a new orthodoxy.

These questions are very much in dispute, but what is not seriously in dispute any longer is that education has functioned to transmit cultural and economic advantages, that education has exhibited stratifying and rationing structures and procedures by segregating learners through well-recognized hierarchies of institutions and curricula. The teacher-education systems have been imprinted with the same cultural and structural features. If the educational systems are to function more democratically then the accepted aims of their personnel and the curricula and organization of their institutions, will all need to be more closely questioned and the dominance of traditional élite groups will have to give way to more democratic and pluralist alternatives. This scaling down of the importance of a particular national tradition will no doubt be accompanied by increased interest in the educational values and practices of other countries. The inevitability of established curricula and organizational procedures is much less evident when culture is taken as a variable. The capacity of contemporary man to get outside his own culture by travel, residence abroad, study, leisure and artistic pursuits and other international contacts must have a relativizing effect upon national cultures and educational systems.

The formal apparatus of democracy however cannot produce creative freedom, any more than legislation against racial discrimination can abolish prejudice. We wish to introduce into our discussion the issue of whether there is not something more significant than democratization towards which modern societies and educational systems are striving, for the most part unwittingly, and which teacher education must recognize if its policies are to be anything other than the reflection of established economic and related orthodoxies. When the means are lacking to impose a social order, that is, when authority loses its absolute power, the rational ordering of social institutions is endangered. But when rationality itself is questioned a struggle breaks out in the very centre of education, in its organization, pedagogy and curricula. Teacher-education policy-makers cannot afford to ignore as blithely as they have usually done in the three countries the possibility that formal education is now beginning to be subjected to such a radical reappraisal. In coming to terms with contemporary uncertainties, the teacher, and all those with whom he is concerned, has to be the sharpest critic of his own assumptions and a full participant in the working out and exploration of cultural values and conventions which are agreed to be maximally appropriate to a social group in a particular time and place.

It is naïve for those responsible for teacher education to fail to recognize the effective pluralism of contemporary society. Teacher education needs integrity and high intellectual standards of inquiry in coming to terms with new values and beliefs, and with new disciplines and methodologies in human knowledge and understanding. The defensiveness of the teaching profession, as the intellectual, social and moral reference-points for the teacher's roles become more indistinct, cannot be unconnected with the failure of teacher-education policy-makers, at least in the societies under consideration here, to accept the explosive unity of modern culture. On the other hand it is already clearly the case that such insights are widely shared within the teacher-education systems and are ready to find wider expression. Apart from the social controls required by any human society, even if these are open to change, cultural and social organization requires principles of coherence. In this study of teacher education we have proposed a typology of policy options which recognizes social order based on constitutional pluralism and systemic integration. In teacher education the re-negotiation of educational objectives and practices must be continuous, and give due part to the creative social value of the wider community.

Meanings and Conceptions

Fundamental for a clearer articulation of aims for teacher education is the question of how society conceives of the teacher's role. Is there a lockstep linking systems of education and systems of thought which predetermines the status of the teacher, and thus the expertise which he is likely to possess? Or is it that, in the contemporary context of questioning and constructing new meanings in all areas of cultural, social and political life, the role of the teacher involves an odyssey of self- and community-discovery throughout a professional career? This would entail the formulating of precise educational objectives on the basis of social and academic specialisms and skills. It is for example as clear that the idea of one powerful and solidary profession committed to a unitary view of what the teacher role involves is obsolete, as it is apparent that the inherited status hierarchies and divisions within the profession and teacher education run counter to a rapidly changing society, in which differentiation increasingly rests upon the performance of specialized tasks. In each of the three societies major reform proposals have envisioned the redeployment of the profession though without tracing the logic of the argument to the differentiation of training and certification or to the more widespread use of ancillary staff that this must entail. Role-specialization amongst teachers could enhance their professional image and offer institutions of teacher education an opportunity to articulate their objectives more closely to future roles.

The proposals for *grade teachers* in West Germany and the employment of pedagogical assistants in some *Länder* are supported by a substantial body of opinion, although such proposals have only been marginally canvassed in the other two countries where their diffusion is limited by restricted concepts of professionalism. On the other hand the renewed emphasis on in-service education is a recognition of the need to rationalize provision of training and re-training opportunities both geographically and over the career-span. The next logical step would seem to be the development of in-service education of an interprofessional nature not only for teachers, but also for teacher educators, administrators, social workers, personnel managers and others. Schools themselves and other social agencies become involved in initial and in-service education of teachers and correspondingly teachers' roles diversify into teacher training, counselling, social work and curriculum development as we have illustrated. These conceptual changes in teacher education call for research and development approaches in teachers' colleges and schools to guide the organizational and curricular planning that will be needed if teacher-education systems are to have available the sensitivity and specialized skills both to service the wider educational system and to ensure their own development.

In so far as teachers are conveying and reinforcing the values and meanings that organize and control the education system they would seem to be in the position of being able to exercise some choice as to whether formal education functions as a series of self-fulfilling prophecies or whether democratic rights are fostered. But we have already noted how teachers themselves are trained in terms of a deeply patterned system of types of knowledge and levels of status. The question of democratization thus resolves itself in the first instance into the extent to which categories of meanings and curricula, as well as of persons, are being de-stratified. It is for example clear that the teacher is himself losing ground in terms of his authority in society; since the end of the Second World War he has had to come to terms not only with informed adult opinion generally, and with rival public sources of information and values, but with an increasingly independent and sceptical youth. We have cited examples of how a lessening of social distance between teacher and taught has been regarded in many institutions as a development to be promoted. In educationally experimental and community schools and within higher education systems these developments are occurring as a critical response to the notion that the teacher has exclusive possession of knowledge. Not only is knowledge being distributed through additional channels, but the generating of this knowledge is a continuous process in the pursuit of which the teacher can often claim no more than the status of *primus inter pares* in relation to his pupils.

The idea therefore that there is some overarching scheme that is pre-existing, and into which the teacher's knowledge fits, must be discarded. In schools, colleges and universities throughout the three countries this insight is being admitted only with great difficulty as the boundaries between knowledge areas are breached and the part played by hierarchical categorizations of pupils and of knowledge-areas in the maintenance of the social structure is more clearly understood. The contribution of recent developments in the sociology of knowledge, and in its application to cultural transmission processes in education, is of major theoretical importance. The pursuit of these ideas in studies of the curriculum is already becoming a powerful, if small focus of critical energy in educational reform. Whether from the point of view of an adequate logic of inquiry, or from the value position of favouring a democratization of education, as well as at least implicitly of the society, the notion that different types of learner should best be confined within different corresponding types of curricula and forms of knowledge is now being challenged from educational and ideological standpoints in the three societies. Culturally and socially distinct subgroups of the population which are disadvantaged by the criteria of the formal educational system are the subjects of research investigations and conflicting doctrines. In England at least it is becoming less likely that a teacher can leave an initial training course without questioning the traditional view that pupils assessed as of low academic ability, or immigrant children, or rebellious adolescents, will profit most from being matched to a curriculum at their level whose aims and academic or vocational outlets diverge systematically from those for other pupils. This kind of problem has been very much under-researched, and we can do little more than raise questions. But such problems are certainly on the agenda for teachers in initial and in-service training for serious consideration over the next decade, and seem likely to entail major redefinition and reorganization of the educational process.

Teachers have been subject to financial policies in the three countries which have kept them in separate groups and made them see their roles in different ways and at different levels. Now there is some convergence of routes into the profession, but at least as important has been the development of opportunities for in-service education which, through formal courses or through informal exposure to fresh ideas and activities, can leaven the whole loaf of the profession, or at least that proportion of it that wishes to avail itself of new learning opportunities.

The idea of permanent or life-long learning is recognition in another form of the impermanency of contemporary knowledge and, at least implicitly, of the evolutionary nature of cultural and social forms. Substantial minorities of teachers now give evidence in all three countries of seeing it as legitimate that they should question, inquire into and criticize the work of the educational system. The teacher sees his role as problematic in a society which often fails to admit its own contradictions. He cannot therefore ignore questions of basic values, for unless he resists the stereotyping of his own role he is merely reconfirming the social values of the past. His problem is rather that the questions he needs to examine in relation to his role are difficult to frame. Educational institutions and programmes are so much a part of history and culture that he can get little perspective for his thinking unless he has the opportunity to develop appropriate intellectual and methodological skills. Very little attention has been given to serious preparation of this kind in initial teacher education in the three countries, but the basis now exists, at least in England and West Germany, for training the profession in appropriate social science disciplines and techniques to ensure a more critical and better equipped generation of teachers in undertaking curriculum research and development that relativize traditional epistemological preconceptions. In particular, comparative studies of the curriculum in which the relationship between culture and curriculum can be envisaged, since both are seen in a wider context, offer a promising though as yet little practised approach. The current development of sociological studies of the curriculum must eventuate in comparative work, if only to afford a scale for assessing the significance of curricular and organizational changes achieved in the national systems. Beyond this lies the possibility of a genuinely cross-cultural perspective upon education, with its potential for the exchange of ideas and the broadening of values and concepts.

We have already reported how even democratically structured curriculum decision-making bodies in England have retained strong loyalties to an inherited epistemology. Similar subject-biased conceptions prevail in the French and West German educational systems where the machinery for questioning them has hardly even begun to exist. There is a danger in the existence of powerful central committees whose concern is not with the curriculum but with a predetermined element of it that begs questions about structures of knowledge and learning. It is being recognized that there is need for a polynucleated development in thinking about knowledge and the curriculum which both functions as a system of professional democracy that is not controlled by the central bodies and also as a generative process that can accommodate the expressed needs of the community. Curriculum development at this level is virtually non-existent, though work to elaborate its cultural and social basis is certainly being undertaken in each of the three countries. Teachers and educational policy-makers are being pressured to recognize their accountability to the broader community, and thus the requirement that schooling should be relevant to a particular society, and they are expected to develop the skills and sensitivities which would allow them to enter with fewer preconceptions into creative communication with the interests represented in the social environment of the educational institutions.

This is a statement of a problem familiar to many teachers. With the development of educational systems they have had to take on new roles in teaching, in caring for and guiding their pupils in a more complex society, in development of the curriculum, in educational investigations and research, and in school administration. What has not been adequately recognized by the policy-makers is the extent to which the expansion of the teacher's role has required commensurate conceptual reappraisal and the development of intellectual and social skills. The introduction of new categories of teacher-training programme to meet social needs singly as they impinge upon the educational system brings about a centrifugal situation in which the safest reaction for many teachers and teacher educators is to stick to their last. Policies favouring the seeking of connections between subjects, disciplines, different types of schools or pupil groups, and the construction of teacher-education courses flexibly adjusted to the needs of the educational system and the interests of the student, are only beginning to reach the stage of implementation. The philosophical questions underlying such developments are concerned with the nature of human community. Once the idea of human beings as interchangeable units belonging to a society that gives them the values and norms by which they must live is set aside, it is for everyone to reflect upon why they live in society and upon how they are to live. Teacher education rarely affords the opportunity to think about such issues as what is one's own identity, what are one's purposes in relating to others, what is acceptable as social relationship, and how society can reach agreement about the appropriate balance of freedom and responsibility for its individual members. An equal danger is run by assuming that these social issues are being adequately resolved as by assuming that their solutions are reducible to traditional formulae.

THE STRUCTURE OF TEACHER EDUCATION

Organization and Institutions

If teacher-education policies are to be rationalized it is evident that they must be seen in relation to options in the wider educational system and as part of the formulation of general social and economic policy. The links between the manpower and skill needs of the societies and the development of education have received considerable attention in national and international reports for more than a decade, and it would be politically naïve to assume that the rationalization of teacher education was not largely motivated in practice by economic considerations. Comparative costings of different forms of higher education have indicated the relatively high cost of traditional university education. Central governments in all three countries have on the other hand secured a greater measure of control over the finance and expenditures of teacher education. The *binary system*, in England, dividing the autonomous and government-controlled sectors of higher education, the 1969 constitutional amendment in West Germany enabling the Federal Government to pass outline legislation for higher education, and the 1968 *Loi d'Orientation* in France that leaves financial power effectively in central government hands, whether teacher education is later subsumed under university or *écoles normales* auspices, are all examples of the developing context of economic rationalization within which teacher education will have to develop.

It is evident that more extensive commitments to improving the quality of education generally will depend upon the deliberate development of teacher education. Policies which merely reproduce traditional specializations absorb resources which could facilitate the emergence of newer disciplines and techniques. Duplication of commitment, as in the continuing existence of a dual system of teacher preparation in the three societies, not only preserves status hierarchies but reduces the level of human resources available to educational systems for considered change. In areas suffering from acute scarcity of resources for research, the initiation of narrowly based and unco-ordinated activities dissipates effort and limits potential benefits. In all three countries, the increased demand for in-service education has raised important and as yet unresolved issues concerning the balance and distribution of resources over the professional life of the teacher, the media and institutions involved in provision and the appropriate machinery for consultation and co-ordination. In so far as recent proposals represent a recognition of such problems, it may be argued that teacher education will be more able to plan rationally the way in which it can serve society. However questions of overlapping provision must also be raised, not only with regard to pre-service and in-service teacher education, but also in terms of the complementary services provided by schools, inspectorates and external agencies such as those concerned with social case-work.

Problems of the degree of coherence with which such policies have been formulated in the three societies intensify in plans to devolve teacher education to a wider range of institutions, to relate it more closely to the ultimate place of work or to de-institutionalize provision, as in the Open University or the West German *Quadriga* experiment. At a curricular level the exploitation of newer learning resources and of technical media, as well as the general re-definition of what constitutes teaching, demand new types of specialization. Teachers' colleges are developing decision-making and evaluation procedures to justify and to maximize their use of resources against pressing claims from other socio-educational agencies and, in training accountable professionals, to equip themselves to be more socially accountable. If the objectives of teacher education are to be envisaged as subsets of broader educational and social objectives, the efficiency with which they can generalize educational innovation is crucial. The danger of many current proposals is that not only do they lack coherence, but they seek to foster a false rationalization by dividing, stratifying and reproducing cultural forms and social structures, and thus militate against the initiation and diffusion of innovation.

Despite the apparently critical role that has to be taken by teachers in the democratization of education, it is none the less evident that mere changes in attitudes and in conceptions of knowledge and of the learning process amongst teachers will not suffice to alter the stratification of educational systems. More wide-ranging policy commitments are obviously required: comprehensive organization, not only of primary and secondary but also of higher education, open-access systems for regular and post-experience study for all categories of learners, including teachers; and unification of the teaching profession as the basis for facilitating educational sequences in organization and curriculum for pupils through both age- and ability-ranges. But of more immediate concern is the development of policy for teacher education itself. An intraprofessional caste structure continues to exist in all three countries, and there is little enthusiasm amongst those who are better placed for abolishing differentials in status. On the contrary, the higher prestige or minority teacher associations strive to maintain their memberships and their own identities and to make known the key points of their policy platforms in particular on salary and professional matters.

Current proposals for the reform of teacher education in England and France, as opposed to West Germany, are not concerned with the democratization of the teaching profession. Instead they maintain most of the traditional horizontal and vertical divisions by reproducing the subject-routes into teaching and distinguishing grades of teacher by terminal qualification. Furthermore they exhibit the traditional schoolteacher mistrust of and the official pusillanimity about the theoretical disciplines which alone can provide a common language for the study of education. In the case of the English James Report, the distinguishing feature from previous major policy recommendations has been the emphasis placed upon the in-service education of teachers. This is now seen not only as up-dating and broadening in intent, but as related to the career structure, to new responsibilities achieved, and to an overview of the priorities of the education system. Whatever judgement is made of the validity, design and coherence of the report, its proposal for permanent education as of right for all teachers is such as to make it path-breaking within teacher-education policy-making in the three countries. There are signs however that even this proposal does not go far enough. The existence of the English *Open University*, the French *Télé-enseignement* and the Bavarian *Telekolleg*, evidence a new concept of decentralization and de-institutionalization of education. The teachers' colleges in the three countries will need to adopt similar organizational strategies, such as home-based learning, flexible time-tabling, systems of credits and options, multi-media teaching programmes, and organized feedback systems, if they are not to fall back into traditional authoritarian patterns.

It is by no means certain that the teacher-education systems of these countries have developed adequate research and other evaluation techniques to keep vital democratization policy questions open. There has been remarkably little research upon teacher education by any of the supposedly interested parties: ministries, teachers' associations, teachers' colleges or the bodies granting funds for educational research. There is a need for the rapid development of such research, not merely to challenge the enormously powerful conventional wisdom of the teacher-education worlds, but to throw macro-policy issues into a more objective light, as the decisions inspired by new cultural values begin to filter through into action. It is perhaps likely that developments now foreseeable on the international scene will give an impulse to more critical questioning. The activities of the established international bodies, like UNESCO, the OECD and the Council of Europe, the pressures from centres for comparative education, the proposals for a European University or Ministry of Education, and the development of the European Economic Community with opportunities for more fluid exchanges of teachers and other professionals, are just some of the new environmental pressures upon national systems of teacher education.

Systems of relationships and organized procedures in teachers' colleges, at least in England and West Germany, are continuing to develop within constitutional forms. The committee system is being extended; democratic decision-making is being institutionalized; organizational and curricular innovation is being rationalized. At the same time increasing anxiety is expressed about student militancy, about educational experiment and about parental or other public intrusion into professional matters. There would seem to be a concept of illegitimate as opposed to legitimate democracy in educational institutions. Where does the right to representation stop, and who is responsible for deciding this? Once the principle of the accountability of the professional educator to the community is admitted, as it increasingly is in schools if not in the teachers' colleges, it seems that there is no logical escape from open dialogue, even with non-professionals. The corollary must be a programme to help teachers develop the sensitivities, knowledge and skills to enable them to work successfully in professional teams and parent-teacher groups, and in a large variety of non-authoritarian teaching situations. The realistic acceptance of such roles for teachers would involve the shattering of the epistemological and structural moulds that presently prevail in the teachers' colleges in the three societies.

Alternative developments are conceivable and already exist in embryo. Curricular studies, deriving from both teaching-subjects and human science disciplines, and experiment in curriculum development and evaluation, can constitute one of the most important elements of teacher education. Experience of curriculum development can become the first stage in acquiring the commitment to implement the new programmes. Such work is happening through teachers' associations, through the English teachers' centres and Certificate of Secondary Education panels, in France through the *Fédération des cercles de recherche et d'action pédagogiques* and in the curriculum work of the Max Planck Institute in West Berlin. When such activities characterize the initial training of teachers, and can be followed through into teacher-monitored research and development in schools confident enough to remain responsive to community needs, a comprehensive programme of curriculum experience can exist for teachers. Rare examples can be found of where schools develop their own in-service education programmes and provide facilities as part of a direct policy to further the professional development of their staff. This strategy seems the most likely to be successful in altering the perceptions and behaviour of the majority of teachers who spare little time to out-of-school professional activities.

If the educational system is bureaucratized to the extent that teacher initiative is stifled, there will either be wastage of creative individuals from the profession or there will be explosive internal reactions. An apparently democratic system can over-determine the professional options of the teacher. This can happen in a school; it can happen during initial and in-service training; it can confine the teacher's activity within one sector of relatively autonomous work, as in a type of school or professional association; and it can separate teachers from other community-workers with whom they could share fundamental common concerns. To reduce this dispersal of energies, policies are needed which would explore links between structures or groups within and outside the formal educational system. Very little institutional experimentation of this type is countenanced by the three educational systems with which we are here concerned. The beginnings are found in the more holistic studies of society, involving both theoretical and practical inquiry and experience, which some student-teachers or teachers in in-service training are now undertaking in England and West Germany. A teacher needs to know about the cultural and social variety of his clientèle, whether or not the *melting-pot* model of the educational system is still considered relevant.

Formal education will continue to depend upon the creative insights of individual teachers, even in democratically organized institutions. The mobility of persons in modern societies allows too many individuals to slip through the net of institutionalized provision. If persons are to relate meaningfully in community, all must be free to choose, to express opinions, to participate and to contribute. This means that educational systems cannot avoid conflict and that they need the skills and procedures to make conflict creative. Such collaboration is rare in the three countries, particularly at the centres of decision-making of the teacher-education systems. To accept conflict as legitimate must mean to accept the relativity of cultural values and the tentativeness of institutional forms. In practice, educational systems that place community considerations first, and subordinate bureaucratic or traditional interests, must envisage the possibility of considerable de-institutionalization of education. This suggests the need for teacher-education policies to facilitate a range of philosophical and experimental activities which could be practical expressions of the basic search for human community.

Control and Decision-Making

If teachers are to be trained as much to question the assumptions underlying their roles as to support existing systems, it is evident that teacher education needs a more developed research capability than exists at the moment. Regional and national co-ordination is necessary if resources are to be allocated more equally and innovations more swiftly diffused. The recent appraisal of the West German educational system by an OECD team was noteworthy for the way in which it redrew the balance of reform as needing to come as much from the periphery as from the centre. Purely national checks on sectors of the educational system are probably now inadequate to the increased cultural inter-relatedness and developing economic interdependence. Within institutions, if bureaucratization and formalization are not to bury innovation, and if today's reforms are not to become tomorrow's orthodoxies, each institution will have to scrutinize its aims and performance as part of a planned and deliberate policy of continuous reform. If teachers are to have greater responsibility for the way in which knowledge is put to work in society, they will need to have more control over entry to the profession. The proposals for a teachers' council in England, though in advance of developments in the other two countries, have to be measured for progress against more recent interprofessional developments. To be effective in terms of wider social and educational goals, the co-ordination of curricular and organizational commitments within teacher education will demand institutional controls and system-wide feedback procedures that will afford protection to all interests.

The test of democratization is not how responsive the authorities are to mass demands, but the degree to which interested parties have representation in policy-making. Moves towards both the decentralization and the de-stratification of the control of teacher education can be discerned in each of the three countries, but their extent is not impressive. Where such democratization has occurred, it has too often been over-institutionalized, as in the academic boards of the colleges of education, the *conseils d'administration* of the *écoles normales* or in the newer constitutions of the teachers' colleges in West Germany. Technical democracy, in which the field for decision is circumscribed, and in which academic freedom is tolerated rather than positively valued, has often been developed in the teachers' colleges as the minimal response to staff and student militancy. Democratization has not yet, except in rare institutions, formed part of a policy of anticipatory socialization for members of a socially responsible and accountable profession.

There are other critical questions to raise, and it is apparent that the teachers' colleges are only in the early stages of developing information systems to cope with self-monitoring functions. It will be hard for these often understaffed institutions to adopt new techniques in the fields of curriculum evaluation, as this has been developing in England and West Germany, docimology, which has been a special concern of French researchers, behavioural objective-testing, attitude surveys or operational research, and yet examples of all of these activities can be located in scattered institutions spread across the three societies. Clearly the teachers' colleges can take little initiative in the broader reform of teacher education, and of education itself, without both a serious effort at upgrading their own staffs and a multi-institutional rationalization of resources. International exchange of ideas and research findings, and the efforts at coordination in policy areas by European regional organizations, are beginning to evoke a climate of interest which could be the prelude to a major reappraisal of aims, curricula and organizational structures.

We can assume that teacher education as a policy area can be subject to deliberate planning, without thereby excluding the capacity of teacher-education systems to change spontaneously through internal growth and through interaction with their social environments. Short of approving anarchical dismantling of all educational institutions, which not even the *deschoolers* have demanded, there is the possibility of developing decision-making procedures which are secure enough to hold until such time as they are legitimately questioned. It is a lesson to be learned from the wider society that social institutions can become redundant; economic institutions in such cases may be shown to be non-productive and eliminated. In educational institutions, partly because they are monopolists with the qualifications they provide, and partly because adequate evaluation of their services would have to be carried out in depth over a period of years, redundancy is hard to demonstrate. Only highly developed social and moral qualities will be able to ensure that the control of educational institutions is sufficient to avoid wasting resources but that the bureaucratization and routinization of education has not been carried so far as to have become exploitative. We encounter the problem that, no less than other bureaucratic processes, teacher-education policy-making is politically protected against inquiry. The issues are hardly broached by formal research, itself closely tied into institutionalized education. Lay groups are rarely in a position to exercise any influence. Teachers' organizations and the Press, on the other hand, are regular participants in national debates on teacher education though students are probably the most influential force for change. The quality of these continuing debates could be much higher and the reforms achieved better calculated if the range of relevant interests were more effectively canvassed and given constitutional standing. Teachers' unions, ministerial working-parties, college governors, students' associations, and countless other bodies, have examined and prescribed for teacher education in each of the countries. What seems to happen is that their efforts cancel each other out, leaving economic and manpower considerations to decide the issues. Experiment is now needed with a whole new range of constitutional forms which would ensure the accountability of teacher-education policy-makers to the society, marshalling information and commanding research and development to take account of the diversity of viewpoints.

The role of authorities, moreover, is the role that those who accept thei authority allow to them. To the extent that it is convenient to have agents who administer funds and execute the policies of social institutions such as those of teacher education, the risk is willingly run that procedural rigidities will build up. But, when this happens, it is important to adjust the balance and to press for greater cultural and academic freedom. The tension expressed in the typology of policy-options is here illustrated. The problem is one of fostering creative developments without losing the control which will facilitate their evaluation and effective exploitation. Educational innovations become routinized partly because this suits the workings of the bureaucratic machinery of education, but partly also because teachers and teacher educators, amongst others, are insufficiently trained to be able to recognize what is happening. In so far as there is a teacher education which encourages reflective activity by teachers and teacher educators and which trains them in theories and methods of criticism of their own roles in college, school and society, it enables them to enhance their roles so as to become conscious agents of social reform, not only as individuals but as members of a profession sensitive to the whole range of aims and expectations for education held in the community and alert to a broader educative society.

TEACHER EDUCATION AND SOCIAL REFORM

Much of what has been written about in the previous section is very understudied in educational research and writing. No one is in a position to be prescriptive on the matters discussed, and we can only conclude that the field is wide open for systematic inquiry to introduce more reliable knowledge into the explosive arguments about the reforms of teacher education. It is hoped that one contribution made by this study may be to have outlined the context for needed sociological research, by identifying critical issues in the broad perspective of a cross-cultural study. In these concluding remarks we will limit ourselves to indicating what seem to us to be some key substantive and methodological transition points to more detailed and developed field research.

This study has attempted to focus upon the teacher undergoing education and training not in order to evaluate the experience of particular cohorts of teachers but to understand the wider social implications of the problematic of teacher education. Because there has been little written in this field, least of all comparatively, the gestalt of teacher education has not been sufficiently recognized; the role of the teacher in school and society, the experience of teacher education, and its curriculum and organization, are studied separately and are rarely brought into any degree of conceptual coherence. We have sought to show not only that a holistic approach is conceptually feasible, but that the reform of teacher education depends upon systemic repercussions of changes induced or originating within its different sectors or components. New types of schools call for new teacher-skills, just as de-institutionalizing education will alter the teacher's role. In our analysis we have sought to encompass divergent possibilities about what teachers ought to become, in order to be able to examine their implications for teacher-education reforms and for broader social change.

To carry out this task we began, in Chapter One, with a broad descriptive approach to the nature and context of teacher education in the three societies. In the following chapter, in order to be able to speak about teacher education as a concept, and in order to be able to compare teacher education in different societies, it was necessary to provide a sociological definition of our subject. Then, in Part Two, we followed this definition and dealt systematically with policy-options in teacher education. A basic device of the study was the typology of policy-options classifying policies in terms of two interacting, but analytically distinguishable tendencies. Either tendency carried to extremes would imply a socially disastrous result. The democratization dimension of the typology asserts the concept of pluralism, but this could not be an unbridled principle in a society of peers. The coherence dimension includes the possibility of rigidity if the requirements of the system are given priority over the needs of individuals. The two tendencies, the creative and the integrative, will always be in tension with each other in a major social institution. We have illustrated all four typological possibilities extensively, posing the question as to whether teacher education tends to maximize its cultural and social freedom, or whether it tends only to reproduce itself in sociological terms, and thus make no effective contribution to wider cultural and social change. In our final chapter, rather than seek to summarize the central part of the book, we have questioned the reproduction hypothesis, and suggested some vital pressure-points for educational and social reform-oriented policies, synthesizing and extrapolating the trends and proposals previously analysed.

A wide variety of research problems has emerged within the areas summarily covered in this introductory analysis. But it is even more patent that refinement of research designs and methodologies is needed for further clarification of the conceptual nature, scope and interrelatedness of the issues involved in teacher-education reform. One important conclusion that we cannot avoid reaching is that all involved in teacher education, in no matter which of the three countries studied, need to develop greater familiarity with and commitment, if not to research itself, then to more rigorous procedures of critical self-study and to the principle of accountability without which effective and fruitful reform is a forlorn hope. In such an appropriate climate, a range of investigations from routine monitoring and surveys to exploratory case-studies, policy-oriented inquiries and basic social research could all help to increase the knowledge, sensitivity and insight available within teacher-education systems.

Certain concluding reflections force themselves upon us though their elaboration must await further work. We have referred to a shift over time in comparative education from a mainly historical to a mainly sociological perspective, but it appears also likely that there will be a movement away from an institution-centred to a societal approach. Early methodological articles in specialist journals stressed the central concerns and implied the boundaries of the field. Now it seems appropriate to extend these in terms of both disciplinary interest and subject matter. Potential applications of the comparative sociological method, by researchers based in education or elsewhere, appear also to include the study of de-institutionalized, on-the-job and community-based learning, as well as the application of a common analytical framework of inquiry to educational and non-educational institutions. There are many starting-points for such parallel studies in the schematic comparisons of educational and church institutions provided by the *deschooling* writers. These comparisons could be taken much further to provide greater understanding of general processes of cultural and social reproduction and change. Similar, and no less valuable studies can be envisaged of other social institutions, including public administration at local and national level, social and cultural agencies, and commercial and industrial bodies, which face fundamentally similar if often ignored problems as to how, through their deliberate development, they can contribute more to liberating than to stifling the human spirit.

Name Index

Adams, P. 166 n
Allen, A. E. 92 n
Anderson, C. A. 25, 29, 45 n, 46 n, 66 n,
   89 n
Antz, J. 111 n, 162 n
Aristotle 124

Bacon 124
Bantock, G. H. 91 n
Barker-Lunn, J. C. 92 n
Baron, G. 90 n
Bataillon, M. 112 n, 141 n
Becker, C. H. 33, 47 n, 67 n
Becker, H. 67 n
Beckmann, H. K. 137 n, 166 n
Bell, R. 141 n
Benjamin, R. 48 n
Benn, C. 44 n, 67 n
Berger, I. 37, 48 n
Berger, P. L. 66 n, 138 n
Bernstein, B. 120–21, 138 n
Bertlein, H. 91 n
Bettermann, K. A. 90 n
Betzen, K. 90 n, 92 n
Biddle, B. J. 88 n, 91 n, 93 n
Birley, D. 95 n
Blackburn, R. 94 n
Blättner, F. 89 n
Blouet, C. 89 n
Blyth, W. A. L. 89 n
Boisset, C. 93 n
Bourdieu, P. 9, 28, 29, 46 n, 51–52, 64–
   65, 66 n, 68 n, 91 n, 113 n, 120, 126,
   129, 137 n, 138 n, 139 n
Brechon, R. 90 n
Brezinka, W. 90 n
Brim, O. G. 110 n
Bulman, I. 164 n
Bungardt, K. 9, 15 n, 46 n, 47 n, 111 n
Burgess, T. 93 n, 113 n, 163 n
Burstall, C. 88 n

Calthrop, K. 166 n
Cane, B. S. 95 n, 113 n, 163 n, 164 n

Cannon, C. 74, 89 n
Capelle, J. 115 n, 138 n, 163 n
Caselmann, C. H. 90 n
Caspari, I. E. 67 n, 141 n
Cass, J. E. 92 n
Caston, G. 139 n
Chapoulie, J.–M. 88 n
Chapuis, R. 166 n
Citron, S. 89 n, 138 n, 141 n, 163 n
Clark, J. M. 68 n, 91 n, 93 n, 167 n
Cockburn, H. 94 n
Cohen, L. 67 n, 112 n, 113 n
Collier, K. G. 67 n, 93 n, 140 n, 142 n
Combe, A. 88 n
Conant, J. B. 67 n, 112 n
Cox, C. B. 114 n
Craft, M. 164 n, 166 n
Crozier, M. 139 n
Curtis, S. J. 44 n, 89 n

Dahrendorf, R. 28
Dale, I. R. 113 n
Dent, H. C. 11 n
Derbalov, J. 48 n, 112 n, 163 n
Dieckmann, J. 89 n
Dilthey, W. 119
Driesch, J. van den 112 n
Dufton, A. 95 n
Dumville, B. 89 n
Durkheim, E. 47 n, 52, 59, 64, 66 n, 68 n,
   71, 88 n, 110, 117, 125, 137 n, 162 n
Dyson, A. E. 114 n

Eason, T. W. 67 n, 162 n
Eckstein, M. A. 66 n
Eggleston, S. J. 67 n, 88 n, 141 n
Erlinghagen, K. 139 n
Etzioni, A. 161 n
Evers, C. H. 167 n

Fackiner, K. 165 n
Fantini, M. E. 141 n
Fauquet, M. 140 n
Ferry, G. 89 n, 94 n, 114 n, 141 n
Fichelet, R. 91 n

Subject Index